THE RICHEST VEIN:

EASTERN TRADITION AND WESTERN THOUGHT

‘My instinct tells me that my head is an organ for burrowing, as some creatures use their snouts and forepaws and with it I would mine and burrow my way through these hills. I think that the richest vein is somewhere hereabout . . . and here I will begin to mine.’

H. D. Thoreau: *Walden*

Charles Le Gai Eaton

THE RICHEST VEIN

EASTERN TRADITION AND MODERN THOUGHT

SOPHIA PERENNIS
HILLSDALE NY

Third edition, 2005
Second edition, Sophia Perennis et Universalis 1995
First edition, Faber and Faber, 1949

For information, address:
Sophia Perennis, P.O. Box 611
Hillsdale NY 12529
sophiaperennis.com

Library of Congress Cataloging-in-Publication Data

Easton, Gai, 1941–
The richest vein: Eastern tradition and modern thought / Charles Le Gai Eaton.—3rd ed.

p. cm.

Includes index.
ISBN 1 59731 026 3 (pbk: alk. paper)
ISBN 1 59731 027 1 (hardcover: alk. paper)
1. Mysticism. I. Title
BL625.E3 2005
231'.095—dc22 2005009314

CONTENTS

FOREWORD

When we reached Charles Le Gai Eaton to request his permission to publish a reprint edition of his book *The Richest Vein*, he graciously agreed, but wondered whether it would 'really be of interest to anyone,' especially as several of the writers discussed in the book are scarcely remembered today. The fact remains, however, that as a very young man (and with the encouragement of T.S. Eliot) Mr Eaton was the first to give a clear account in English of the 'traditionalist' school of writers in his chapter on two of its major representatives, René Guénon and Ananda K. Coomaraswamy.

Traditionalism has since been championed by others, pre-eminently Frithjof Schuon and Titus Burckhardt, as well as S.H. Nasr, Huston Smith, Martin Lings, and many others being actively published today. The past decade has also seen the completion of the monumental 23-volume *Collected Works of René Guénon*, an achievement that could only have been dreamt of at the time the present book was written. But precious little has been published *about* these authors; and this is perhaps not so surprising, for their writings tend to repel minds over-saturated with modernism, inexorably attracting only those who retain a sense for the sacred and a receptivity to the traditional metaphysics that till yesterday in the grand scheme of things formed and fashioned the best in men and civilizations—a circumstance only made the more challenging today by the need to assimilate what Schuon called the 'relatively absolute' claims of all valid spiritual Traditions in a world that has shrunk in ways that could not have been imagined even a century ago. But those who treasure traditionalist works inevitably seek to furnish their libraries with any title that bears upon them. This demand, alongside the inherent and lasting interest of Mr Eaton's writing, is sufficient reason to republish this work, and we hope it may reach many new readers and stimulate them to look further into the writers he so engagingly characterizes here.

In the preface to the 1990 edition of his second book, *King of the Castle: Choice and Responsibility in the Modern World*, Mr Eaton writes:

> The story begins many years ago in the mid-1940s when a passionate study of Eastern mysticism (not yet fashionable at the time) led me from the agnosticism of childhood and adolescence to beliefs which cried out for clarification. I can only think coherently on paper, so I wrote a number of 'essays' on Hindu Vedanta, Chinese Taoism, and Zen Buddhism.... [They were] published with the title *The Richest Vein*, taken from Thoreau's *Walden*: 'My instinct tells me that my head is an organ for burrowing.... I think that the richest vein is somewhere here about ... and here I will begin to mine....' Letters began to arrive from people who had read the book and imagined that I was something I was not. 'I have been trying to picture what you are like,' wrote one correspondent: 'I see you as an elderly man with a white beard, meditating on a mountain in the Himalayas....' As I had started on the 'essays' at the age of 25 ... I felt a fraud; indeed, I was a fraud, but I began to understand for the first time the heavy responsibility which falls upon those who choose to write of anything but trivial matters.

Mr Eaton went on to publish many articles for *Studies in Comparative Religion* and other journals, and in addition to *King of the Castle* (first published in 1977), two widely-acclaimed works: *Islam and the Destiny of Man* (1985) and *Remembering God: Reflections on Islam* (2000). It will be evident to the reader of these two books just how earnestly Mr Eaton accepted the responsibility he alludes to above.

INTRODUCTION

In violence and the loosening of all familiar bonds, tradition has perished in the West. The strands, deep-laid and unseen, that held a civilization together, stretching and contracting with the times, vigorous yet elastic, have snapped, and each man is left to choose whether to abide by that lonely thing, his own personal integrity, or to replace the old certainties with a new fanaticism. An unparalleled freedom, in thought if not in action is the gift, turned burden, of the modern age. A freedom no sooner won than feared and even hated; the dangerous freedom of a spiritual and psychological vacuum. For centuries there has been at work this process of levelling out the ruts in which human thought and action once moved, and now that their traces are almost erased we enjoy, unprotected, the liberty of a pathless desert.

In this desert, it is presumed that every man must be his own pathfinder; he must, as the phrase goes, 'think for himself', and originality is prized so highly that one might suppose the most insane private fiction superior to traditional human thought in its entirety. The presumption, however, has never been fulfilled; most people, although they have accepted in theory the gospel of 'thinking for oneself', just as they have accepted all the other dogmas of our time, incorporating them into an unconscious network of rationalistic and scientific superstitions, have never really upheld the principle that each man must plod round the desert in his private circle; if they had, the multitude of beliefs which have grown up, swiftly as any crop of weeds, upon the body of so-called facts 'discovered' by modern science, could never have passed, as they have, virtually unquestioned. The age of faith is always with us; only its object changes.

Substitutes for the old patterns of thought are not hard to find to-day; any private illusion sufficiently potent to win a hearing will serve its turn, and the problem is not to find an answer to the questions we ask concerning ourselves and the world we live in, but to select the congenial voice from the multitude that cry for our attention. Not only is there the rich variety of modern beliefs and theories, but we are also offered, in an appetizing, fashionable presentation, beliefs of a less private nature and of a more ancient origin. The distinction between old and new is not always as sharp as it might be; in modern dress, and stripped of anything that might really shock the scientific mind, the ancient ideas compete, or try to compete with the brash younger generation, until one gradually begins to realize that all these apparently conflicting doctrines might seem to a stranger—to a visiting Martian, perhaps—the products of a single collective mind and a single moment in time. The babble of voices merges into one, the almost unanimous voice of the age in which we live.

It is, in fact, easy to mistake for true alternatives what are really no more than variations upon the same theme, and to suppose that because a hundred different paths seem to branch out before us, they must therefore lead to different goals, whereas they may well reunite, after a divergence of a few yards or a few miles, to form a single concrete highway to destruction. If there exists a real alternative, a totally other and different way, it must lie outside the closed circle in which modern thought, with all its variety and all its fundamental sameness, moves, and that means that it must lie, as it were, on our blind side. Every age has its variations, but every age is confined to a particular field of vision, determined chiefly by the assumptions (usually called 'facts') which seem to it self-evident; what lies beyond this field of vision must always seem to the age in question to be contrary to the self-evident facts, and therefore unreal.

INTRODUCTION

The events of the last thirty-five years have done a good deal to shake Western complacency, but they have done nothing to dislodge the fundamental assumptions by which the modern world lives. In some cases, a naïve optimism has been replaced by an equally naïve pessimism, but these are two sides of the same coin. The effects of shock do not last very long; the shock of the 1914–18 war, that of the economic troubles between the wars and, more recently, of the atom bomb, necessitated certain adjustments in our outlook, but we adapt ourselves fairly easily to changed circumstances, and such adjustments cost us very little. Our chastened mood, which would not, in all probability, outlast a few decades of peace and prosperity, is certainly not sufficient in itself to make possible a solution of our difficulties; and though necessity may be the mother of invention, a multitude of inventions contrived to stave off a multitude of disasters will never add up to one real solution, nor will the desperate need to deal with the immediate situation lead us automatically to the discovery of a new world and a new way of action.

There are certain historians who maintain that civilization comes into being and progresses in response to the challenge of difficult circumstances and that all that is of value in human history has been wrung from us by the harsh necessity of dealing with dangerous or intolerable situations. The theory depends upon a false equation between value and civilization on the one side and an outer complexity combined with inner agitation on the other, and it assumes that the man whose life is cumbered with distractions and luxuries stands on a higher level than he who pursues his human way, through the common human experiences, to his true and final end, without leaving behind him on the earth any of those scars by which historians measure the greatness and glory of a civilization.

This challenge-and-response theory of history is productive of two particularly misleading notions. The first is the idea that a human society in grave difficulties will find, in the heat of the battle with adversity, a real cure for its ills. Now men who are hard pressed will make use of the powers which they have already developed—will, in fact, develop them still further—and if the crisis was itself largely due to the powers in question and to the way of action which they represent, it can only be aggravated by their further development. The drunkard who finds life increasingly difficult will almost certainly make further use of alcohol as the only means he has of coping with his difficulties. If a human society is moving in the wrong direction, if its substance is warped, it will, by its response to the challenge of adversity, increase the pace of its false progress and become still more warped. The one hope for such a society is that it may succeed in rising above the immediate necessities of the moment and learning, from an unbiassed study of other, less catastrophically inclined societies, to recognize the nature of the vicious circle in which it is confined.

But the challenge-and-response theory has another unfortunate result, for it makes such an unbiassed study quite impossible; it is infected through and through with the almost universal Western conviction that any civilization that is not in a perpetual state of agitation must be 'stagnant'. So hectic and unbalanced have our lives become that we can only think of stability as a form of stagnation, and we are aroused almost to fury by the spectacle of any human society in which the new generation follows in the footsteps of the old, and the old in those of their remote forefathers, who walked the way that, from immemorial time, had been regarded as the human way. We are horrified to see how certain age-old abuses are handed down from generation to generation, and we refuse even to consider the possibility that the abolition of these ancient abuses may call into being others, at least as terrible, and that, when these in their turn are cut off, there may spring from their roots, embedded in the very conditions of human life, a new and perhaps more noxious growth, until the feverish process of hacking down the perennial weed that always sprouts again is in full swing and the society in question earns from us the title of 'progressive'.

Not only is it hard for those whose whole attention is concentrated upon the struggle for existence of the society of which they are members to survey the human scene with detachment, but they must inevitably come to regard everything in the light of the immediate problem and either to ignore all that transcends the human struggle or to try to make use of it for the purpose of attack or defence. We see this clearly in certain modern arguments in defence of religion; it is pointed out that civilization cannot survive without a religious basis, and it is then assumed that the religious interpretation of human life is sufficiently justified once it has been shown to be socially useful. It would be hard to find a stranger reversal of the normal order of things or a more blatant case of putting second things first; it is a short step from this to pragmatism and the theory of 'useful fictions' and 'illusions necessary to life'. Men are as likely to come to faith in God because they have been told that such faith, whether founded in the truth or not, will make for a happier and a better world as they are to grow wings simply through recognizing the usefulness of such a development.

It is a platitude that happiness is not found by those who seek it too deliberately, but we still have to learn that a good and ordered human society will never be built by those who make the creation of such a society their principal aim; the truest creative work is done, as it were, absentmindedly, and a good society can only arise as a by-product of action, thought and feeling which aim beyond the contingencies of human life, having their goal in eternity. No man ever achieved sanctity through wanting to be a saint; but 'Seek first the Kingdom of Heaven . . .' is not only a maxim for saints; it is an essential condition of all political action, if that action is to escape the fruitless and monotonous round of chasing its own tail in an increasingly narrow circle.

The Kingdom of Heaven, however, is neither sought nor found through sentimental aspiration, and the first essential, if we wish to re-orientate our own society, is that we should move some way towards understanding those cultures which were, in the past, or have remained to this day, faithful to the age-old principles of human life and action. It might even be as well if we were to give serious consideration, for the first time, to the warnings which the Western world has received, time and again, from the representatives of the ancient, traditional cultures. However chastened our present mood may be, we are still too inclined to think that our civilization 'came off the rails' fairly recently and that, on the whole, it was moving in the right direction until this mysterious accident took place: if we would consider, for one moment, the possibility that the direction taken by the Western world at the beginning of modern times may have led inevitably to our present troubles, and may lead to still worse ones in the future, we should be ready to listen more respectfully to those many warning voices.

Every schoolchild knows of the persecution to which the early scientists were subjected; he has heard all about the wicked reactionaries who struggled to keep mankind in bondage and ignorance, when the age of light and freedom was dawning, and he has been told—for the retailing of such absurdities enlivens the history lesson—of the dire prophecies made by the representatives of the old order in the face of every one of those inventions and advances which led, in ordered progression, to the glorious present-day. He may, in later life, become sceptical concerning the true value of the achievements he was taught to admire, but his schooling effectively screens him from thinking of those old prophets except with derision; they were discredited, those prophets, for no thunderbolt fell from on high to strike down the impious pioneer or heretic; but then, the mills of God grind slow.

These prophecies belong to the past, but others, of a similar kind, may be heard to-day on the lips of 'superstitious savages', who resist the introduction of progressive measures designed entirely for their own good—the West has been as generous in giving other, less 'mature' races the benefits of progress and enlightenment as it has in bringing them gin, syphilis and tuberculosis. To the missionary or colonial administrator whose life-work it is to raise the 'standard of living' of a primitive people, the opposition of the local priest or witch-doctor seems not merely frivolous and absurd, but actively wicked; the fact that the people in question, while enjoying unknown and unwished for comforts and amenities, may lose the one thing that gave their life meaning and coherence scarcely occurs to him, for his education and background make it inevitable that he should ignore what cannot be seen or touched or statistically assessed.

In comparison with other colonial administrators, the British may justifiably claim to have interfered very little with the native customs of the territories under their control; but we, like all other Westerners, are firmly convinced that if a particular measure is good in itself, its consequences cannot fail to be excellent. Because our own way of life is disjointed, we think that everything can be judged purely on its own merits, even when we are dealing with a primitive society that is still coherent and integrated. We argue, for example, that the introduction of Western medical services and agricultural methods into a 'backward' culture represents an unqualified advantage for the people concerned, without for a moment stopping to consider whether the introduction of such alien elements may not bring about the total disruption of the cultural pattern into which they are inserted and, in consequence, the death of the tribe or community as a harmonious and functioning whole. To heal the sick and to reduce the incidence of famine is obviously desirable, but it becomes decidedly less desirable when it is done at the cost of destroying the spirit from which the victims of our charity drew, not merely their reason for living, but life itself.

Every aspect of a culture that has retained some measure of coherence is linked to every other aspect, and it is no more possible to root out the cruel and displeasing elements in a primitive culture, while retaining the admirable ones, than it is to divorce Western medicine from the Western mentality and way of life. Certainly, there exist forms of society as monstrous as certain species of giant orchid; there is no travesty of human life that may not be found as an integral factor in some human society, but it is very seldom that such things can be lopped off, like the misshapen branch of a tree, without destroying the life of the whole organism. It is not unreasonable to prefer a living community, with all its abuses and anachronisms, to the human wreckage represented to-day by a large part of the negro population of South Africa and the Polynesians of the Pacific Islands.

The study of the social forms of so-called primitive peoples, and of the myths upon which these social forms are patterned, will help us, perhaps to an incalculable extent, to understand the anomalies present in our own civilization and to feel our way towards the source of all harmonious and ordered human living; but such a study, to be effective, must be undertaken in a spirit very different from that of the orthodox anthropologist who too often maintains an attitude of complacent superiority to the people he is studying and imagines that he can discover their secrets without, to some extent, learning to share, or at least to respect, their beliefs. Nor shall we derive much profit from our investigation if we insist upon believing that the myths of a primitive people are nothing but stories, fantasies and garbled history, and refuse even to consider the possibility that they may be valid statements about the nature of reality, illustrations of metaphysical truths once recognized the world over. It is, however, the major traditional societies—infinitely more complex than those which we call primitive, but based upon the same principles—that offer the richest field of study; and this brings us, inevitably, to India.

In Hindu India there existed, until fairly recently, a great culture which had altered very little, under the surface froth of dynastic changes and princely conflicts, since the time when the Vedas and the Upanishads were first committed to writing; a culture in which there were many abuses, such, for example, as the over-developed and petrified caste system, but which had remained faithful either to the traditional doctrine in its pristine simplicity or to the ramifications of that doctrine. Certainly, there were signs of decay, but decadence and corruption are, in the Hindu view, inevitable in this dark Kali Age, when the cosmic order—indeed, the universal manifestation—approaches the end of the present 'Great Age'; the framework, however, remained intact until the alien wind blew upon it from out of the West.

INTRODUCTION

It is far too early to tell how profoundly Western ideas may have penetrated the basic structure of life in India, but it is clear that the process of penetration has by no means ceased with the abdication of the British Raj; the country, now regarded as 'politically mature' because its traditional forms have been more or less undermined, has been left to the tender mercies of Westernized Indians who are unlikely to show such moderation as we did in tampering with the old way of life. It remains to be seen whether the next generation of India's rulers will uphold so fervently the Western catchwords—Science, Education and Progress. We have done our best, or worst, and now have troubles enough of our own.

It would be perverse to start by objecting to the imposition of Western ways upon the East, and then to advocate that of Eastern ones upon the West, although not, perhaps, as perverse as it might appear, for the two kinds of civilization are not stricly comparable, that of India, for example, offering but one of the many possible examples of a traditional culture and way of life, while that of the West is, in the fullest sense, 'abnormal', whether we choose to regard this epithet as complimentary or otherwise, in that its whole attention has been concentrated exclusively upon aspects of human existence which other cultures have always regarded as of merely secondary and relative importance. But there is no question of the West attempting to remodel itself upon a foreign pattern. 'In the beginning', runs an American Indian proverb, quoted by Ruth Benedict, 'God gave to each people a cup of clay, and from this cup they drank their life'. We have broken so many cups, in an effort to improve their design, and this is no moment to try and steal one for our own use. A study of Eastern ways—of life as well as of thought, since the two are so closely interconnected—will not offer us any kind of blueprint applicable to our own society; it will not even show us an established path which we might follow in our personal lives; what we may reasonably hope to come to, by means of such a study, is a growing understanding of the foundation upon which the life of all traditional human societies is based, the foundation upon which our life in the West was once established, before, in pursuit of the mirage of a material heaven on earth, we broke loose and became a wonder and an abomination to the rest of the world.

I have tried to suggest that the most essential need of the moment is not that we should concentrate all our attention upon the task at hand, but that we should stand back, as men have not done in the West for a very long time, and that, since many are agreed that they can see no way out of our present difficulties, we should take up a new position, one from which we may look out upon a wider landscape and see, beyond our former horizon, a way clearly marked; our own way, and not an alien one, but a way to which we must have remained blind had we not made use of the alien standpoint.

I have tried to show that we cannot hope to come to any kind of understanding of another culture unless we are prepared to respect the way of life in which it finds expression and to accept, restraining all desire to alter or improve, that way of life as valid in itself and appropriate to the people in question; to recognize also that material luxury and complexity, diversity of belief and variety of emotional and sensual experience, are not the only tests of value in human life; to admit that a society is not necessarily backward, humanly speaking, because it has remained stable and almost unchanged throughout recorded history, indeed, that it may have retained many things that we have lost in our single-minded concentration upon a single aspect—and that the most exterior, least essential one—of life in the world.

It is not easy for us to recognize or to accept any of this. Reality is, for most of us, the sphere in which our impressive achievements have been wrought, and those other spheres of being which were once thought of as more truly real than the sensible world of daily experience, seem, if not illusory, at least vague and purely subjective. It is the price of a wholly one-sided development that one comes to doubt the very existence of any other side to things; a man whose eyesight had developed out of all proportion, in such a way as to cause the dwindling and even the disappearance of his other senses, might be prepared to admit the possibility of a knowledge of the world not based on sight, but the senses of hearing and of touch, of which he might be told, would seem to him trivial and unreliable in comparison with the clarity of vision. It is such an attitude as this that must be shaken off if we are to approach with the slightest measure of respect or of understanding a way of thought which regards the visible world as an insubstantial veil before the invisible, the world of the senses as dependent upon something beyond the grasp of the senses, the knowledge derived from observation and experiment as unsure and misleading compared with the certainty attained by wholly other means, and myths and analogies as sounder statements of objective truth than any rational theory or scientific hypothesis. We need not necessarily be convinced that the correct performance of a ritual, which binds human action in time to its prototype in eternity, is more important than the raising of a people's standard of living, but we must be prepared to regard this as a reasonable possibility if we are to gain anything from a study of traditional belief and doctrine.

In what follows, I shall first deal with certain aspects of three Oriental doctrines, making no attempt to relate them to modern Western ideas, but using occasional quotations from Western authors when these help to clarify, without distorting, the doctrines in question. I am in no way qualified to give a full, orthodox exposition of any Eastern doctrine, for, as we shall see when dealing with the title of Translator, qualifications of a very special kind are essential for anyone who undertakes to transpose a traditional doctrine from its normal setting to a foreign one; all I can do is to offer certain suggestions and indicate certain lines of thought which may play their part in clearing away some of the obstructions that still, in spite of all the work that has been done in the last half-century, block the Western approach to a real understanding of the Oriental doctrines.

In the second part of this book I shall be concerned with five Western writers, all, in their different ways, opposed to the main trends of the modern world, and all, with one exception, considerably influenced by Oriental ideas. The first, Max Plowman, may be said to have criticized the world he lived in 'from within', without crossing over the frontier into foreign fields of thought and feeling; in many ways, he was a living example of the finest human type that our Western world produces; not a 'thinker', not an intellectual, but a man of tremendous personal integrity and of passionate, sometimes quixotic, faith. The second, L. H. Myers, was a man of far more complex character; one who tried, in his personal experience, almost all the illusions of our time, and found no satisfaction in them; he studied the Oriental doctrines, but turned away, without denying them, to beliefs which flow, like Christianity itself, from the Jewish tradition, with its intense sense of relationship and of a living presence in a living world. The third, Aldous Huxley, turned to the East out of a deep-rooted disgust which seems, at times, to be focused not only upon the anomalies of the modern world, but upon human life itself.

Finally, I shall describe the work of two writers who offer us the traditional doctrines of the East in their pure, unadulterated form, and make no concessions to modern belief and prejudice; the first is a Frenchman, René Guénon, who demolishes, with clarity, precision and arrogance, every illusion cherished by the contemporary world; the second, Ananda Coomaraswamy, was a Ceylonese who lived and worked most of his life in the United States.

Protest, criticism, opposition—these were never more necessary than to-day, and there was never a better moment than the present one for bringing home to as many people as possible the realization that the troubles to which our world is subject and the disasters with which it is threatened are only the symptoms of a deeper disease; and because so many of the remedies proposed lead only further into the desert and only accentuate the tendencies which have brought us to this point, it was never more necessary to emphasize that there are other ways of living than our own and to make audible the distant voices of those who, in time past, took another road, unbeguiled by the promise of ease and enrichment in return for the surrender of their ancient heritage.

PART I

CHAPTER ONE

APPROACH TO THE EAST

'. . . it would hardly be an exaggeration to say that a faithful account of Hinduism might well be given in the form of a categorical denial of most of the statements that have been made about it, alike by European scholars and by Indians trained in our modern sceptical and evolutionary modes of thought.'

—A. K. COOMARASWAMY.

We are accustomed to putting our trust in experts. If we require information on some point of biology, we go to a biologist for it; and there are many fields of modern thought that are virtually closed to the interested amateur—fully to understand the latest theories on the physical structure of the universe, for example, requires, not only a special mentality, but also a long and intensive training. Quite naturally, we have come to rely on the specialist and to feel confident that, within his own compartment of knowledge, he knows more than we can ever hope to learn or to understand. So it is disturbing to discover that, in matters of Oriental belief and doctrine, the Orientalist is not always the most reliable of guides.

What, after all, is an Orientalist, in the accepted sense of the word? He is a man who has set himself to study, objectively, as another might study the habits of a certain type of microbe, the history, customs, language and literature of a particular Oriental people. The historical part of his study will almost certainly be based upon two assumptions; firstly, that political activity, springing from a diversity of beliefs as to how the life of the community should be regulated, is a sign of advance in civilization; secondly, that, since our own society represents, for him, the highest point so far reached by humanity, the proper attitude to adopt towards all other social forms is that which a mature man adopts towards his own youth. He will take it for granted, in studying Oriental customs, that the doctrine upon which they are based represents a very early stage in the human search for truth. When he comes to the literature —inevitably, a sacred literature—of the people of his choice, he may react in any one of three ways; perhaps he will be impressed by its poetic value, and regard its religious and philosophical content as irrelevant; or he may find, here and there, something that recalls to him certain Western philosophical ideas or that seems conspicuous for its depth of 'religious feeling' and, lifting it from its 'archaic' context, treat it as we treat the unexpectedly bright remark of a small child; or, finally, he may be actuated simply by the ambition to add a little more information to the sum total of human knowledge.

To see what is lacking in the spirit in which the Orientalist undertakes his work, we must consider what the title of 'Translator' implies, for instance, in Tibet. The 'Translator' is the man who brings a foreign doctrine to his own people, in a form which they can assimilate. In order to do this, he goes first to the country in which the doctine originates, and he may well spend the greater part of his life there; he studies under the qualified teachers; he is initiated; he follows, with the other disciples, the way that leads, step by step, to a full, personal realization of the meaning of the doctrine. Then, and then only, armed with the sacred books, as a student with his notebooks, he returns home. He gathers disciples around him; he initiates them, handing on the grace that has been transmitted to him, and he instructs them in the doctrine, translating the sacred texts, which he no doubt knows by heart, into his own language, not necessarily word for word, but in such a way as to preserve their full meaning.

Of what value, beside this, is the work of the Orientalist, who frequently confesses, when translating the more obscure passages of a sacred treatise, that he has not the remotest notion what it is all about? It may be argued that it would not be possible for him to devote years to sitting at the feet of a teacher; but, in that case, why does he adopt a profession that can hardly be called rewarding from a financial point of view, and which involves years of dry labour over texts to which he lacks the essential key? The answer seems to be that we suffer, in the West, from a monstrously over-developed sense of curiosity, and the fields in which it may be exercised are not so wide that we can afford to ignore any dark corner that remains unexplored. People of a different background may ask why we spend time and trouble so lavishly upon studies from which we do not really expect any reward—the American Indian, for example, cannot understand why we should be interested in his sacred dances, when we do not share the beliefs which they are designed to illustrate—but the fact is that our capacity for labour and study, having lost its true object, has run wild; a knowledge of facts, no matter how trivial or irrelevant they may be, is valued for its own sake just because our power of knowing is great enough to reach out to the understanding of divine things, and when it descends to the pursuit of inessential knowledge its appetite is insatiable.

Unfortunately, we are dependent upon the Orientalists for translations of the sacred scriptures of the East; and it is hardly surprising if many of these translations, however accurate they may be in a word-for-word sense, are rendered almost useless by the fact that the translators have, in most cases, very little notion of the fundamental ideas and precise symbolism behind the texts.

One example of the nonsense to which this ignorance leads must suffice us: in the second section of the first Adhyáya of the Brihadaranyaka Upanishad the activity of the Creator is described in terms of a tremendous concentration of power and of will, out of which creative power goes forth; this is the performance of what is called 'tapas', often translated as penance, but in fact denoting a state of concentration—the generation of an inward power, a glowing inner heat—which is the necessary preliminary to creative activity of any kind. In one of the standard English translations of the Upanishads, the key sentence in this passage is rendered as 'He tortured himself', which not only makes nonsense in itself, but is actively misleading, suggesting, as it does, the picture of some half-crazy 'fakir' indulging in an orgy of masochism. The translator would no doubt insist that the Sanskrit word here employed sometimes means 'tortured'; the fact that it quite obviously has a different meaning in this case, and that an elementary knowledge of the ideas in question makes clear what it does mean, would perhaps seem to him irrelevant.

If the Western Orientalist is an uncertain guide, what of the native Indian scholars who have written, for the benefit of the West, on the Hindu doctrines? These writers may be divided into two main groups. The first is that of the professors, men whose life-work it is to develop Western educational methods in their own country and who have had some training in Western science and philosophy; it is in the light of this training that they analyse the doctrine of their own country. No teacher faithful to the Hindu tradition could bring himself to participate in a method of education which must seem to him worthless, if not actually dangerous, nor would it occur to him to make public the teaching of which he is the depository otherwise than by word of mouth, in conversation with disciples who have proved themselves temperamentally and intellectually prepared to receive his instruction. An Indian who becomes a university professor or, for that matter, a teacher in a school of the Western type, however excellent his motives may be, forfeits the right to interpret his own tradition.

The second group consists of men inspired by a missionary zeal which is very uncommon in the East. Vivekananda, a disciple of the great Ramakrishna, who, after his master's death, toured the United States lecturing and preaching, was really the founder of this group, and there are many people who have gained their only knowledge of Hinduism from his books. He was a man of predominantly emotional character, and, under

Western influence, he became both sentimental and dogmatic; whether from personal conviction or simply in order to make Hinduism more acceptable to American religiosity, he falsified the teachings which he considered it his mission to propagate and succeeded only in adding one more rootless cult to the number of those already flourishing in America. It is impossible to insist too strongly upon the fact that the whole idea of propaganda and missionary work on behalf of the Hindu doctrines and the promiscuous dissemination of those doctrines, without regard for the individual needs and aptitudes of the people amongst whom they are disseminated, is utterly foreign to the spirit and practice of the Hindu tradition.

The choice is narrowing down. To whom else can we turn for reliable information? There are, in England and elsewhere, a number of enthusiasts for what is sometimes called the 'Wisdom of the East'. Western idealism, in its more emotional and ineffectual forms, burns brightly in them, and, being progressive, they are generally opposed to whatever remains of tradition in the West and, in particular, to the Roman Catholic Church; but they are attracted, indeed fascinated, by certain elements in Oriental belief; they would say, perhaps, that the West has concentrated too much on material things and the East too much on the spiritual, and that what is to be desired is such a happy marriage of the two mentalities as would make it possible for us to retain all the benefits of materialism, while gaining a new spiritual depth; they would like to have the best of both worlds, and so it is only what they happen to regard as the 'best' in Eastern thought that interests them; unfortunately this 'best' is often a ghostly and insubstantial thing, a lovely but fragile blossom cut off from the sturdy plant upon which it grew.

Finally, there are the occultists and Theosophists, who have woven for themselves a complicated fabric of borrowed ideas, symbols and terminology. So long as they do not claim to represent any authentic Oriental doctrine, there is no cause for complaint, although the fascination exerted upon them by certain psychic phenomena and their excessive preoccupation with what is sometimes called the 'intermediate world'—the twilight territory on the confines of human experience—has led some of their number to the borders of insanity and across; but it is important to realize that these cults are essentially Western and essentially modern and that the manner in which they employ traditional symbols, whether of the East or of the West, is peculiar to themselves.

All this is very discouraging for anyone who wishes to undertake a serious study of the Oriental doctrines. And yet, it is as it should be. In a world in which everything, in the realm of knowledge, is made too easy of attainment and in which we have come to think it our right that the wisdom of the ages should be handed to us on a plate, sliced, cooked and made palatable by the very best authorities, it is as well that the traditional teachings of the East should remain far from easy of access. An Indian 'guru' would no doubt insist that the study of these teachings, except under the personal supervision of a Master who passes on as much as his disciple is able to receive and to assimilate, is fruitless; but we who, in the West, lack the opportunities for this form of study and yet believe that it is only through a knowledge of the Oriental doctrines that we shall rediscover the roots of our own tradition and our own characteristic way across what Eckhardt called 'the storm of the world flow', must make what use we can of the means at our disposal.

As to the means, it is surprising how far a little common sense will carry us and how many pitfalls it will help us to avoid. It is, for example, only common sense to suppose that the sacred texts upon which the life of a great race, with a great cultural history behind it, has been based, perhaps for thousands of years, are something more than 'meaningless mumbo-jumbo' (a phrase that has actually been applied to the Hindu scriptures), and to admit, when a particular passage baffles us, that this may be because we lack the key to its meaning or because it has been mangled in translation, instead of at once assuming it to be nonsense.

It is also reasonable to believe that, when certain medieval mystics and theologians, and, before them, Plato and Plotinus, used phrases and figures of speech which correspond very closely to those used in the Upanishads, they and the Indian teachers were speaking the same language of the spirit, even though the dialects might differ; to believe also that, when the Pawnee Indians of North America carry out the Four Pole Ritual, placing the fire, which represents their Lord, Tirawa, in the centre, or when the South Sea Islanders say:

> *He existed. Taaroa was his name.*
> *In the immensity*
> *There was no earth, there was no sky. . . .*
> *Existing alone, he became the universe.*
> *Taaroa is the root, the rocks.*
> *Taaroa is the grain of the original sands. . . .*

or when, finally, Irish myth and legend recounts that 'in the beginning' there was only the boundless Lir, existing alone, and that from him sprang, with the dawn of a new Day of time, the sacred Hazel, then we are justified in relating these things to the corresponding teachings concerning the Four Quarters and the central fire, the manifestation of the universe out of the solitary Brahman and the growth of the World Tree in the branches of which nest all existences, as they are presented in the Upanishads.

The Westerner who is trying to come to an accurate understanding of the Oriental doctrines will find his task made easier by a study of the equivalent symbols and rituals present in other cultures; but the language of symbolism is a universal one (Professor Jung has shown, in the field of Analytical Psychology, that many of these symbols are deeply ingrained in the very substance of the human mind), and even in our own everyday lives we occasionally come across remnants of the very symbolism that seems to us so strange when we first encounter it in the Eastern books; the game of chess, for example, in which the pawn who reaches the 'farther shore' becomes a 'Crowned Queen' and a 'Mover at Will', will teach us more of the orthodox Brahmanical doctrine than many an Orientalist's heavy volumes.

With these aids to understanding, and by winkling out from amongst the academic Orientalists, the Westernized native scholars and the apostles of the 'Wisdom of the East', the few exceptional men who are to be found in each group, it is possible to make real progress; but, before proceeding, it is essential that certain very widespread misconceptions, particularly with regard to the Hindu doctrines, should be cleared out of the way. And the first of these attaches to the word 'Maya', frequently translated as 'Illusion', which has led many people to suppose that the Hindus regard the world of human experience as unreal and meaningless.

'Maya' refers, in the first place, to the power and art whereby all things are produced; it might, with reservations, be translated as the divine art by which God makes a likeness, subject to space and time or to other limitations, of the eternal prototypes or ideas inherent in His nature, much as the human artist makes a likeness, subject to the limitations of stone or wood or the flat canvas, of the ideas present within him. According to Shankara, greatest of the orthodox Hindu commentators upon the Upanishads, 'Maya' is 'the power of the Lord, from which the world springs'. But the world process itself is described as 'maya', and Shankara explains in what sense this is to be understood; 'This whole multiplicity of creatures', he wrote, 'existing under name and form, in so far as it has the Supreme Being itself for its essence is true; if regarded as self-dependent, is untrue'.

'Maya' has, in fact, a double function; it both reveals and veils the ultimate reality; reveals it, in that it expresses certain possibilities inherent in that reality, and veils it in that it conceals the totality of the real. When Shankara says that the world is 'untrue' if regarded as 'self-dependent', he means only that it derives its existence—its *raison d'être*, in the fullest sense of the phrase—from the meaning which, as a symbol, it shadows forth. When we consider, for a moment, the gulf that separates the so-called savage, for whom everything is instinct with life and significance and who thinks in terms of symbols rather than of facts, from the modern Westerner, for whom everything is simply what it appears to be, we can see why the world we live in to-day has been described by an American writer as 'a world of impoverished reality'. A world devoid of meaning and significance is, in the strictest sense, 'unreal'; and it is only in this context that the Sanskrit word 'Maya' may justifiably be translated as 'illusion'.

A second obstacle to any true understanding of the Oriental doctrines (or, for that matter, of orthodox Christianity) is the notion that the supremacy accorded to contemplation in the East (as in medieval Europe) denotes a 'slothful' and 'passive' attitude to life. So completely have we reversed the normal values of human culture that we not only regard the world of the senses as alone real and objective and that of the spirit as nebulous and subjective, but we think of contemplation as something dreamy and unpractical, a kind of leisure pastime between bouts of blind activity.

The traditional craftsman or artist, whether in the East or in a 'primitive' society, gives us an example of the normal relation between contemplation and activity. Before undertaking his work, whether this consists in the moulding of an image or the building of a house, he makes, as a free man, the son of Heaven as well as of Earth, what is often described as a 'journey to Heaven', and studies the divine forms there; in other words, he enters into a state of contemplation and observes the perfect and archetypal model of whatever it is he is to make. Then, returning to his normal place in the world of the senses, he makes of himself a passive instrument; his hands and brain, as servants of his spirit, copy the model as best they can. Here, plainly, it is the contemplative act that is truly active and free, and the work which he undertakes, as a result of this act, that is passive and servile (the modern worker or factory hand is, obviously, reduced to a purely servile, 'coolie' role, since the contemplative act is not for him to make). Activity is always passive, whether, in relation to a spiritual impulse, born of contemplation, or, if it has broken away and become independent, then in relation to the drag of desire or appetite.

If we replace the terms active and passive with another pair, male and female, we shall see that Spirit is traditionally regarded as male in relation to the Earth and the activities of the Earth. In innumerable myths, the Earth is impregnated, either by the Supernal Sun or by seed from the Heavens, and is, in consequence, fruitful, and most so-called fertility rites are but the symbolic enactment of this drama. Many primitive peoples believe that sexual intercourse is only incidental to conception (the more hidebound of the anthropologists claim that these 'savages' have 'failed to observe the connection between intercourse and conception'), and that the real impregnation is by the spirit (or 'by the Sun'); a child born of a purely human coupling would be, from their point of view, a bastard, whereas the child of Heaven and of Earth, born of the spirit's conjunction with nature, is truly legitimate.

It is in this sense that modern culture and modern industry may be called illegitimate. Human activity, unravished by the thrust of the spirit, is effeminate—busy, agitated as a clucking hen, but never truly active—and never free. The wheels turn faster and faster; and men's minds become so preoccupied with the problem of keeping them turning that they drift ever further from that source from which alone significance and purpose flow into the world of movement and activity. It is as though the turning wheels drew us, in their turning, more and more to the surface of ourselves, tempting us to remake ourselves in their image, automatons, useful adjuncts of the machine. What counterweight have we in our own society to balance that drag to the surface? And what else but impudence is our condemnation of those other societies in which the contemplative discipline, whereby Heaven and Earth are brought into fruitful conjunction, is valued and respected?

The instrument of contemplation is the intellect, but not that intellect with which we are familiar in our ordinary lives. In the modern view, man apprehends the objective world through his senses and he understands it or 'makes sense of it' by means of a mental faculty which may be called either reason or intellect; he is not admitted to have any other means of obtaining knowledge. This view is completely opposed to the traditional doctrines of the East, as it is to those of medieval Europe. The Sanskrit terms for 'mind' and 'intellect' are 'manas' and 'buddhi' respectively, and the two are considered to belong to different levels of reality and to operate in different fields. It is through 'manas' that human reason and discursive thought operate; it is a purely individual faculty, subject to all the limitations of the individual, and the material upon which it works is derived from the senses. 'Buddhi', on the other hand, may be likened to a direct ray of light which strikes the human mind from without; it is not an individual faculty, but much rather a universal light in which the individual participates to a greater or lesser extent, according to his degree of awareness.

'Manas' is, then, the middle term, set between the senses, which connect the human being with the world around him, and the intellect, which connects him with the eternal principles. Western science and philosophy, in modern times, have claimed supremacy for this middle term, maintaining that truth is only to be reached through the theories which the mind builds upon the evidence supplied by the senses; but neither modern philosophy nor traditional doctrine has ever maintained that the senses are to be trusted or that 'seeing is believing'—for our eyes plainly tell us that the sun, rising above the edge of the world, moves across the sky, and that the sky itself is a solid dome inlaid with stars. Modern man, however, busies himself correcting the observations of the senses, with the aid of reason and theory, whereas the traditional teacher, whose aim it is to lead us beyond the phenomenal and the contingent, is content to use such observations as stepping-stones, symbolizing realities beyond the sphere of the senses and of the reasoning mind.

Here we see two diametrically opposed attitudes. Our contemporaries are interested only in how things work, whereas the ancient philosopher was concerned only with what they mean; if he failed to 'discover' that the earth circles round the sun, it was because such matters did not interest him; he was prepared to accept human experience as he found it. The one attitude springs from a belief that there is nothing higher than 'manas', the mental faculty; the other from a conviction that the human being has direct access, through 'buddhi', to the ultimate truth. There can be no possible compromise between these two points of view, and they have no common meeting ground.

The failure to perceive exactly what is meant by 'intellect' has led many Westerners to complain that the Hindu doctrines are inhuman and arid, in that their emphasis is upon knowledge rather than upon love and worship. Once we realize that, by intellect, something of the intuitive, rather than of the rational order is meant, we must see that the 'knowledge' of which these scriptures speak is a total awareness, attained only through the dedication of all our powers, and that it is not, in any sense, a matter of entertaining certain ideas or of being informed of certain facts; it is a transforming knowledge, for, at its touch, the whole personality takes new shape. Aware only of the ordinary world in which we live and of the feelings and impressions which that world calls up in us, we are what we are; aware of something totally different, we cannot but become different. The Sanskrit word 'vidya' means, not only knowledge, but vision and awareness in the widest sense and a release into boundless freedom; 'avidya', its opposite, is confinement within the narrow bounds set by the mind and the senses.

If the language describing the way which leads to this awareness is austere, it is hardly more so than that of the Christian mystics who speak of the naked intent—the aim devoid of feelings, images or preconceived notions—which must be brought to bear on the Divine or of the Catholic 'spiritual directors' who warn the beginner in contemplative prayer never to confuse 'feelings', however gratifying, with spiritual perceptions, and who recommend a 'dry, naked prayer'. Emotionalism in religion is always a sign of decadence and heresy.

But in all the Oriental doctrines, except, possibly, in Buddhism of the Hinayana school, which is essentially a monastic discipline, intended for the few, there is a recognition of the diversity of ways which lead to the one goal of knowledge or enlightenment. In theory and, to some extent, in practice there are as many ways as there are human individuals, for no man can set out on a journey except from the place in which he finds himself, and no man can build except upon the foundations with which he is supplied. The question of 'adequacy' or 'fitness' is central in all orthodox teaching in the East; the medicine that will bring one man to enlightenment might poison the very springs of another's life; the ideas and symbols which one man will assimilate almost effortlessly might prove a fatal stumbling-block to another. Always, in the early stages of any spiritual discipline, there is a very real danger of the man who undertakes it becoming unbalanced; perhaps certain inner forces may be aroused in him before he is equipped to deal with them, or perhaps he may repress, prematurely, some natural impulse which is quite strong enough to wreck the structure he has built over it; possibly, again, he may have come too soon to aspects of the doctrine which are beyond his powers of understanding and, misinterpreting them, been led away into a blind alley. All this should make it clear why such emphasis is laid upon the need for personal instruction under a qualified teacher.

The Oriental doctrines are, potentially, wide and universal as truth itself (that is why they appear 'unsystematic' to anyone trained in Western philosophy), and they contain that which corresponds to the spiritual needs and capacities of every type of human being, but that does not mean that they may be altered so as to bring them into line with, for example, modern science or American humanism; it is one thing to adapt a particular doctrine to a particular human personality, but quite another to adapt it to ways of thought which are in direct opposition to it, or, in other words, to adapt truth to error.

The diversity of individual 'ways' (and, in consequence, the diversity of aspects which the doctrine contains) are generally grouped by the Hindus under three main headings; the way of knowledge and mental effort (jnana marga), the way of love and worship (bhakti marga) and the way of works and sacrifice (karma marga). These three ways correspond to three main human types, the intellectual, the passionate and the practical, or again, to the man in whom mental activity predominates, to the man who lives by his feelings and emotions, and to the man of action; but just as these three types are seldom found in a pure form, so the three ways merge into each other, and just as the man of action must necessarily be impelled either by ideas and principles or by his feelings and reactions, so the follower of the 'karma marga' is at the same time a follower, to some extent, of one of the other two ways—his work and his sacrifice are inspired either by the love of God or by knowledge of the divine laws. It is also worth noting that, in the same way that sensitive and emotional characters require the framework either of social custom or of religious belief if they are to maintain a certain order and balance in their lives, so the follower of the 'bhakti marga' needs the framework of the traditional doctrine which is his heritage or he may fall into sentimentality and lose all sense of proportion.

A very brief consideration of the history of Christianity should be sufficient to suggest that, in the Western world, the way of love has generally taken precedence over the way of knowledge; and certainly in modern Christianity (since the Middle Ages, that is to say) religious emotion and moral ideals have thrust the doctrine so far into the background that it is almost forgotten, and the vast number of Christians think of their faith exclusively in terms of 'feeling religious' and 'being good' (it is only fair to say that, in the last twenty years, there has been something of a reaction against this, and theologians such as Maritain, Berdyaev and Karl Barth are in the forefront). In spite of this, the Westerner generally approaches the Oriental doctrines from their most austerely 'intellectual' side.

Out of every ten people in the West who have studied the Hindu doctrines, at least eight have confined themselves almost entirely to the extreme point of view represented by Shankara's commentaries upon the Upanishads and the Brahma-Sutras. This may be due to a fundamental sense of superiority, very difficult to shake off, which makes us feel that only the best is good enough for us and that leads us, when we condescend to study an alien faith, to ask at once what is the 'highest' that this faith has to offer and to ignore all that savours of popular superstition. It may be that Shankara presents the Vedantic doctrine—the doctrine, that is, of the Vedas and the Upanishads—in its purest and most rarefied form, but it remains questionable whether any of us in the West or, for that matter, more than a very few in the East, are able to receive the pure essence of the teaching.

When those who have not reached a stage in their personal development at which a particular interpretation of the doctrine answers a genuine spiritual need encounter such an interpretation, they must inevitably misinterpret it. This fact, and not a desire to keep the cream of the faith to themselves, is the reason for the reticence which teachers in Eastern countries have always shown in communicating their knowledge to others. The writings of Shankara provide a case in point; they were composed as an aid to the student in his study of the Upanishads under a qualified teacher, and even in India the results of their publication have been far from fortunate.

Writing half a century ago of those of his co-religionists who, through overweening spiritual pride, attempted to follow the extreme 'Vaidic path' (which was the path of Shankara), the learned Hindu author of the 'Tantra Tattva' complained that 'Many a spiritually disposed man who . . . has attempted to become a Yogi along the Vaidic path has ended by becoming neither a believer nor an unbeliever, but a queer being, half-man, half-lion. By constant meditation upon a misty nothing, his mind and heart become such a vacuity that there is neither faith, reverence, devotion nor love in them'. He likens such men, who, through their failure to achieve anything upon their ill-chosen way, judge the Vaidic path to be useless, to one who supposes a tree to be without fruit when he has searched no higher than its roots; he adds that only he who is capable of reaching its topmost branches will find the fruit, but that one may yet obtain it 'if one has but faith in the existence of the fruit, and takes up one's abode in the tree's shade'. He remarks that those who try prematurely to over-leap the 'dualistic world' will fall to earth with broken bones; certainly, he says, the world is 'false', but the question is 'Who may and may not say it is false?' meaning that only those who have become aware of a more intense reality have earned the right to speak of this one as false.

The same author, a Hindu writing for Hindus, adds a further warning, which is worth quoting since it shows a side of Hinduism of which the Westerner who has confined his attention to such authors as Shankara is too little aware. After complaining that everyone wants to be a Yogi, because pride will not allow them to take a lower place, he continues, 'The kind of dissatisfaction with the Sangsára (that is, the world-flow) which one occasionally feels before entry upon the path of spiritual knowledge is not dispassion, but only passion in a different guise. Hence the fool who, on feeling such dissatisfaction, wants to forsake the Sangsára . . . only sticks in the meshes of that net, and resting half within and half without it loses his life. . . . It therefore becomes an intelligent person not to make futile efforts to tear the net, but to endeavour to move about happily in the water within the net. If by the grace of the Devi (Mistress of the Universe) you gain the strength which will enable you to dive into deep water . . . then Maheshvara (the Lord), who holds the thread of this net, will Himself undo its top-knot. . . . Just as death does not wait for anyone's permission, so liberation does not wait for anyone's comment'.

Speaking of Liberation (we shall see later how this term is to be understood) as the fruit of human development, he says 'When the fruit appears the flower dries up of itself and falls. . . . But how wonderful must be the intensity of the greed and the impatience and hurry of those who, on seeing this, understand the flower to be of no use and proceed to destroy it the moment it has blown?'

These quotations should be sufficient to show that the Hindu doctrines are not altogether, in Albert Schweizer's phrase, 'world-and-life-denying'; the discipline which they teach is a discipline strictly adapted to time and condition, and its aim is in no way to produce spiritual abortions. When a man can say, with Jalalu 'din Rumi the Sufi, 'I am cramped like an embryo in the womb: I have come to be nine months old; this migration has become urgent', it is time enough for him to put the world and all the things of the world behind him.

But discipline of some kind there must be, at every stage; and all discipline is to some extent ascetic. Asceticism is opposed, not to enjoyment, but to attachment; it requires a process of simplification and calls upon us to renounce those things which we cannot bind up into the integrated whole of our lives, those things, in fact, which we cannot rightly use. It is the pursuit of objects, and not our enjoyment of them, that is condemned as dissipating our vital energies. 'Claim nothing!' says the Isa Upanishad, 'Enjoy, do not covet His property'. And Meister Eckhardt, the great Christian mystic of the fourteenth century, tells us, 'It is permissible to take life's blessings with both hands provided thou dost know thyself prepared in the opposite event to leave them just as gladly'. It is interesting in this connection to observe that one Indian rule which demanded strict continence in its followers, recommended them, if a woman were to offer herself to them, to go in to her; for to resist would be to become involved with their own self-centred wills. The neo-Brahmin hero of Somerset Maugham's novel, *The Razor's Edge*, follows this precept.

There is a point at which asceticism and abandon meet. Asceticism seeks to release men from the self-centred individuality which is intensified by the search for pleasure and riches in the world; abandon would release them from a similar intensification of the ego-sense which comes from resistance to —and a defensive attitude against—the natural impulses of our own hearts; in self-denial, the emphasis rests too often upon the word 'self'. To a lesser extent, we find the same paradox in Christianity; St. Catherine of Siena was at one period of her life tormented by visions of fiends who filled her cell 'with obscene words and gestures inviting her to lust'; so long as she opposed them, they continued against her; but when at last she surrendered her self-will and was prepared to accept them, they fled away; she who had been tightly bound up in her own defensiveness relaxed, and was at once free. De Caussade, a Roman Catholic divine of the eighteenth century, in a book called *Abandonment to Divine Providence*, advocates self-abandon to the will of God even to the extent of joyfully accepting insanity should Providence so decree.

These two methods of attaining freedom; that of ascetic renunciation and that of abandon, meet in the Eastern doctrines when we are counselled to accept whatever comes to us, whether from within or without, but not to run after it or mourn its departure. It is a question, always, of moving with the rhythm of life and of our own being, instead of setting up the turmoil of a counter-motion which springs from our own self-will. But this submission is the most difficult thing in the world; Arjuna, in the Hindu Bhagavad-Gita, is commanded to accept whatever fate may bring him, but he is called, in his actions, to a terrible and uncompromising purity of intention; the Taoist follows the Way of Heaven, trying to run like water in the channels carved for him, but, in a world which, for the most part, runs counter to that way, obedience to the Tao is no easy path; Zen Buddhism would make a man free as the wind, but it takes its illustrations from fencing and wrestling.

But generalizations, when one is dealing with so wide and varied a scene, are dangerous, and before we can make a closer study of the place which man occupies in the setting of the Oriental doctrines, we must consider one particular doctrine, that of the Hindus, in greater detail. There is a story that Socrates once met an Indian philosopher and told him that he was occupied upon an inquiry into the nature of man; 'No one', answered the Hindu, 'can understand things human who does not first understand things divine'. It is with this primary and essential understanding that the Vedas and the Upanishads—the traditional scriptures of India—are concerned.

CHAPTER TWO

THE SOURCE OF LIGHT

He, the highest Person, who is awake in us while we are asleep, shaping one glory after another, that indeed is the Bright, that is Brahman, that alone is called the Immortal.—KATHA UPANISHAD.

First and last, according to the doctrine of the Vedanta, within the centre and yet enclosing the circumference of the circle in which all things have their being, is the infinite Brahman. Since It is infinite, there can be nothing before or after It, and nothing outside It. All things that exist, that have ever existed or that could ever exist are a partial and fragmentary showing forth of the possibilities which It includes within Itself.

This Brahman is not 'One', not simple unity, for the ideas of oneness and unity are notions conceived in our limited minds, and Brahman is limitless; It is called 'That', since no qualifying name is truly applicable to It, and it is described as 'non-dual', since such terms as unity and duality are equally meaningless in relation to It. It is beyond all that we can think or say of It (yet nothing that we think or say can fail to be true of some aspect of It); 'The eye does not go thither', say the Upanishads, 'nor speech, nor mind. We do not know'. And again, 'The ignorant think that It lies within knowledge; the wise man knows It beyond knowledge.' Every attempt at definition is considered to be misleading, for by defining anything we limit it; ' "That" is to be described by "No!" "No!" '. Every word is inadequate, and we are silenced; every thought is inadequate, and the mind is stilled; every feeling is inadequate, and our senses are suspended; only then does the essence of all our faculties, that which lies at their root and from which they have grown, emerge from the shell of words, thoughts and feelings to reveal its true nature and find its true fulfilment. The moment passes; life flows again into the channels of words, thoughts and feelings, but the more avidly these worldly powers try to hold on to what has been revealed, the more surely does it escape them. The cry of 'Not this! Not that!' echoed so frequently in the Upanishads, is a confession, not of ignorance, but of the breakdown of human language before the memory of that experience.

When words are used to communicate the shadow of what has been seen, they are used not to define but to indicate, each word an arrow pointing beyond itself; they should be written upon water, lest the word, remaining too long before our eyes, should beguile us into stopping at it and into mistaking the sign for that which is signified. It is the same with concepts as with words; in the West we have sought to enclose reality within theory and concept; in the East the concept is, as it were, open at both ends, a pipe through which the living waters may flow. These pipes may be seen by every passer-by, their names learnt by rote; but the water will only flow for the man whose long devotion has fitted him to receive it. Rites and ceremonies, systems and moralities, theories and dogma—all these are rungs on a ladder which lead far beyond them to a region where speech, action and even thought are lost, not in the clouds, but in matchless clarity.

However far beyond our horizon—the horizon of the ordinary man—that clarity may lie, we must never attribute to it the mistiness that is before our eyes when we peer at things beyond their range; the mist is within us. But our point of view—with its limited horizon—has its own truth, a relative one, but none the less valid so long as it is assigned to its proper place and so long as we do not try to impose upon the final truth the limitations of our ignorance. Nothing is more confusing to the student of the Hindu scriptures than the sudden changes in the point of view from which reality is envisaged; at one moment, Brahman is spoken of as It is in Itself, and all else becomes shadowy and unreal in comparison; at the next, since we can only start out from the place in which we find ourselves, the writer takes up our point of view, from which the light beyond the horizon seems darkness and the real, unreal.

Naturally, statements that are valid from one point of view are invalid from another. What is true for the dreamer is untrue for the waking man; yet the dreamer can only be instructed in terms of his dream, the awakened man in terms of waking life. And when there are dreams within dreams, and an awakening beyond waking, a multitude of different points of view must arise, and so a multitude of relative truths which lead, in the growing light, to the One Light of which all others are a reflection, whether bright or dim.

A relative point of view (as opposed to the absolute one, which takes its stand in the Supreme Brahman) arises as soon as the process of creation is to be considered; but to make the picture of this process more complete than it could be if we confined ourselves to viewing it from a single position, a number of different points of view are taken up, rather as though one were to photograph the same object from a number of different angles in order to make up a composite picture; hence the diversity of 'creation myths'. But one thing is constant in almost every account of the creative process; the Brahman that is, to the knower of It, an all-inclusive splendour, seems from our point of view—that of beings who have come up into existence out of a pre-natal darkness and are not yet on the 'path of return'—the very opposite; ignorant of our source, we think of it as darkness; clinging to our small possessions, we think of that plenitude as privation; and so the Brihadaranyaka Upanishad says, 'In the beginning, nothing whatsoever was here. All this was veiled by Death, by Privation. . . . "That" took on Intellect, and thought "Let me be Selfed!"'

This text may be more easily understood if we call to mind a modern psychological theory; 'Consciousness', says C. G. Jung, 'is derived from the Unconscious'. Just so, Consciousness or Intellect is described by the Upanishads as arising within the absolute Brahman; the great 'I am!' is spoken, and from the 'That' of which nothing can be said there arises Being, the Divine Intellect or Selfhood, called by us 'The Lord' (Ishvara), and the first step in the process of manifestation has taken place. 'The Father', says Meister Eckhardt, 'is the manifestation of the Godhead', which comes to the same thing, stated in Christian terms.

But although we, who are creatures of time, can only speak of this process in terms of time and in the images of human mortality, it must be realized that the derivation of God from Godhead, and the stages which follow it, do not take place in time; it is an order, not of succession, but of arrangement; Brahman is prior to Ishvara only in the sense in which the greater is prior to the less, including and transcending it. To quote Eckhardt once again, 'God and Godhead are as distinct as Heaven and Earth, and so the Godhead is above God', and this was said, not in some learned treatise, but in a sermon preached before an ordinary medieval congregation.

The same Upanishadic text continues, 'He, the Self, manifested Light. Of Him, as He shone, were the Waters born'. Even in the West, we frequently speak of consciousness as a light which shines upon the mind and senses, and it is clear that, in this passage, 'born' might be replaced by the word 'revealed'. This All, which was, from our point of view, veiled in darkness and therefore non-existent (if we understand by 'existence' a 'standing out', which is, after all, its literal meaning), is illuminated by the shining of the Divine Self (as it is, in part, by the awareness of our individual selves), and the dawn light of creation reveals a few of those possibilities of existence, infinite in number, which lay dormant in the absolute Brahman. A boundless expanse of waters is the commonest symbol for this infinity of 'possibilities', indeed it is one of the most universal of symbols; and hardly less universal is that of the sun, denoting the light by which all things are revealed or brought to birth.

To complete the picture, a third symbol, also taken from the world of the senses, is added to those of Sun ('Supernal Sun') and Waters ('Primordial Ocean'); it is that of the Wind ('Vayu', in the Hindu scriptures) or Breath of God, the 'spirit of God' which moves upon the face of the waters in the Hebrew Genesis. This wind—according to the symbolism which we are considering—breaks up the smooth surface of the sea, and so shatters the still reflection of the bright sun. Waves rise and clash; the ocean stirs in tumult, and short-lived islands of foam are formed. Where once there was only the sun above and the sun's exact reflection below, there are now innumerable facets of water to reflect the heavenly brightness; there is a sparkling diversity of flashing and reflecting surfaces. The one light has become many lights.

Traditional symbolism is never a closed system, for its terms are fluid and susceptible of different applications, but it is always precise. We shall see later that the movement of the Waters, and therefore the manner in which their surface catches the light, is causally determined; we shall see also to what significant conclusions the fact that each tiny reflecting surface is connected to the sun (which has 'brought it to light') by a particular ray, leads; and should this symbolism seem strange and alien to our mentality, we may take note of the words of Dionysius, quoted by St. Thomas Aquinas—'God sends out upon each creature, together with a certain flashing, a distribution of his luminous "raying", which is the font of all light'—and see if this point of Christian doctrine does not help our understanding of the Hindu symbolism.

In place of 'Sun' and 'Waters', the Hindu scriptures speak sometimes of 'Purusha' and 'Prakriti'; terms that may be roughly translated as 'Person' and 'Nature' respectively, or as 'Essence' and 'Substance'. Purusha is the light which at once reveals and gives form, and in this it typifies what, in the Far East, is called 'actionless activity', in that it acts simply by its presence, by shedding its light. Movement, on the other hand, belongs to Prakriti, which multiplies the single, unchanging light into a diversity of shifting, dancing reflections. It is by the interaction of these two principles, Essence and Substance (the Scholastic terms), Purusha and Prakriti (the Sanskrit names) or Sun and Waters (the universal symbols), that the multiplicity of things is produced from the divine Unity.

It is clear that the frequently quoted Hermetic saying, 'As above, so below', equivalents for which can be found in every tradition, depends upon the doctrine of reflection. What is 'in Heaven' exists, as a reflection, whether perfect or imperfect, on Earth, since all the things of this world are shadows of the realities included in the divine Unity; these realities correspond, fairly exactly, to Plato's 'ideas'; and the medieval Christian theory of aesthetics, based as it was upon the belief that the beauty of any object depends upon the perfection of its proper form, its ugliness (and uselessness, for the two things cannot be divided) upon a deformity or lack of form, is also in line with this teaching. What has been said of inanimate objects applies also to man, whose goal, as we shall see when considering the Hindu teaching with regard to 'dharma', is to realize to the fullest possible extent his due form and so to actualize the divine idea which his existence bodies forth.

Here also is the explanation of the discipline of craftsmanship as practised both by the Oriental artist and by the 'primitive' artisan. By his 'journey to Heaven', the artist comes to know, within the very heart of his own being, the form of the thing he is to make; to confine himself to making a 'copy of a copy', as would be the case if he simply drew or carved a representation of what met his eyes, would seem to him contemptible; he has a higher notion of human dignity, and believes that man may take, in his daily work, the same models that were the Creator's when He made the world.

When this same artist or artisan, being civilized, becomes a coolie or a factory-worker, something far more serious than a sacrifice of quality to quantity takes place, though that is bad enough. The things made are now dead things, cut off from the source of life and being; they are not even truly useful, for man is both spirit and body-mind, and to be useful an object must serve both his natures, which means that it must have been made by a man who exercised both his natures in the making of it. Just as the good man affects all those around him, so does the object that is well made and truly formed affect those who make use of it; and just as the evil man contaminates those around him, so does the deformed object contaminate those who use it. It is sentimental and idealistic in the worst sense to suppose that we can divorce ourselves from the material objects amongst which we live or to think that men can live a truly human life unless the things which they use and come into contact with in their daily lives have upon them the mark of Heaven.

But it is not only these commonplace objects that must either remain attached to their divine prototypes or else fall into chaos and deformity; the manner in which they should be used is determined, in a 'primitive' or traditional society, by an archetypal divine activity. 'We must do what the gods did erst'; this, and not, as the moderns suppose, a desire to placate the deity or to procure a 'psychological effect', is the meaning of ritual. In such a society there is, under the normal conditions of life, a method of action which is regarded as orderly and regular, and there are others which are considered disorderly and irregular; it is believed that the former helps to maintain the total equilibrium of the world, and that the latter make for universal chaos. For an action to be orderly means that it is ordered to its true end and is thus in conformity with what the Hindus call 'rita', the order of the Whole.

Enough has been said to show that the 'creation myth' discussed above embodies not merely a theory, but a way of action. In the modern world, though we may be prepared to consider the theory, we are unwilling to give serious consideration to the applications which follow logically from it. Yet many of our objections are based purely upon misunderstanding; we may ask, for example, why, if the different human societies which believe that, in their methods of building a house or in the postures they adopt in sexual intercourse, they are imitating the 'action of the gods', are really doing so, these methods and postures should vary from one part of the world to another; to ask this question is to forget that a direct imitation of the divine powers is impossible to the creature of flesh and blood, but that our buildings and our intercourse, according to the traditional view of the matter, correspond, within the limitations of human life, to certain types of divine action—action which we can imitate only in accordance with the particular conditions imposed upon us by racial temperament, geographical position and so forth. The Eskimo and the Negro will not build the same kind of dwelling, for their needs are different, as are the materials with which they work, but both may be making copies, so far as these needs and these materials permit, of the archetypal House of God.

All this may seem far removed from the metaphysical abstractions which are generally thought to form the substance of the Vedanta; we like to keep the different aspects of our lives in separate compartments, leaving the metaphysician to amuse himself in his study, the artist with his designs and the lover with his playmate; and those who realize that such a state of things breeds sterility all round—that the metaphysician becomes a dry stick, the artist frivolous and the lover bored, when they are left to themselves—run too easily to the other extreme, trying to break down the natural divisions which exist in human experience and allowing everything to merge and coalesce, so that no kind of order remains; it is by this process, for example, that metaphysics is reduced to a sentimental 'philosophy of life' or that sexuality is surrounded with a vaguely mystical aura of false idealism.

In the traditional doctrines of the East, the divisions are recognized and respected, but there is a connecting link which binds together the different levels of human experience, and there is a sense of hierarchy which maintains a proper order between these levels. There is no question here of the 'lower' being sublimated into the 'higher', but all the elements of our make-up are required to conform, each in its own terms, to the order of the whole and to reflect, each upon its own level, the realities of which all life is, as it were, a revelation. Intellect, mind, emotion and sensuality are regarded as so many tongues with which the human being may praise God; these tongues are different, but the meaning which they express in their different ways is the same.

But the moment has come to ask why, if Brahman is, as the Hindu teaching asserts, perfect and complete in Itself, the process of manifestation should ever come about. Why should the mysteries hidden in the Godhead have to be played out on a stage, subject to so many limitations?

Several answers are provided, answers that seem to conflict with each other, until one realizes that the answer one receives depends upon the point of view from which the question has been asked. For the 'knower of Brahman', there is no question; the innumerable spheres of creation are, for him, little more than optical delusions, for everything is Brahman and there is nothing apart from It, although to us, whose sight is afflicted, our world seems separate and outcast; similarly, for the Buddhist who has reached the final vantage point, the world and what he calls 'the Void' are one, illusion and knowledge are one, bondage and release are one. This, though true for the 'knower of Brahman' and for the man who has inwardly become the very Buddha, though his outward appearance and personality continue to play their part on the world stage, is not true for us; and the question that no longer has any meaning for them, is real to us.

The Upanishads, for the most part, adopt this absolute position. Brahman, they insist, is so all-inclusive that it cannot be set over against diversity as something opposed to it; It is a unity of which even the utmost diversity is a partial aspect; a unity to which the words of Blake might be applied—'Everything possible to be imagined is an image of the truth'. But through 'avidya' we are in bondage, say the Upanishads, to a half-truth, and we allow ourselves to become the slaves of a nature that is the product of our own distorted vision. Brahman is like a magic box from which whatever we choose to imagine comes forth to plague us, and 'Man binds himself with himself as a bird is bound with a snare'.

But the doctrine of 'avidya' does not explain the existence

of beings capable of illusion and able to think of themselves as separate from their source. We have to come to a more human point of view before we can find an answer that is humanly satisfying; and from this point of view the Hindu scriptures ascribe creation to the 'play' ('lila') of the Divine. It is said that the ultimate Being has revealed an image of Itself in a spirit of joyful play, and this prodigal creation is an expression of the fundamental nature of that Being. It is dancing feet—the feet, it is said, of Shiva Nataraja, King of the Dance—that set the dust of multiplicity whirling. It is interesting to compare with this the words of Eckhardt, when he speaks of God's delight in creation; 'The joy and satisfaction of it are ineffable. It is like a horse turned loose in a lush meadow giving vent to his horse-nature by galloping full-tilt about the field: he enjoys it, and it is his nature. And just in the same way God's joy in his likes finds vent in his pouring out his entire nature and his being into this likeness. . . .' And again, turning back to the Eastern scriptures, we find in the Rig Veda (7.87.2), 'The Gale that is thyself thunders through the firmament like an untamed stag that takes his pleasure in the fields' (quoted from Coomaraswamy; *A New Approach to the Vedas*).

There may appear to be a discrepancy between those accounts of the world process which make it something purely subjective (as in the Hindu teachings on 'avidya' and in a good deal of Buddhist doctrine) and those which recognize an objective creation. But the discrepancy is more apparent than real. A doctrine which maintains that the ultimately real is a unity in which the antithesis of subject and object is transcended, and that our life and the environment in which it is lived out are both reflections of this unity, cannot allow the antithesis anything beyond a purely practical role in the scheme of things.

Modern psychology, in the West, has done a good deal to break down the notion of a hard and fast line dividing the subjective sphere from the objective; in some of its branches, it has made such wide use of the theory of 'projection'—the theory that we project upon our environment a great deal that really belongs within the psyche—that the environment itself has been left as little more than a skeleton which we are presumed to clothe in flesh. But this psychology has also recognized a reverse process, whereby outside things are absorbed and treated as though they were a part of our inner selves, and it seems in practice to produce a chart on which, if we mark out two poles to represent subject and object, the line of demarcation between their respective spheres is continually shifting. It is a short step from this to a recognition of human experience as an indivisible whole in which the elements (the thoughts, feelings and so forth) which, for convenience, we call subjective and those which we call objective merge into each other.

For the Hindu doctrines, experience is indeed an indivisible whole, and the real 'subject', 'the witness in the heart', is a light which shines from above on to the field which we divide so neatly into 'subjective experience' and 'objective fact'. It is from this point of view that the theory of cycles and world ages may best be approached, if we are to realize that this theory is less easily disproved than might at first appear. Each Day of Brahma—the Day which begins with the shining of the Supernal Sun on the Primordial Waters, and ends with the reabsorption of all things into the original Unity—is divided by the Hindus into a thousand 'Maha-Yugas', and each of these is in its turn divided into four 'yugas' or world ages, strictly comparable to the Golden, Silver, Brass and Iron Ages of Western mythology, but called, in India, the 'Krita', 'Tretá', 'Dvápara' and 'Kali' ages, these names being derived from the four throws of the dice game.

The course of the 'Maha-Yuga' or cycle flows downwards from a state of completeness, integration and ordered perfection to one of privation, disintegration and chaos, till it reaches the very brink of dissolution into nothingness and is only saved by the divine intervention which brings the cycle to a close and initiates a new one. The initial stage is one in which quality predominates over quantity, and in which diversity is included in unity; the final stage is one in which multiplicity and division have reached their maximum, and in which, since diversity of form comes from above, a terrible uniformity reigns. For example, humanity, at the beginning of the cycle, enjoys the richest possible diversity and yet lives in the utmost harmony; towards the close, men become as alike as peas in a pod, yet are in perpetual conflict with each other because they have lost the unity of spirit which alone makes fruitful communication between different beings possible. At the beginning men lie open to all the influences of Heaven; at the close, they are open only to those of the infernal regions.

This theory, commonplace a few centuries ago, now seems strange to us, but it clearly shows why the races that still hold to it set such store by their traditional ways and rituals. For we are said to be in the Dark Age, the 'Kali Yuga', and tradition is the one thing that has been handed down to us from those early days of pristine perfection. So long as the connecting link of tradition is maintained, the world order cannot altogether disintegrate; but when that tradition, which is believed to linger on in the great religions and in the myths and rituals of 'primitive peoples', is totally lost, the end will be upon us. It should be added that, when the pace of the descent becomes altogether too fast and furious, an 'avatara' or descent of the divine principle into human life is believed to take place, in order that the balance of things may be restored.

Obviously, there can be no question of proving a theory of this kind, but can it be disproved? The changes said to take place are not confined to a single aspect of things; they are changes in what we have called the experience-whole—in man, in his environment, and in the ideas which he forms regarding his environment. And if any relics of earlier world ages remain, they, like everything else, must have undergone a change bringing them into line with the present state of the cosmic order. Or, to take another example, scientific calculations as to the age of the earth are based upon the assumption that the properties of matter were the same a million years ago as they are to-day; if, as the Hindu theory implies, those properties were quite different, then all such calculations are invalid.

However, this is not the moment to enter upon a lengthy discussion of the relative merits of the traditional theory of cycles and the modern theory of evolution; the important point is that a great deal of Hindu doctrine is comprehensible only in the light of the former theory. From this point of view, it may be said that there exist three main types of human society in the modern world; first, there are the traditional civilizations, such as that of India, in which the pure doctrine handed down from the primordial age is still the possession of a few men, but in which the masses have fallen into superstition, that is to say, they no longer fully understand the rituals which they continue to practise; secondly, there are the 'primitive' peoples who are, according to this theory, not primitive but decadent, and to whom the higher elements of the traditional doctrines are completely lost, although the doctrine itself lives on in myths and legends which can no longer be interpreted by the people who cherish them; and finally, there is the modern Western world, which denies any validity to tradition (there are, as René Guénon has remarked, denials that resemble cries of rage).

The cycles which, according to the Hindus, follow each other throughout the Day of Brahmá, and the Days of Brahmá, which are infinite in number, do not start out with a clean slate. To return for a moment to the symbolical representation of the creation as a movement of the Waters in the light of the Supernal Sun, the wind which stirs the Waters, and so determines the direction of their movement, is a wind out of the past, generated by the events of the preceding Day (it is, of course, only figuratively that one can speak of this in terms of time, since time, as we understand it, comes to an end at the close of a Day).

Whatever the inimitable Freud may have had to say of 'repression', he certainly never went so far as to conceive the reality behind appearances as something having a hunger for expression and containing an infinity of possibilities which may, in innumerable spheres of being, take form and enjoy existence. Yet, according to traditional doctrine, the infinite possibilities contained in the womb of Being require an infinite number of theatres in which to play out their various roles. From our point of view the treasures emptied out of that magic and bottomless pit onto the fields of time degenerate in the course of a cycle of human experience; the gold and gems of the 'Krita Yuga' are succeeded, in this 'Kali Yuga', by pebbles and trash; but, from a point of view beyond time, every cycle must fulfil its predestined course, revealing not only the glories of God, but also the lower possibilities of existence, the dregs, which have their right to play their part, as have, in our human society, the madman and the criminal; for, in terms of our narrow utilitarianism, the ways of God are indeed past finding out.

It is from all the possibilities that have found expression in a particular cycle that there are crystallized the seeds of the cycles to come; and, in the Night of Brahmá, when, as it is said, all things are encysted and hidden, it is the unfulfilled potentialities that gnaw and irritate until a new outlet is found for them and a new Day dawns. What we do in our own time not only determines our own future and the modes of existence in which our own being will find expression, but also, since we are not in any real sense separate from the whole, contributes to the sum of circumstances which direct the course of worlds beyond our imagining. It is an inconceivably vast system of inter-dependent spheres that the Hindu doctrines propose, and the repercussions which they attribute even to the slightest of our gestures are limitless.

In relation to the tremendous diversity of created things, the divine functions and qualities must inevitably appear to us under the form of multiplicity; and the further we are from the single source of light, the greater the number of different aspects under which we perceive its action in the world and the greater our need to take, as an object of worship, some particular and limited aspect of the universal Brahman. It is in answer to this need that the pantheon of Hinduism, with its innumerable gods and godlings, has come into being, so that those for whom the idea of the One Lord is too vague and too remote may rise, first through worship of a godling, friendly and close, and then through that of a god, splendid and omnipotent, to the realization that 'all the gods are one', and even beyond to That in which Lord and creature are one. But there are three particular aspects of the divinity which take precedence over the rest; the trinity of Brahmá, Vishnu and Siva.

Brahmá is essentially the creative principle; his role is entirely positive, for he is revelation incarnate and is never represented as destroying what he has created; at the beginning of his Day, he is born in a Lotus which rises up from the Waters or from the navel of the reclining Godhead, and he undertakes his task in a spirit of piety and devotion.

Vishnu is a far more complex divinity, and is frequently used as a representation of the Godhead in all Its universality, but his function, when he is considered in relation to the other members of the trinity, is primarily that of preserving the universal order and balance; he adjudicates between the forces of Light and those of Darkness, and he keeps all things in being until their time is come. In his incarnation as Krishna, he defeats the great serpent Káliya, who had set out to destroy the world, but it is not his role to annihilate the serpent force; Káliya tells him, 'As you created me with strength and endowed me with poison, so I have behaved. Had I acted otherwise, I should have violated the laws laid down by you for every creature according to its kind; I should have challenged the order of the universe . . .'; and so Vishnu, as Krishna, limits the serpent's power, adjusting the frontier line between demons and men.

Siva, although, like Vishnu, he is frequently represented as ambivalent, comprehending within himself all the divine aspects and qualities, is, on the whole, a darker figure and is called the Destroyer of the Universe. But what, from one point of view, seems to be destruction, is transformation from another; and although Siva seems a terrible figure to us, who cling to what we have and fear the unknown, he is also the bringer of peace and the leader on the way to Liberation.

Both Vishnu and Siva have many worshippers specially devoted to their service (Brahmá, the creator, is too one-sided in character to be taken as a symbol of the universal Brahman), but perhaps the most popular object of worship, at least in modern Hinduism, is the Mother of the World, the Maya-Shakti or creative power that veils the eternal in transient forms of existence, spoken of as Parvati (who is the consort of Siva) or, in her more terrible aspects, as Kali, the Black One, and, again, as Durga or Uma. That the creative principle should be regarded as female is in keeping with the Oriental belief that contemplation is proper to the Male and activity to the Female, and the gods of the trinity are often represented as rapt in trance while their various Shaktis, their consort-energies, build and transform the worlds of time.

It is impossible to summarize the conflicting characteristics of Kali, who seems, at one moment, an ogress, at another a young girl of surpassing loveliness; she is a mother who not only cherishes, but consumes her children, a goddess who shows forth the wrath and the majesty, the gentleness and the compassion, the beauty and the terror of the Lord. She is represented as a black figure, her long tongue out to lick up the world, with sharp fangs for her teeth, yet with a body that is lithe and beguiling, and breasts big with milk, holding the sword of physical extermination and of spiritual decision and the scissors with which she cuts the thread of life (but also the thread of bondage); she carries also the bowl of abundant nourishment and a lotus to symbolize generation.

European sensibilities are generally shocked by the symbolism of Kali, yet it is hard to see why they should be. A really vivid representation of Christ bringing 'not peace, but the sword' would no doubt seem equally shocking. We who have been taught by Christianity that, to find our lives (or, in an alternative translation, 'our souls'), we must lose them, and that 'The word of God extends to the sundering of soul from spirit' (St. Paul), may take these counsels for 'figures of speech' and keep our imaginations closed to them; but in India it is fully recognized that the loss, whether of life or of 'soul', is destruction, and that destruction, even though the necessary prelude to all change and advance, is always terrifying to our emotions. Even at her most monstrous, Kali, decked with skulls and dripping with the blood of her victims, is midwife to the spirit and, as such, is cruel only to be kind.

But whatever forms the ultimate Being assumes for its worshippers, until they are able to know it as it is, and however various the ways which may be taken, whether through the jungle of passion or over the ascetic's desert, through water, signifying enjoyment, or fire, signifying purgation, the Lord behind the various masks is the same, and the Brahman, of which both Lord and creature are partial manifestations, set over against each other in mutual relation during Brahmá's Day, is eternal, infinite and unchanging, the source and goal of all that is.

CHAPTER THREE

THE GOLDEN PERSON

Having assumed light, he goes again to his place, the Golden Person, the lonely bird.

—Brihadaranyaka Upanishad.

Thus it has been said: That Golden Person who is within the Supernal Sun, and who from his golden station looks down upon this earth, is even he who dwells consuming food in the Lotus of the Heart.

—Maitri Upanishad.

It is said that, 'once upon a time', all things were held imprisoned in the coils of the Serpent called Ananta ('Endless') or Vritra. 'Once upon a time', that is 'agre' in Sanskrit, 'at the summit', 'in the first place', not merely once, but for all time; and for Serpent we may substitute Dragon, Rock, Tree or, to speak philosophically, First Principle. But a Second Principle was (and is) born, a son who will supplant his father, and his name is the Dragon-slayer. With his sword, which is both a ray of light (here we see the connection with the symbolism of Sun and Ocean) and a phallic weapon, he strikes the great Serpent of the deep and compels him to disgorge the riches of creation; or, in another formulation, he cleaves the Rock, so that the waters of life flow free, or fells the Tree and cuts it into logs.

In truth, slayer and slain are one, but, upon the stage on which creation is played out, they are enemies, and the slayer has committed a sin; it is such a sin as the heroes of Greek drama commit—one that could not be avoided, and yet for which atonement is required. The dismemberment of the Serpent was the First Sacrifice, whereby all things were brought into existence; the atonement is the Second Sacrifice, whereby all things existent are reintegrated into one whole.

This notion of the twin Sacrifices and of the rhythm which they imply is of central importance in the Hindu doctrine, particularly in relation to its teaching regarding man's life and his final end; it also shows why the Upanishads appear to invert the whole teaching of the Vedas, since the latter are primarily concerned with the First Sacrifice, the former with the Second. From the point of view which usually finds expression in the Vedas, man is thought of as having come up out of the darkness into the Light-world, or he has been lifted out of the formless chaos of the Waters into the Sun boat (the Sun's reflection in the Ocean), a boat which is the support of life and enjoyment; 'When I with Varuna embarked, drave out our ship into mid-ocean, rode on the crests of the waves; would that we yet swung there in the smooth-gliding swing for gladness, whereaboard Varuna set Vasistha in the clear-shining of the days, when Heaven and Earth, the Dawns and Dusks were warped' (Rg Veda, 7.88. Translated Coomaraswamy).

Such is the joy of release, when potentiality passes into act; and when, in another formulation of the myth, the settlers, released from the dark world by the First Sacrifice, cross a river to reach the farther shore, upon which the sun shines, their first act is to perform on this farther shore, this earth of enjoyment, a ritual imitation of that Sacrifice, so that the riches of existence may continue to flow.

But nothing remains stationary, and man's course does not end here; the womb was a dark prison compared with this daylight life, but now, ripe for a further journey, man begins to see this daylight as dark compared with a world of Light beyond. In terms of the earlier myth, the wealth which the Serpent was forced to disgorge is now dispersed in multiplicity, buried under the human mind and personality; the time has come for atonement, a Second Sacrifice, in which man surrenders his partial existence and is reintegrated into that ultimate reality in which there is no distinction between potentiality and act, Darkness and Light. And this is the point of view of the Upanishads.

This, then, is the rhythm of manifestation. What was unformed and inchoate takes on form, labours to perfect that form and to fulfil the possibilities which it encloses, and so passes out into the formless. The coming into form and the passage out of it are both essential movements of the spirit, and it is natural that, while from one point of view (that of most of the Vedas), the attainment of form or of existence is the highest good, from another (that of the Upanishads and of Buddhism) the goal is release from form—now perfected and finished—and the attainment of a good that cannot be confined within the limitations of any specific mould.

So long as we are not 'caught unawares' by the onward sweep of this process, both Sacrifices are to our advantage. By the first, we emerge from total unknowing into the partial knowledge provided by human experience; by the second, we break from the shell of limitation into a total awareness. It is significant that the Supernal Sun is spoken of, in innumerable myths, as a Serpent who has cast his skin; although that from which we came and that to which we go is, in truth, a single and unchanging plenitude, it is a mark of our evolution in time that we should start by thinking of it as a dreaded Serpent and end by seeing it as the life-giving Sun. It has not changed; but we have.

In our daily awareness, under the form of multiplicity, we daily dismember the Ancient Serpent who is also the One Light; and this is our sin, which we expiate by the Sacrifice from which the dismembered deity rises up whole again. 'There is thus', writes Coomaraswamy (*Hinduism and Buddhism*, p. 9), 'an incessant multiplication of the inexhaustible One and unification of the indefinitely Many. Such are the beginnings and endings of worlds and of individual beings: expanded from a point without position or dimensions and a now without date or duration, accomplishing their destiny, and when their time is up returning "home" to the Sea in which their life originated'. 'In other words', says the same author, writing of those who are taken up out of the Sea into the 'Sun-boat', 'we come forth as those who cannot swim and return as accomplished swimmers, at home in any waters'.

But we can only accept and rejoice in the Second Sacrifice if we have learned 'who we are'; only so can we know this death for a new birth, and only so can we partake in the victory and resurrection of the deity who was dismembered by our partial experience. 'Become what thou art' is the stern necessity laid upon all existent beings; and to become what, in truth, we are is to know 'who' we are—to become aware that, in the most frequently quoted of all the phrases in the Upanishads, ' "That" art thou!'

Man, in the Upanishads, is regarded not as a creature of the natural world, but as the vehicle or expression of an immortal and changeless spirit, the Atman, 'benign and tolerant, the silent witness in his heart'. All meaning in human life derives from and flows back to the Atman, which is itself unmoving. 'He who dwells within the seed, whom the seed does not know . . . and who rules the seed within, he is thy Self. There is no other seer but he, there is no other hearer but he, there is no other perceiver but he, there is no other knower but he'. This Self is the principle of all our life and of all our powers; the principle without which nothing in us could function. It is the eternal Subject; we may climb above our feelings and our thoughts so as to see them as objects, processes laid out beneath us, but the Self can never be an object and there exists nothing that could transcend it.

This Atman is uninvolved in its journey through human experience, just as the sun remains unaffected by the things upon which it shines; 'On being born, that Person, assuming his body, becomes united with all evils; when he departs and dies, he leaves all evils behind'. This Self is a pure awareness, and none of the storm and stress of which it is aware can really change it; all that we normally regard as 'ourselves'—the currents of thought and emotion, the movement of desire and will —all this is but the field in which the tent of the Self is, for a few years, pitched. We think that, because we have marked off a small area of ground beneath the tent, it is personal ground; but, according to the Upanishads, this, which modern science would say is all that there is of man, is nothing but the interplay of the forces of the earth; forces conditioned by their own laws, and no more exclusively ours than is the wind which eddies around us. Man, the true man, is elsewhere, and what he has been lent is not him or his.

'Now as a man when embraced by a beloved wife, knows nothing that is without, nothing that is within, so this person, when embraced by the Self, knows nothing that is without, nothing that is within'. And, 'He therefore that knows it, having become quiet, subdued, satisfied, patient and collected, sees self in Self, sees all as Self. Evil does not burn him, he burns all evil'. But the Self, say the Upanishads, with the perpetual demand which, by its very existence, it makes upon us, is obscured by the passage of time and by the changing multiplicity of things; 'as people who do not know the country walk again and again over a golden treasure that has been hidden somewhere in the earth and do not discover it', so we pass over the 'Golden Person' within us. 'In a glorious golden scabbard hides the stainless, indivisible, luminous spirit'. Yet however deep this unseen spirit lies, it is the pivot around which all our existence revolves; 'Life falls from Self as shadow falls from man'; everything that we experience is a development, a manifestation of that Self. 'It is I alone knit and enliven the body'; all is fixed in that centre, 'as are spokes in the hub of a wheel'.

It should be clear, from what has already been said, that 'Atman is Brahman'. The pivot of man and the pivot of the cosmos are the same. This, then, is 'who' we are; this Self, this Golden Person (who is 'within the Supernal Sun', yet also 'dwells consuming food in the Lotus of the Heart'), this Brahman—'That art thou!'

But the gulf which separates us, as we are, from the realization and full accomplishment of that unity, is tremendous, and we picture it as being spanned by a single narrow bridge, the 'razor-sharp bridge' of the Upanishads, the 'Brig o' Dread' of the Celtic tradition or that bridge provided for the North American Indian by the pathway of light which leads over the ocean to the setting sun. Here again we have to keep in mind the fact that this symbol, like so many others, may be employed in two contrasting ways; in the Vedas, it is generally the bridge that leads from the dark shore of chaos to the bright one of existence, and over it are driven the 'hidden kine' (the possibilities as yet unexpressed); in the Upanishads, it is the bridge connecting the worlds of time and eternity, over which the wayfarer passes on his journey.

That which is within, the Atman, seems to us far above; that which is closer to us than anything else, seems infinitely distant, and we can only think of ourselves as connected to it, if at all, by a thin thread; this is in fact the 'thread-spirit' (sutratman) of the Upanishads, upon which all beings and all worlds are said to be strung like the beads of a necklace. But the idea is not exclusively Oriental; 'I give you', wrote William Blake, 'the end of a golden string, Only wind it into a ball; it will lead you in at heaven's gate, built in Jerusalem's wall'. Gold is the colour assigned to the sun, and it is not difficult to see that this 'thread' is the same as that 'ray' of the Supernal Sun which connects the reflected image to its source. And this ray, as we have already seen, is called, in the Hindu tradition, 'buddhi'.

'Buddhi' is described as the first manifestation or determination of the 'Atman'; it represents the 'Atman', in what might be called a viceregal capacity, in relation to each particular individual. The nucleus of a living being ('jivatman') is determined —if we keep to the terms of this symbolism—by the intersection of 'buddhi' with a particular field of vital possibilities, which comes to the same thing as saying that it is the point at which a ray of the Supernal Sun strikes the surface of the Ocean; a kind of crystallization of certain of these vital possibilities is said to take place at this point, and this crystallization is the psycho-physical individual; for the rest, other elements of the environment are drawn in and assimilated and, in this little patch of light, a cycle of experience runs its course. When the light is extinguished, the nucleus breaks up and the various elements go back into circulation.

This might seem to suggest that there is no real relation between the individual, functioning upon a particular level of existence (in this case the human one), and the being of which he is supposed to be an expression; but this is by no means so. In the first place, both the particular level upon which the being reveals itself and the point, upon such a level, at which the crystallization takes place are strictly determined by the nature of the being itself. Secondly, it is assumed in all the Oriental traditions that the being simply uses the vital possibilities of its chosen environment in order to express its own nature—these possibilities are the material in which it works, and its work is to show forth, in a transient mode, the forms which it contains within itself.

Two things follow from this. Firstly, there is no such thing as chance or accident; whatever happens to a particular living being, though the event may seem to come upon him from outside and he has no control over it, is in fact in accordance with his nature and comes to him only, one might say, because he has summoned it, although here one must obviously take care to make sure to whom one is referring as 'he', for it is the total being (the Self), and not that fragment of it represented by the human personality, that has issued the summons.

Secondly, although the human personality, as an outward manifestation in the world, cannot be torn out of its environment and lifted up into Heaven (one might recall, here, the words of the Gospel, 'No man hath ascended up to heaven, but he that came down from heaven'), yet the principle, of which this personality was merely the illustration in terms of human life, remains ever-present in the Self; in the same way, although the physical body disintegrates at death and its elements return to the earth from which they had been borrowed, the 'body of glory', its principle and prototype, can never be lost.

The principles, then, of which all that evolves in the psychophysical fields of this world is an image wrought in the material of our experience, are eternally present at the centre of the being. But this centre must be more closely defined. The Hindu doctrine conceives each particular sphere of existence as expanded from a point to which no dimensions can be ascribed; this expansion unfolds what lies hidden in the 'point of power'. Man, as the microcosm, has his own centre, from which his powers and qualities fan out like the spokes of a wheel to the rim which is his outward form. The so-called World-wheel, which is itself a microcosmic image of the great wheel of universal manifestation, has also its centre, its spokes and its rim.

It follows that, the closer anything approaches to its centre, the greater is its intensity and the more closely is its diversity integrated into unity; the further it is from the centre, the wider is its extension and the looser is its integration. Just as the spokes converge towards the centre, so do the powers and qualities manifested in a particular sphere of existence converge towards their immediate principle; the rim of the wheel might be defined as representing the furthest possible extension, short of disintegration into nothingness—the Light at the centre is reflected at the rim, but beyond is only the outer darkness of dissolution.

But although the Light is single and there is but one centre—that 'point without dimensions'—for all things that are extended, we in our ordinary experience do not know our own centre to be one with all the others, any more than we know our Self to be the changeless Atman. So long as we are thinking in terms of the extended, manifested world, the centre of our being is only a cross-section of that Axis about which the innumerable wheels of existence revolve, an Axis extending between the two poles of manifestation ('Purusha' and 'Prakriti', 'Supernal Sun' and its image reflected in the 'Ocean'), which, in the words of the Rg Veda, 'pillars apart Heaven and Earth' and makes possible the evolution of all the worlds between. So long as the centre of our state is only one point on this Axis, so long is the central Light of our experience only a reflection of the Supreme Light; and if the movement of man's spirit is represented in terms of this diagram, we must say that it is a movement first towards the centre of an individual state, and that only from this central position is it possible to 'see', in the zenith, the primal Light.

In all traditional teaching, therefore, the first step in any spiritual advance is towards the possession of the human state in its fullness. 'Not till the soul knows all there is to be known', said Meister Eckhardt, 'can she pass over to the unknown good', and nothing short of a complete interior realization of all the possibilities belonging to our own particular sphere of existence will serve as a stepping-stone, either to the possession of other spheres, or to that ultimate station from which the 'knower of Brahman' surveys the total 'world picture, painted by the Self on the canvas of the Self'.

The meaning of such an 'interior realization' as this may be clarified by a brief consideration of what the psychologist C. G. Jung calls the process of 'individuation'. Jung starts out from the fact that most of us, at least in our conscious lives, are in possession of only a very small part of our humanity. He divides men into four main types—or rather, into eight, since each type may be either 'introvert' or 'extravert'—and he shows how each has over-developed certain of its powers and a certain aspect of its experience, at the expense of other powers and other aspects. In the man in whom thought predominates over feeling, for example, the light of consciousness is focused, not on the centre of the total individuality, but on the region of mental activity, and a lack of balance results; Jung speaks of the total individuality as a circle, and so it may be said that, in such a case, the man is conscious only of a segment of himself, the rest being in darkness.

Jung maintains that those elements in ourselves which we have failed to develop fall into the unconscious (this 'unconscious' is called, in universal tradition, the 'Lower Waters', in which the possibilities of formal manifestation lie hidden, awaiting birth) and become, as it were, hostile or even demonic powers within us until they are given the recognition which is their right. He tells us that, in order to rescue these deformed and frustrated elements in ourselves and to integrate them into our conscious experience, we must descend into the darkness and meet, in strange shapes, all that we have neglected in our one-sided lives.

That no real advance beyond our present state is possible until its potentialities have found expression and been exhausted is a platitude of Oriental teaching; in the Hindu tradition, the story of Narada illustrates this point. Narada was an ascetic who had devoted his whole life to a single-minded endeavour to know the 'Lord of Maya'; to achieve this knowledge, he descended into the waters of transformation (as in Christian baptism, the way to a change of state always lies through the waters), but he emerged as a young princess who married, had many children and fulfilled the course of her life; then, waking as from a dream, he returned to the form of Narada, aware at last that he could not by-pass life (or Maya) and the demands that it makes. Every tradition makes provision for a 'Descent into Hell', whereby the inferior possibilities of a particular state may be exhausted; whether Jung's psychology offers a real technique for this descent and for the subsequent return is open to question, for tradition speaks also of a 'Fall in the Mire', a dissolution of the personality in the 'outer shadows', from which there is no return; but he has certainly restated in modern terms a very ancient doctrine and demonstrated the necessity for a re-orientation of consciousness if we are to come into possession of our integral humanity.

Jung, however, stops short at this point, and regards it as an end in itself, whereas the traditional doctrines, in the West (where it represents the term of the Lesser Mysteries) as in the East, consider it only as a means to an end. The establishment of our consciousness at the centre of a given state of existence is said, in these doctrines, to open to it a way up the Axis of the Universe, through numberless higher states of existence, to the One Light or Supernal Sun and, through the Sun-door or Janua Coeli (of which the leaves are the opposites, past and future, good and evil, in terms of which the Universe is laid out), out into the limitless freedom beyond. The Axis is itself 'that ancient narrow path whereby the contemplatives, knowers of Brahman, enter in, liberated hence on high to the world of heavenly light' (one might consider, in this connection, the fairly obvious symbolism of the 'Indian rope-trick').

This symbolism must, however, be qualified; it is all too easy to forget, when we speak in symbols, that we are speaking, not of things as they are in themselves, but as they appear from a certain angle. That miracle, dramatized for us in the 'rope-trick', in which a man, climbing the thread-spirit or the Axis of the Universe, is lost to sight in the Empyrean, might suggest a dualism—an opposition of upper as against lower, of light as against darkness—that is by no means intended, since the ultimate Brahman is no more light than It is darkness, no more above than It is below. 'That', which is beyond the Sun-door, there, out of our sight, is also the very stuff of all that is here before our eyes; and the 'knower of Brahman', far from having turned his back upon the spheres of manifested existence, has encircled them and possessed himself of them.

It is said that, by virtue of climbing the Axis of the Universe, the being identifies himself with it and, as he climbs, absorbs it into himself as a spider absorbs the thread it mounts; he himself becomes the Axis, it is around him that all the worlds revolve and it is he who surveys, from his commanding, central station, the fields of conditioned existence extending in every direction. So, in Islam, the Sufi is able to say, 'I am the Pole!'; and, of the man thus magnified, Allah says, 'My earth and My heaven contain Me not, but the heart of My faithful servant containeth Me', for this man is 'the eye of the world, whereby God sees His own works'. And, in the Hindu tradition, Brahmạn says to this man (though 'man' no longer, for his humanity remains upon the earth he has left behind him), who sits on 'the seat "Far-shining" ', 'The Waters verily are my world, and are thine!' For he is Master of all the possibilities of existence, and the play (lila) of the Lord is his play also.

But before we can examine more closely the meaning of such terms as Liberation and Lordship, a slight digression is necessary. It would be unprofitable to discuss matters which lie so far outside the range of our ordinary experience without considering, for a moment, their significance for human life as we know it. We saw that the contemplative is said to identify himself with the Axis of the Universe, and this means that he conforms to it; in the precise meaning of the word, he 'conforms' his own nature to that model, and, since it is in the central Axis that the forms, of which all things in time and space are copies, inhere, this is the same thing as saying that he fashions himself in the likeness of his own divine image; and this is his fulfilment of the command, 'Become what thou art!', his fulfilment of his 'dharma'.

It is not only the rare contemplative who is concerned with 'dharma', a term translated as 'rule', 'order' or 'way', the 'dharma' of the Universe being the order by which it is held together and accomplishes its destiny, and the 'dharma' of the individual the way by following which he contributes to the order of the whole and takes his proper place in it. Every living being depends upon it for coherence; in so far as a man fails to conform to his 'sva-dharma' (own 'rule' or 'way', peculiar to himself as a particular, unrepeatable individuality), he falls into disorder and confusion. 'He who denies spirit', says the Upanishads, 'denies himself; he who affirms spirit, affirms himself'; the same might be said of 'dharma', which is not a law imposed from without, but inherent in the individual; the denial by a man of his vocation and proper destiny (in many cases, 'dharma' might almost be translated as 'function') is essentially an act of self-frustration, and it might even be possible to apply the terms of modern psycho-analysis to this 'repression'.

When we consider the effects attributed to the thwarting of the destiny of a particular instinct, it is easy to see that the fulfilment of a destiny inherent in our nature is by no means a matter of indifference; it is a necessity, if we are to remain 'sane' (healthy and balanced). If the repression of an instinct or even of thoughts can have such a dire effect upon the whole personality, what must be the result of repressing the spiritual principle? If the modern world has been wrong in denying the existence of such a principle and of the vocation which it implies, what must be the fruit of such a denial? A universal sickness, bitterness, frustration, and a dim yet agonizing sense of possibilities unrealized and needs unsatisfied. And what is the condition of the modern world? There is no need to labour the point.

There might at first seem to be a conflict between the law which requires the fulfilment of all the possibilities belonging to a particular state of individual existence and the concept of 'dharma', but the latter implies, not a choice of certain possibilities and a rejection of others, but a rule for the development of all these possibilities in accordance with the universal order and rhythm. A piece of music, for example, may be played in the correct manner—with the notes in their right order, given their correct time and emphasis—or it may be 'scrambled', so that, although the requisite notes are played, they are without form or significance, and complete disorder results. It is so with the potentialities which we contain within ourselves; they may either find expression in an ordered and significant form, or they may tumble out in confusion, without rhyme or reason. Moreover, if some are refused their right expression in their right time, they may become unruly and demonic, forcing an outlet for themselves at the expense of others; how often, for example, is a frenzied sexuality the compensation for a failure to fulfil other needs which have quite as much right to expression as has the sexual instinct. A disorderly development of our potentialities—one that is not in accordance with 'dharma'—means, inevitably, an over-valuation of some things, an underrating of others and, in consequence, a distorted sense of values.

In the Hindu tradition, great attention is paid to music, dancing and the rhythm of words, since all three may serve man as means of integration; the world process is regarded as rhythmic through and through; consequently the order of human life is also rhythmic, and in sacred dances or music, or in the recitation of 'mantras', the human personality is knit together, just as the body is maintained by the rhythmic activity of heart and lungs. It is by rhythm, 'by the metres', that the imminent god who is dismembered by our partial knowledge (as in the legend of the Dragon) composes or 'puts himself together' again; and it is by the ultimate rhythm of the Days and Nights of Brahmá that the Universe is brought to birth and finally transformed.

We can see now in what sense anything that is contrary to 'dharma' is discordant and disintegrating. It is by 'vrtha' (a Sanskrit word meaning 'heresy' or 'choosing for oneself') that discord is produced and rhythm is shattered. The man who is fully obedient to 'dharma', conforming himself to his divine image, has surrendered his private will, and he fulfils his role as obediently as the actor plays the part laid down for him; such a man is described as being spontaneous, because his every act and every movement is directed, not by forethought and desire, but by the ruling of the immanent principle, which is in fact his own Self, and so expresses perfectly what it is meant to express in the order of the world. The connection between this and the traditional theory of art, referred to above, should be clear.

In the Hindu tradition, the universal degeneration which takes place in the course of time is defined in terms of a loss of 'dharma'. The 'Krita Yuga' is said to stand 'four-square', conforming perfectly (within its natural limitations) to the divine order; but only three-quarters of this attachment to 'dharma' remains in the 'Tretá Yuga', while one quarter is open to disorder; in the 'Dvápara Yuga', the forces of order and disorder are equally balanced, while in the 'Kali Yuga' the latter are paramount. The fact that, according to this teaching, disorder is bound to triumph in this age in which we live does not mean that individuals are therefore free to follow their own tastes and ignore the divine law; here the words of the Gospel, 'Offence must needs come, but woe unto him through whom offence cometh!' are particularly applicable. There is no being that can escape the divine power; all, even the devil himself, must serve it after their fashion, whether willingly or unwillingly, and darkness and disorder contribute, in a manner beyond our limited understanding, to the harmony of the whole; but while it may be a matter of indifference to the Lord of created beings whether a particular being chooses to foster disorder or to oppose it, it is by no means a matter of indifference to that being himself.

Those who serve the powers of darkness fall, according to the Hindu doctrines, into the hands of these powers; their role is a nightmarish one, their dance a dance of death; not that the divine mercy is denied to them, but they deny it (according to the Islamic teaching, each sphere of hell offers to its inmates a pleasure to which they become attached, for if they suffered nothing but agony they would call upon the Mercy of Allah, and that Mercy could not be denied them). Whatever the conditions of the time, the choice of the 'outer shadows' is always personal and deliberate. In *The Diary of a Country Priest* the French writer, Georges Bernanos, speaking of hell, says that it 'is nothing, never will be anything but a half-formed shape . . . a stunted thing on the very verge of all existence . . .', and of those who choose this nothingness, he says, 'one day in the eyes of eternal God they will be no more than a mass of perpetual slime over which the vast tide of divine love, that sea of living, roaring flame which gave birth to all things, passes vainly'. In the Hindu tradition, the various hells correspond rather to the Christian Purgatory, but there is a recognition also of the possibility of just such a spiritual suicide, just such a loss of being and just such a dissolution in the bottomless mire as that of which Bernanos speaks.

Although, from our personal point of view, our attempts to restore order, to forge again the almost shattered link that binds man to the source of his life, and to push back the forces of destruction are, according to the theory of cycles, doomed to failure or, at the best, to no more than a passing success (for the process of decay may be temporarily reversed), this fact can never be taken as an excuse for surrender. It is not for man to concern himself with the success or failure of his action; all that concerns him is the action itself, and it would be presumption on his part to assume his task to be hopeless and so to abandon it. We cannot know what will be the ultimate effects of any action we undertake; all that we can be certain of is our own intention in undertaking it; but it is in accordance with the

Hindu theory to believe that the seeds of triumph may lie concealed even in the blackest failure and defeat, and that these seeds must, in accordance with an inescapable law, bear fruit one day.

It is also implied in the theory of cycles that it is only the efforts of men who still cling to the good and who, in spite of their times and, as it were, against the tide, establish a personal contact with their source, that make possible the preservation of a last vestige of balance in the world; and the work of these men might be likened to a desperate rearguard action which keeps the enemy at bay until that time when, by the divine intervention, perfect order is restored and a new Age begins.

In spite of this emphasis upon heroic action, the Hindu scriptures are frequently described by Western critics as 'amoral', no doubt because the Westerner, in modern times, is irritated if not infuriated by any doctrine which gives precedence to personal spiritual development over philanthropy and the 'public good'. It is, however, the belief of the Hindus and, for that matter, of the Christians, that the man who has established in himself a true relation to the divine acts as a channel for a grace that floods over the fields of time. In spite of the fact that our active philanthropy (even the Marxist communist has only the good of his fellow-creatures at heart) is swiftly turning our world into a wilderness peopled with wild beasts, we persist in our contempt for the monk who confines himself to praying for the world, and for the 'rishi' (the Hindu holy man) who, in silent contemplation, casts about him a reflection of the divine Light; we persist also in our belief that there is no higher ideal than that each man should do good 'according to his lights', even though the most elementary observation shows us that the deliberate evil-doer is rare indeed and that ninety-nine out of a hundred of those who play their part in destroying the world do so in the firm conviction that right is on their side; two fishwives in a brawl defend, each of them, human justice, and two nations at war uphold, each of them, human righteousness. Self-interest will not carry an aggressive man very far, but self-righteousness will take him to the ends of the earth.

It is hardly to be wondered at if religion, in the West as in the East, has been sceptical of the pretensions of the ordinary, decent, unregenerate man and has demanded that this man should be changed, should surrender himself, before he embarks upon a course of promiscuous charity; it is only the politicians who believe in the perfectibility and the righteousness of man, and they, when no longer subordinate to the spiritual power, are blind leaders and have no authority. If the Christian speaks of a surrender to God and the Hindu of a surrender of the self to a higher principle which is the source and centre of every being, the difference is not as essential as it might appear; Christianity speaks of the 'synteresis', the divine spark imminent in man, and Eckhardt says that 'the bottom of the soul tops heaven's summit', implying that there is no impassable barrier between the human and the divine orders.

The Hindu Upanishads have little use for 'works without faith'. 'Give with faith; if you lack faith, give nothing'. This warning is based upon the fact that the good we try to do out of an abstract idea of duty or in mere obedience to the law is one-sided and will call out its opposite in compensation. The sacrifice we make, unless some measure of the divine love has entered into us, will generate the resentment that cancels the good it has done; whatever evils are abolished by compulsion will reappear in some different form. Outside the sphere of love and faith, there is no escaping this law of compensation. But just as, in the personal life, a sacrifice made from love is an action 'beyond the opposites', stimulating no reaction, leaving behind it no bitterness, so the man who lives the good life because it is the natural expression of his devotion to the supreme spirit is living out his whole nature and finding a true fulfilment; he is storing up within himself no demons, no profusion of suppressed, unlived impulses, but is completely what, in his outward life, he appears to be.

It is the aim of the Upanishads to show us how we may become such a being as finds his natural expression in the harmonious life, in nobility and in charity. Given that inner change (depending upon the surrender of 'self' to 'Self'), everything else slips into place, and those things that could never be conquered by force of will fall away of their own accord. 'When the demons came to it, they were scattered as a ball of earth would be scattered when hitting a stone'. Against that immovable mark, all things partial and conflicting are broken; 'Day and night do not pass that bank, nor old age, death and grief; neither good nor evil deeds'; for self-will and its burden are destroyed.

The fact that both good and evil deeds are said to be cancelled when the Self is known has been a further stumbling-block to Western critics, but this liberation from the burden of the past is itself to a large extent dependent upon past conduct; the Upanishads recognize the psychological law by which one kind of life leads a man forward to the realization of his true nature, and another draws him into a vicious circle of his own making. And yet, just as in Christianity the sinner may find salvation before the righteous man, so long as his heart has not become hardened, so, in the Upanishads, the evil man may find Liberation, not because ill deeds lead to Heaven, but because they may be the misguided efforts of a good heart, whereas righteousness may be the refuge of a hard one.

It is only the 'Sage', whose human nature is the instrument of the transcendent Self, who can say that good and evil lie behind him—that they are terms which have no further meaning for him; 'When the Sage meets Spirit—phallus and what it enters—good and evil disappear; they are one'. Then, having found his place, he 'does not assert himself; playing with spirit, enjoying spirit . . . he takes his rank'; so that, after the long experience of suffering and division, beyond the recurrent cycles of death and generation, he comes into the light and knows himself for what, under all his passing disguises, he always was.

The way in which a particular being lives out his life in the world depends upon the extent to which he has realized or actualized within himself the immanent spirit; naturally, according to the Upanishads, the posthumous conditions of that being are equally dependent upon the extent of his Self-awareness. At the moment of physical death, the powers of which the various senses are the instruments are said to withdraw into the mental faculty ('manas'), which, in its turn, withdraws into the vital breath ('prana'); the vital breath is then re-integrated into the 'living soul' ('jivatman'), and the latter, with its various powers and faculties now latent in it, departs in a 'fiery vehicle'. So far, the process is the same for the ignorant person as for the contemplative Sage, but now the ways divide.

The being in who awareness of the Self has never dawned will now follow the Pitri-yana, the 'Way of the Patriarchs', to what is symbolically described as the sphere of the Moon; this sphere may be called the 'cosmic memory', where forms that have completed their cycle of development are dissolved and the germs or possibilities of future cycles are stored; from here the being must return to existence in one form or another (a process that is metaphorically spoken of in terms of 'reincarnation') and although this existence may be, in comparison with our present one, either better or worse, he will have in it the same chance of achieving 'Deliverance' by a realization of the true Self that is outside all limiting forms.

The being who has achieved a certain degree of awareness, without actually becoming, during his life, a 'knower of Brahman', is said to follow the Deva-yana (Way of the Gods or Angels) and, passing beyond the sphere of the Moon, to be freed from the limitations of a particular form; he journeys upwards through certain heavenly states, spoken of as worlds or Regions, coming into effective possession of them through his self-identification with the various principles described as their respective Rulers, and he may stop short in one or another of these states, remaining in it until that final dissolution when, at the end of Brahmá's Day, all things are plunged into Brahman. He may attain 'Deliverance' from any of these stations on the Way, or he may reach the supreme centre of all the worlds without actually making effective for himself the identity of this centre with that absolute and single one of which all others are a reflection.

Whatever the state, short of 'Deliverance', which a being has reached on his journey, there is 'no Deliverance without omniscience'; however universal his mode of existence may seem, in comparison with our own, it is still a limited mode and, as such, veils him from the ultimate Brahman; and unless he has attained at least such a 'virtual Deliverance' as will become effective upon the dissolution of all things and their reintegration into Brahman, he will only suffer this reintegration 'unknowingly', 'passively', as in the state of dreamless sleep (a state which is contrasted with that active reintegration into Brahman, which is called 'Deliverance'), and from this he must return to other states of existence, for there is no real end to the journey short of the absolute 'universalization' of the being in identity with Brahman.

Finally, we must consider the case of the being who attains 'Deliverance' either immediately after death or actually during his lifetime. For him, there is no need to make the progressive journey through other states of existence; since he is at one with Brahman, all these states are already virtually in his possession, even though he may occupy but one of them and refrain from animating the others; all states and all worlds are contained in his nature (which is the nature of Brahman) as 'possibilities' subsisting simultaneously in an eternal present, and he does not need to live through them in order to know them in their fullness; indeed, to speak more accurately, one cannot say that there is for him any distinction between potentiality and act, for the place where he now stands, asleep and yet 'utterly awakened', beyond the dualities of night and day or life and death, is prior to any such distinction.

What more can be said of this state beyond all states? The Buddha, when questioned regarding it, 'maintained a noble silence'. The Upanishads tell us, 'This Brahman is silence'. All words are misleading. And yet the refusal to define 'Mukti' (Deliverance) or 'Nirvana' (Extinction) has given rise to so many misconceptions in the West, including the preposterous notion that this supreme plenitude is an 'annihilation', that some slight attempt at definition must be made.

In the first place, although the delivered being has passed beyond 'name and form', his 'name' (with the 'form' which it calls up) is written, to use the Christian terminology, in the 'Book of Life', 'revealed in its perfection, in its flower, where it first burgeons forth in the ground of its existence' (Meister Eckhardt; here, as in many other cases, his words may justifiably be applied to the Hindu conceptions), and this 'name' or individual prototype is included in the possibilities which the delivered being possesses in his own nature; he is infinitely greater than that which can be bounded by a name, but his name is not lost to him.

Secondly, this being is said to have become a 'Mover at will'; using, for the last time in this study of the Hindu doctrines, the pregnant imagery of the Supernal Sun and its rays, we may say that he is not only within the centre, at one with Brahman, but can move at will up and down the rays of the intelligible Light, through all the spheres of existence, manifesting himself wherever he chooses, without needing to leave his place—which is no place and yet all places. We find a similar terminology in the Gospel according to St. John, when it is said that he who enters in through the door that is Christ 'shall be saved, and shall go in and out, and find pasture'.

In this state, which is the true and final end of all that has being, we are, in Eckhardt's phrase, 'fused, yet not confused', 'founded, yet not confounded'; and he says also, 'When I go back into the ground, into the depths, into the well-spring of the Godhead, no one will ask me whence I came or whither I went'. This also, according to the Hindu doctrines, is the end and the completion; this is the silence.

CHAPTER FOUR

THE GREAT WAY

But Tao, when uttered in words, is so pure and flavourless!
When one looks at it, there is nothing to see;
When one listens to it, there is nothing to hear.
Yet, if one uses it, it is inexhaustible.

—Tao Te Ching. 35

It is time to descend. From the mountain-heights the way leads down to the yellow plain and the yellow rivers. The spoken dialect alters with the change in scenery, and in place of the abstract language of metaphysics we have the network of wit and paradox in which the Chinese temperament delights; in place of the doctrine in which human life is dwarfed before the massive presence of the ultimately Real, is a teaching deeply concerned with the nature of man, that nature which, says Chuang Tzu, 'can be hot as fiercest fire, cold as the hardest ice. So swift is it that in the space of a nod it can go twice to the end of the world and back again. In repose it is quiet as the bed of a pool; in action, mysterious as Heaven. A wild steed that cannot be tethered—such is the heart of man'. And the Hindu 'rishi' who, in one-pointed concentration, flashes to his goal like an arrow to its target is replaced in China by a more vegetative Sage—a little man fishing in a muddy stream, with meditative eyes and a merry smile.

But the difference in the manner of approach should not blind us as to the identity of the goal. It is easy to be deceived; in the Hindu scriptures, the difficulties which face us are relatively superficial, and, once we have mastered certain basic principles and grasped the key to the symbolical formulations, we may proceed without too great a danger of losing our way; the Taoist writings, on the other hand, present a superficial simplicity which leads the unwary to suppose that the meaning is as simple and as straightforward as the language, in which it is veiled rather than expressed. In India, foolish and inept questions as to the nature of things are answered only by silence; the Chinese prefer to answer such questions with a witty paradox; the 'rishi's' silence may persuade the questioner to find the answer for himself, whereas the Sage's paradox is likely to send him away cheerfully convinced that he knows all there is to be known.

The Chinese spirit, at least as it shows itself in Taoism, is compounded of the lightest gaiety and the most profound, all-seeing sadness; and if it seems careless, it is with the carelessness of the man whose back has broken under his burden—and who has then learned to dance. Beneath the deceptive *naïveté* is a complexity that excludes nothing, and an account of human nature that seems as optimistic as that of Rousseau conceals a stern doctrine of obedience and self-surrender. The words of the Taoists seem like those of a man so full of years and experience that he can speak only in riddles, and their books are the most cryptic in existence; they use five words where a Hindu would use fifty and a European philosopher five hundred.

Amongst the most cryptic, and certainly the most famous of these books is the *Tao Te Ching*, ascribed by tradition to a certain Lao Tan or Lao Tzu ('Old Master'). Here, in eighty-one verses—about the length of the Introduction to a modern religious or philosophical work—is a book that has fascinated the West more than any other work of Oriental teachings; an analysis of the mystical life, a treatise on government, a text-book for philosopher-kings, a tract against busybodies, a system of psychology; it has been called all these things; and, since Chinese written characters lend themselves to a variety of different interpretations, no two translations (and there must be a dozen, in English alone) agree. A second source that must be considered in any study of Taoism is the *Chuang Tzu Book*, which may bear to the Master Chuang much the same relation as do Plato's Socratic Dialogues to Socrates; it is a collection of stories, dialogues and aphorisms, interspersed with philosophical exposition, and it abounds in satire.

Although many of the stories in the *Chuang Tzu Book* are aimed against the Confucianists, it is important to realize that both Taoism and Confucianism stem from the same ancient tradition, embodied in the *Book of Changes*; whereas the Hindu doctrines provide both for the inner life and outward conduct, these two aspects of existence have tended to become separated in China, and it may be said that the Taoists take over where Confucius leaves off (the highest rank in the Confucianist hierarchy corresponds to the lowest one in the Taoist hierarchy). There is, therefore, a sense in which Taoism, from the point of view of the ordinary man, is incomplete and requires Confucianism; the doctrines of Taoism are necessarily the property of the few, while Confucianism, by itself, comprises little more than a rule of conduct, and it is no doubt for this reason that Mahayana Buddhism, a more complete and more universal doctrine, gained so firm a footing in the Far East.

Before proceeding to a consideration (confined, by necessity, to its more superficial aspects) of Taoism, or rather of those teachings which may be called specifically Taoist, although they exist in a less developed form in the other traditional doctrines, it is essential to take note of the metaphysical framework of these teachings; a framework which is simply the Chinese 'transcription' of the main principles of the universal tradition. 'The Tao that can be expressed is not the eternal Tao; the name that can be defined is not the unchanging name'; here, then, we have the Chinese equivalent of the nameless Brahman. 'Tao was always nameless; when for the first time applied to function, it was named'; in other words, it is only in relation to our limited existence that we may justifiably translate Tao as 'Way', 'Law', 'Significance'. Of Tao in itself nothing can be said, except that it comprehends all things; 'That to which a name is given is but the mother that rears the ten thousand creatures, each after its kind'.

In the process of self-development, however, 'Tao became One' (not only 'became', but 'becomes', since the process is eternal); and this is equivalent to the Hindu statement that Brahman took on Selfhood. 'One became two'; only from duality, by the interaction of opposite principles, can the 'ten thousand creatures' and all multiplicity arise. The twin principles are called, as they are in themselves, the 'Active Perfection' (Khien) and the 'Passive Perfection' (Khouen), and, as they are in relation to manifestation, 'Heaven' (Tien) and 'Earth' (Ti), by which we must understand, not the sky above us and the earth under our feet, but the principles of which these are a local expression. It is not difficult to see that we have here the 'Purusha' and 'Prakriti' of the Hindu doctrine; the two poles between which all existence is extended.

The whole of existence is expressed in terms of duality or of what are called the 'opposites' or 'contraries' (so the Greek Heraclitus; 'The world order is a harmony of opposing tensions —as in the Lyre and the Bow'), those contraries that form the leaves of the Sun-door and crush between them, as they swing to, the wayfarer who is not yet fit to pass out of the Universe. When we come to consider these contraries in our own sphere of life, in the world as we know it, we see them as two opposed forces which the Chinese call Yang and Yin; the former is full of fiery vigour, light, generative and male; the latter, called the 'Motionless Grandeur', is dark, productive and female (it may be noted that they are generally spoken of inversely as 'Yin and Yang' since, from the point of view of created beings, darkness precedes light). These twin forces are never found in separation from each other; they are complimentary as well as opposed, and existence itself depends upon the tension maintained between them; a preponderance of one over the other causes disharmony and a loss of balance, and both are swallowed up and unified, as are the principles of Heaven and Earth, in the 'Great Extreme' (Tai-ki).

The complimentary movements of Yang and Yin represent, in a wider sense, the dual process which brings the Universe to birth and dissolves it again; evolution and involution; the out-breath and in-breath of God, whereby He speaks the primal Word and takes it again into Himself. This is the everlasting, alternating rhythm which controls and orders all things, and it is known to every traditional doctrine; the alchemists of Europe, faithful to the Hermetic teaching which they inherited from Egypt, spoke of the two processes of 'coagulation' and 'dissipation'; the Hindus speak of 'creation' and 'destruction', and the Chinese of 'condensation' and 'dissolution'; 'birth' and 'death', in their widest sense, are universal terms, but there is another word for death, dissolution or destruction, and that is 'transformation'; what is destroyed from one point of view is, from another, newly created; death to one order is birth to another. In this connection, the saying of the alchemists that 'The dissolution of bodies is the fixation of the spirit' may be related to the Hindu teaching of the reintegration, through the death of that self-will which is the motive-power of separate individuals, of the immanent god who was dismembered by the existence of those individual wills, and it might be said, in these terms, that the condensation of individuals in the world of multiplicity is the dissolution of that god, and that the dissolution of individuals is his condensation. There is, between all the orders of reality, a ceaseless 'give and take'; and the giving is always a sacrifice, the death of one order, that another may be infused with life.

It is in the light of this doctrine and in the realization that the dual process is yet a single and continuous one (we die and are reborn in every moment of our experience) that we may best approach the Taoist teaching that man should remain 'soft' and 'open' (should not, in fact, contract or suffer 'condensation' to too great an extent) , although it would be rash to imply that there are no other possible interpretations, equally valid, since the axioms of the *Tao Te Ching* may be differently applied at every level of experience. The process of ageing, whether it is the ageing of the world (described, in the traditional theory of cycles, as a process of 'solidification') or of individual men that is in question, is always accompanied by a certain hardening, a certain loss of pliancy; 'In life', say the Taoists, 'man is soft and tender; in death, hard and tough'. Again and again they emphasize that the distinctive quality of the living is neither strength nor endurance, but pliancy, adaptability and openness.

'The wise men of old', says the *Tao Te Ching*, 'were cautious, like one who crosses a stream in winter; modest, like one who is a guest; yielding, as ice when it begins to melt; receptive as a hollow in the hills; simple, like wood that is not yet wrought'. It is interesting, in this connection, to note that, in 'primitive' societies, a mother is unwilling to hear her child too highly praised, for such praise might suggest that the child is perfected and fully wrought, and to be 'finished', in this sense, is to be on the brink of death; in the same way, the 'primitive' craftsman leaves something uncompleted in any piece of work he undertakes; the article that is fully wrought has no further place among the living.

'I alone am tranquil, and have made no sign, like an infant that has not yet smiled; unattached, like one without a home. Others all have more than enough, I alone seem to be in want. . . . The world is full of people that shine, I alone am dark. . . . The men of the world are clear, so clear; I alone am as if beclouded . . . restless as an ocean, blown adrift, never brought to a stop; all men can be put to some use, I alone am intractable and boorish'. And the reason for this: 'But I value no sustenance that comes not from the lavishing Mother'. The power of the Mother is 'intangible, invisible, yet latent in it are all forms; shadowy it is and dim, yet within it there is force'.

Such is the description which the *Tao Te Ching* gives of the man who waits upon the power of Tao; in perfect calmness he allows the forces of Heaven to come to fruition through him, and his only progress is the progress of nature, unforced, unstrained, a gradual unfolding no stronger than the action of a flower. This doctrine has been presented in a characteristically Western and 'scientific' form by the psychologist, C. G. Jung; he speaks of the Unconscious as the creative source of the human psyche and says that within it lie infinite possibilities of development; the man who has cut himself off from that source, says Jung, lives a partial and uncreative life, always threatened by the very forces which, if he had learned to co-operate with them, might have brought him an inexhaustible strength. And he adds, 'One must be able to LET THINGS HAPPEN. I have learned from the East what it means by the phrase Wu Wei: namely, not-doing, letting be, which is quite different from doing nothing. Some occidentals, also, have known what this not-doing means; for instance, Meister Eckhardt, who speaks of "sich lassen", to let oneself be. The region of darkness into which one falls is not empty; it is the "lavishing Mother" of Lao Tzu, the "images" and the "seed". When the surface has been cleared, things can grow out of the depths'.

Jung's Unconscious is a decidedly ambiguous and ill-defined term, and he refuses to accept the distinction which the Eastern doctrines make between that which is above consciousness and the shadowy territory beneath it (it is characteristic of our age that all the things that lie beyond the confines of our everyday experience should be lumped together as though they all belonged to the same order), and his definition of Wu Wei does not touch on the principal meaning of the term, which is that of 'actionless activity', comparable to the activity by which the sun, simply by its shining, brings all things to birth; but the need to 'let oneself go', in Jung's sense, is certainly one side of the picture which Taoism presents, and it is a side that has considerable importance for modern man, whose surface is entirely cluttered up with defensive works and instruments of war.

The Westerner, in his hectic world, feels a desperate need for such defences and, in building them, closes himself up within himself; in his struggle to adapt himself to his environment, to fulfil certain ambitions or to create and maintain a particular picture of himself, which he imagines to coincide with his real nature, he constructs a brittle surface façade which, while to some extent protecting him from the dangers of his environment, blocks all development from within; against such a finished structure, the tender shoots of a new life are powerless—powerless, that is, until, confined in the darkness, they have become misshapen, violent and destructive. In his haste, the 'civilized' man solidifies too early; he uses his will as an instrument for forcing nature, and, as a result, her store is closed to him; he can no longer draw upon the rich possibilities of that source out of which his surface personality crystallized.

Jung has attempted to show the man of our time the way back to the source of his powers. The Taoists were also concerned with the fertility which is one aspect of the Tao, which is said to be 'like an empty vessel that may be drawn upon without ever needing to be filled. . . . It is like a deep pool that never dries'; to give without stint, and never be decreased by what it has given is the nature of this Tao. But the comparison must not be pushed too far, nor must Jung's confession of his indebtedness to the teachings of Taoism be taken as evidence that his psychology is in line with these teachings. The modern psychologist is concerned with individual creativeness and with the enrichment of the human personality; the concern of the ancient doctrine is with the universal order and with man's place in that order; the former thinks only in terms of the fulfilment of the individual; the latter sees such a fulfilment as a fragment abstracted from the universal pattern of evolution and involution. The surrender which Jung demands is a surrender of that deliberate selectiveness in accordance with which we accept only a part of ourselves and a part of our own experience; what the Taoist requires, although he acknowledges the necessity, as a stage on the way, for a controlled and guided descent into the depths, is the surrender of individual self-will and a perfect submission to the divine order.

From Tao come forth all created things, but once they have emerged, although free, they remain under its guardianship and find a course in which it is their destiny to run— a circular course that will ultimately lead them back whence they came. There is a perfect harmony in this circular motion, until created things desert their proper course and attempt to set up an order of their own. 'See, all things however they flourish return to the root from which they grew. Going back to the root is called peace; peace is called submission to Destiny; what has submitted to Destiny has become part of the eternal pattern'. And of Tao it is said, 'If I am forced to give it a name, I call it "Supreme"; "Supreme" means moving onward; moving onward means going far; going far means returning'.

It is the aim of the Taoist to move in perfect accord with the original power—'The original power which goes so deep and goes so far, that joins with all creatures in turning back, and so brings them to the Great Harmony'. He is possessed of a sense of order, an order of concentric circles which depend for their perfect revolutions upon the maintenace of connection with their centre. When connection is lost, everything falls apart; when rediscovered, everything is kept, as by a law of gravity, to its natural course.

The sense of an ordered harmony is present in all Chinese doctrine. In the *Golden Mean* of Tsesze, a Confucian work, it is defined in a manner to which the Taoists would offer no objection; 'What is God-given is what we call human nature. To fulfil the law of our human nature is what we call the moral law'. Morality is not the forcing of human nature, but its harmonious development in accordance with the order inherent in it, an order which is 'God-given'. And this is the Taoist version of the same idea; 'Man follows the laws of earth; earth follows the laws of heaven; heaven follows the laws of Tao; Tao follows the laws of its own nature'. Right conduct, then, depends upon the restoration of our human nature to that pristine spontaneity which it is said to have enjoyed before it fell from its true orbit. Tao is, as it were, the fly-wheel which keeps all things rotating in proper time, and it is in breaking loose from Tao that our lives have become violent and disordered.

Obviously the expression 'human nature' does not mean in the East quite what it means in the West. We generally define human nature as the way of acting, feeling and thinking that is typical of a particular epoch, and our only method for determining what is normal to that nature is the statistical method; human nature, we say, is the nature of the 'average man', who is, in his turn, an abstraction made from the statistical majority. In the East, the question is not approached from this empirical angle; the Taoist would say that, just as it is the nature of a knife to cut effectively or of a ship to be seaworthy and to make the best use of the wind, so it is the nature of man to fulfil the function laid down for human-kind. Knives may fail to cut, ships may sink; but it is still the essential nature of a blade to be sharp and a vessel to be sound; and so human nature is not simply what happens to us when we 'let ourselves go' but a rule, a standard, to which we may or may not conform.

Human nature, then, is the divine image, the perfection proper to man; and in so far as man fails to conform himself to that image he is not wholly human. The Taoists naturally maintain that the impress of this image upon individual men has, through the ages, become less and less sharp. In the primordial age, men are said to have possessed their human nature in its fullness, but this is no longer so in our time; the 'Great Way' has been lost to us, and its rediscovery is, for each individual, the work almost of a lifetime. 'When the great Tao is lost, spring forth benevolence and righteousness'; man is a fallen being, and he attempts to replace the Way that has been lost with law and morality. The manner of living that is simply the spontaneous fulfilment of his own nature so long as he remains linked to his source has become an outward morality, imposed upon him in a frantic effort to stop the rot. The Taoists, however, believe that this outward compulsion is a measure that aggravates the condition it was meant to remedy; we cannot defy the laws of life and then expect to evade the consequences by an 'act of will' or by 'self-control'. We cannot stop the process we have set going by crying 'Halt!'

Here, once again, we are close to the teaching of the Upanishads. The greatest moralizing campaign will produce exactly the requisite amount of 'sin' and violence to balance its good effects. The balance can never be upset, for human existence depends upon its maintenance. But, instead of swinging at the extremity between relative good and relative ill, and trying to stay the pendulum at one extreme of its arc, it is possible for us to reach the actual point of balance and to centre ourselves once again on that point.

The sense of a pre-established order from which man has, by his own will, broken away, is to be found in every traditional doctrine. St. Augustine stated it in terms that would not be out of place in the *Tao Te Ching*; 'Because men have become exiles even from themselves, there has been given also a written law. Not because it has not been written in the heart, but because thou wast a deserter from thy heart'. The laws of self-will and the laws of the heart are in mutual opposition (it must be remembered that, in all the traditional doctrines, the 'heart' is the seat, not of those emotions which serve self-will, but of intuitive knowledge; it is the centre of the individuality).

In returning to the law of his heart, the Taoist sets himself under the same law which keeps the heavenly bodies in their orbits and regulates the growth of every plant and every creature. And because he no longer depends upon the power of his individual will, he becomes a channel for the inexhaustible power of Tao. 'By adhering to the Ancient Way, you can master the existence of the present'; by adhering, that is, to the power in which the world begins and through which it endures, man comes to work with that power. But the price of drawing upon the illimitable Tao is submission to its rhythm. Of Lao Tzu, it is said, 'The Master came because it was his time to be born; he went, because it was his time to depart'. The rhythm which regulates the seasons of the earth presides over man's coming and his going and orders the course of his personal destiny; if he struggles against that destiny, tries to grasp at what is not yet ripe and to cling to what is due to depart, he wastes himself in the most unprofitable of battles and is denied participation in that power which, according to Chuang Tzu's pleasing illustration, enabled the 'Yellow Ancestor' to enjoy twelve hundred concubines without injury to his health.

Chuang Tzu remarks, 'If the bronze in the founder's crucible were suddenly to jump up and say, "I don't want to be a tripod, a ploughshare or a bell. I must be the sword Without Flaw!" the caster would think it was indeed unmannerly metal that had got into his stock'. In this matter, a modern psychologist, Hans Prinzhorn, echoes the ancient teaching; there is, he says, an innate power in every individual which, throughout his development, will make itself felt in a definite direction, leading him towards his own unique form of maturity, 'irrespective of all that is added from without by education and guidance'. We are predestined to act as a particular vehicle of life, and only harm can come from attempting to adopt a mode of existence foreign to our nature; that innate power will make itself felt, fruitfully if we learn to co-operate with it, destructively if we ignore it. Envious self-comparison with others is futile; we have each been given the medium in which to work out our lives, and to work well within the bounds of that medium is our first duty. To imitate some model of so-called general validity or to twist ourselves inside out in the effort to comply with a particular social norm or school-book virtue is to neglect our true task for a chimera.

Prinzhorn, although a naturalistic psychologist, owning his intellectual descent from Nietzsche and Ludwig Klages, restates the ancient Oriental teaching when he says that each man's goal 'inheres in the individual human being as does the fully developed plant in the germ', and this point of view has been very fully developed by the modern Spanish philosopher, Ortega y Gasset. It is in the work of the latter that we can see most clearly the gulf that divides the modern doctrine concerning destiny and vocation from the ancient one; Ortega y Gasset maintains, for example (in *Tríptico*), that the man born to be a thief must either become one or else be guilty of thwarting his own inherent destiny, but this is to assume that the destiny of a particular individual is a matter of chance and may well be in conflict with the equally pressing destinies of others, whereas the Taoist believes that conflict and disharmony in the universal order spring from the failure of individuals to conform to the pattern of development laid down for each of them.

The modern philosopher thinks in terms of innumerable separate individuals, connected only in so far as they share in a common psycho-physical nature; the Taoists see the man who submits to his own inner law as—to use an illustration found both in Plato and in the Indian scriptures—a puppet, the course of whose existence is controlled by the puppet-master who holds in his hand the wires of all created beings and regulates their movements, in so far as they consent to be regulated; in consequence, it is only individual self-wills, never individual destinies, that conflict with each other. It is because this consent whereby the being is re-attached to its own centre, is the only way in which a state of harmony may be restored, that the Taoists object so strongly to the practice of 'tampering', whether the interference comes from a social authority or is directed by one part of a man's nature against another. 'Nothing is worse for the soul than struggling not to give play to feelings that it cannot control', says Chuang Tzu; 'This is called the Double Injury, and of those who sustain it none live out their natural span'.

To suggest that such a teaching is 'dangerous' or that it would make the maintenance of any ordered human society impossible is to miss its point. The Taoist does not assert that men 'should' give play to feelings that are socially or personally harmful, but simply that where these feelings exist they will work in a certain fashion and that the very fact of their existence points to a distortion of human nature which no amount of 'tampering' will mend. We cannot abolish an earthquake by complaining that it is 'harmful'. And those who do violence to themselves breed violence wherever they go.

As with man's nature, so with the world. 'For the world', says the *Tao Te Ching*, 'is a divine vessel; it cannot be shaped. He who shapes it damages it; he who grasps at it, loses it'. Do not tamper with the world or with men's hearts, says Chuang Tzu, and let your love be so unobtrusive, so undemanding, so unwilling to interfere, that it passes unnoticed and its beneficent influence works unobserved. Most of our interference, he adds, is like 'trying to stop an echo by shouting at it'. Or like a child, we might say, whose efforts to erase a mark he has made on the carpet, make it ten times worse. When we have sown confusion, we cannot be too careful in using the very methods that brought it about in the effort to remedy it.

The violence that we use in our dealings with the world—

and against ourselves—is the violence of the bad craftsman. The Taoist does not wrench open the door of felicity—it opens at his touch, for his touch is gentle and skilled, and he knows how to wait; 'The greatest vessel takes the longest to finish'. And he observes that water, the softest of things, conquers the hardest, rock; for, while the rock crumbles away, without inner resource, the waves of the ocean are eternally renewed. Haste and violence, he believes, defeat their own ends. 'To kill in place of the supreme Executioner is to hack in place of a greater carpenter'; in which case, adds the *Tao Te Ching*, 'One can scarcely avoid cutting one's hands'.

Patience is not a modern virtue; the man-made wastes of the American dust-bowl, not to mention the increasingly voracious consumption of the mineral resources of the earth, are a sign of the times. In the matter of human growth, the forcing processes of modern education are already bearing a bitter fruit; and the human will (though not so much the will, in its true sense, as a kind of itch which makes us incapable of letting well alone) is, as Jung has pointed out, for ever 'interfering, helping, correcting and negating'.

Above all, we seem determined to drag everything out into the open, that it may be catalogued and assigned to its pigeonhole, although all that is best in us develops in a kind of secrecy. 'One must have chaos in one, to give birth to a dancing star,' said Netzsche, and it is by our refusal to accept this inner chaos and to wait upon the slow process of its integration, that we doom ourselves to sterility. We are led, for example, for the sake of having firm and serviceable opinions, considered so necessary to human intercourse, to expose certain insights, certain perceptions that are hardly more than a dim foreboding, before they are ripe for exposure. The wintry air kills them. Like all dead things, they become hard and brittle, deprived of the pliancy of life.

This is why the Taoists say that a man should remain a little murky and confused, a stammerer amongst the easy dialecticians. He should beware of imposing a rigid law of consistency upon himself, for few of us can pretend to understand the source out of which our riches come and, lacking that understanding, we cannot be certain what to accept and what to reject. Many an ugly duckling of the mind has grown into a very fine swan. We have to await, with a little humility, the emergence of values and possibilities, from whatever quarter they come, and watch the slime from which no man's heart is free, without horror and without refusal, putting faith in the obscure alchemy of human growth.

That which is formed in accordance with Tao endures; 'What Tao plants cannot be torn up, what Tao clasps cannot slip.' What we make of ourselves by effort is broken by time; it is nothing more than a surface structure, and conforms too often to an abstract pattern, laid down either by personal vanity or in accordance with the theories of moralists and educators. The only unique pattern is the one that forms itself in accordance with its own unique law—for every particular reflection of the universal Tao is unique, and only what is unprecedented and unrepeatable has a place, which nothing else can fill, in the pattern of the ages.

To a world in disorder, the advice to 'let things be' is not, taken by itself, very helpful. The Taoists, however, condemn the methods of the moralist and the reformer just because they have an alternative method to offer, and that method involves the following of a Way which, although it does not require the distortion or suppression of any element in the human make-up, demands a constant discipline of watchfulness and receptivity. 'To live in contact with the world and yet in harmony with the Light' is no easy achievement. Chuang Tzu speaks of the danger of what the moderns call 'repression', but he speaks also of 'freedom from desire' as the first condition for establishing attachment to Tao (this condition might be described as the bridge leading from subservience to 'the world' to submission to Tao). 'You do not understand what I mean when I say "passionless" ', he adds; 'When I say "passionless", I mean that a man does not let love or hate do damage within, that he falls in with the way in which things happen of themselves, and does not exploit life.'

The rule of Tao does not involve the destruction of anything inherent in the human being, but it shows the channels in which each element of our composite nature should run, each expressing its possibilities within its limitations, without overflowing into other fields, as do our natural desires, when, undirected, they flood the personality and subordinate all else to their special purposes. Western humanism has also upheld the ideal of the 'Complete Man', whose component elements operate in an ordered and harmonious manner, but humanism assumes that the work of ordering and integration can be undertaken by the self-centred will or by human reason. The Taoists believe that only when man is centred upon the true pivot of his being do these elements fall into place. 'Let Tao rule the world, and the spirits will not show their evil powers'; the evil spirits are aroused by our will to go in a direction which is contrary to our destiny (that destiny, equivalent to the Hindu 'dharma', which is one with the Great Way), but when Tao rules they play their part and work creatively, or, as the *Tao Te Ching* puts it, 'Their powers converge towards a common end'.

The 'common end' is, for the Taoists as for the other Oriental doctrines, first the restoration of that primordial state in which the human personality is perfectly conformed to its principle and, ultimately, the attainment of that supreme and total awareness which is the final goal of every being; but the precise methods by which the Taoists themselves strive to reach this end are not revealed in their writings (or, if they are to some extent revealed, as in *The Secret of the Golden Flower*, it is in a manner that requires the interpretation of a qualified teacher). They have, however, a maxim which should be kept in mind whenever the question of specific methods arises; 'When the right man uses the wrong means, the wrong means work in the right way. But if the wrong man uses the right means, the right means work in the wrong way'; and they go so far as to call the methods described by writers of the past as 'the lees and scum of bygone men', for, they say, 'all that was worth handing on died with them; the rest, they put into their books'.

There is a legend, told in the *Chuang Tzu Book*, of a meeting between Lao Tzu and Confucius. The great moralist spoke of universal love and of the impartiality of the reasonable man, but Lao Tzu said, 'To speak of loving all men is a foolish exaggeration and to make up one's mind to be impartial is in itself a kind of partiality. If you indeed want the men of the world not to lose the qualities that are natural to them, you had best study how it is that Heaven and Earth maintain their eternal course. Thus you too shall learn to guide your steps by the inward power . . . and no longer need to go around laboriously advertizing goodness and duty, like a town-crier with his drum'. The secret of the stability of the cosmic order is the secret of Tao; it cannot be taught, for it is inexpressible in the terms which men use to communicate with one another, but no man is likely to discover it for himself without the support and guidance of a teacher.

The guidance of the teacher, the Sage, is unobtrusive, and even when, in ancient times, the Sage was also the ruler, he kept himself always in the background. It is said that, when the really great ruler achieves a success, people think that the thing has come about of its own accord. A certain Fan Li is held up as the perfect model; he had won a great victory and was offered half the kingdom as a reward if he would return in triumph with the army; but he 'stepped into a light boat and was heard of no more'. And so it is said, 'When your work is done, then withdraw. Such is the way of Heaven'. Equally unobtrusive was Lieh Tzu who, to his dismay, found himself being served first in an eating-house; 'It meant', he reflects, 'that my inward perfection is not properly secured; its fiery light is breaking out through my bodily frame and turning men's thoughts astray, so that they defer to me in a way that gives offence to the honourable and the aged and at the same time puts me in an unpleasant situation'.

Of the common people it is said, 'There must be no scorn of what makes home for them, no contempt for what means life to them'; the power of Tao works through their simple beliefs, as it does within the Sage's heart; the old Sages, says the *Tao Te Ching*, 'used their power not to awaken the people to knowledge, but to restore them to simplicity'. And again, 'When the government is dull and inactive the people will be happy and satisfied'; for the order of the Tao and that order which is outwardly imposed by human organization are incompatible. The ideal people 'know how to make, but not how to hoard; they live and move thoughtlessly and at random, yet every step they take tallies with the Great Plan'.

In our time, when governmental organization and spiritual disorder have reached a point beyond which it hardly seems possible for human life to endure, the maxims of the Taoists are, to say the least of it, refreshing, but it would be a ludicrous misconception to assimilate them to the nineteenth-century doctrine of *laisser-faire*. The insistence upon leaving the people undisturbed and exercising the powers of government as little as possible is linked to a doctrine which is perhaps particularly difficult for the modern Westerner to grasp; the doctrine of the Sage or, above all, of the 'Wang' (Priest-King) as Mediator between Heaven and Earth.

Readers of Sir James Frazer's *The Golden Bough* will be familiar with the belief, common to many primitive peoples in different parts of the world, that the supernaturally endowed King controls the forces of the natural world. The King is commonly regarded as the dynamic centre of the universe; by turning his head or raising his hand he may alter the whole balance of cosmic forces and, by his misconduct, he may so disturb that balance as to bring destruction upon his people. In many cases he lives in virtual imprisonment, fulfilling no other function but that of universal fulcrum; his every action is regulated by the most exact 'taboos', and his authority is less over his tribe than over the rain, the wind and the fertility of the earth.

This belief, which regulates the life of so many 'savage' peoples, is the decadent or (if we cling to the evolutionary hypothesis) the undeveloped form of the Hindu doctrine of ritual gesture and of the intimate connection between the rhythms of human dancing and music and the cosmic rhythm, and in China it finds expression in the doctrine of the mediator.

So-called 'Sympathetic magic' is always based upon a knowledge of the close connection between all the orders of reality and of the manner in which realities of one order symbolize (and therefore participate in) realities of another. And although such practices may have degenerated, here and there, into little more than wizardry, they have, fundamentally, nothing to do with what is normally called magic, their object is not to force supernatural powers to serve human ends, but to forge, by means of an imitation in human mode of a divine activity, a link between the divine and human orders and to permit a supernatural influence to flow into and merge with a human action.

The *Tao Te Ching* says, 'It is the function of the King to unite'; for the Priest-King who—to return for a moment to the symbolism used in connection with the Hindu doctrines—has made himself one with the Axis of the Universe, uniting in his own person the influences of Heaven and of Earth, is the supreme 'Pontifex'; indeed, he is himself the single Bridge of Light. So the poet Longfellow wrote:

Well has the name of Pontifex been given
Unto the church's head, as the chief builder
And architect of the invisible bridge
That leads from earth to heaven;

only, for the Eastern doctrines, this bridge is also the channel through which the influences of Heaven descend to make fruitful the Earth. The King is sometimes spoken of as personally ascending the Axis (climbing the 'tree' or 'mast') and bringing down the treasures from above, these treasures being the grace which is figuratively spoken of as 'rain' (here we see the true meaning of 'rain-making' rituals).

It is for this reason that the function of the Emperor in ancient China was essentially a sacred one; he is said to have maintained order in his empire by the ritual circumambulation of a building called the Ming-Tang; the edicts for each month were issued from that one of the twelve apertures of the Ming-Tang which corresponded to the month in question, and the nine divisions of the building were taken to represent the nine provinces of the ancient Empire. 'The ancient sovereigns abstained from any action of their own, leaving Heaven to govern for them. . . . All prosperity comes from good government, which derives its efficacity from Tao, through the mediation of Heaven and Earth'.

Clearly, in these terms, order could only be fostered by the Emperor if he was truly established in the 'Unchanging Centre' (Tchoung-young), the single point at which Heaven and Earth meet and by participation in which a being becomes himself their bond of union, for only so could his gestures, motivated not by his individual will but by the power of Tao, of which he was an instrument, both reflect and maintain the universal harmony. It is naturally assumed by the Taoists that such was the case in ancient times. But although the function of 'uniting' was pre-eminently that of the Emperor, the 'wu wei' or 'actionless activity' of the perfected Sage is really the same function in, so to speak, a less official guise. The Sage, it is said, 'relies on actionless activity and carries on wordless teaching'; he 'holds to the centre', and 'since all things have been made, he does not turn his back on them: since they have life, he does not appropriate them: controls them, but does not lean upon them'.

When it is remembered that, in the case of the contrasted principles 'Essence' and 'Substance' (or 'Purusha' and 'Prakriti', 'Heaven' and 'Earth') it is always assumed that only 'Substance' moves, changes and is active, while 'Essence' acts simply by being present, illuminating and measuring (as, in the Hindu tradition, the Sun's rays are said to 'measure' the space in which manifestation is unfolded) the wide expanse of possibilities, it should be clear that the Taoist 'actionless activity' is just such an action by presence. It is believed that a Sage, lost in contemplation, the world and all its concerns forgotten and far behind, quite literally holds all things together and sheds upon all beings a vivifying radiance. He stands, in the exact sense of the word, in an 'essential' relation to the world.

Whether we, who are of the world and fear the abyss of 'being nothing and being all', envy or pity his state, is unimportant, for, as yet, we know neither what we want nor how to will. Our aim is life, which we can think of only in terms of limitation, and the sage's condition may seem to us indistinguishable from death; but, 'he who aims at life achieves death', says the *Tao Tē Ching*, anticipating a similar maxim in the Christian Gospels; and there is a sense in which to be prepared to lose everything, even life itself, is to receive life more abundantly. To hold on to nothing is, by some strange magic to receive everything, and to shut out nothing, say the Taoists, is never to be shut out.

There is a tale of Chuang Tzu's that glorifies this freedom and compares it with the imprisonment of those who mark out an area of life for themselves and struggle to hold on to it against all the forces of time and change: A certain frog lived in an abandoned well; 'How you must envy my delightful existence!' he said to the Giant Turtle of the Eastern Sea; 'When I go into the water I can make it hold me up under the armpits and support my chin; when I jump into the mud, I can make it bury my feet and cover my ankles. As for the baby crabs and tadpoles, none of them can compete with me. . . . To have at one's command all the delights of a disused well, that surely is the most that life can give!'

The Giant Turtle tried to get into the well, but before his left foot was well in, the right got wedged fast. So he wriggled free and retired, saying: 'As you have been kind enough to tell me about your well, allow me to tell you about the sea. Imagine a distance of a thousand leagues, and you will still have no idea of its size; imagine a height of a thousand times man's stature, and you will still have no notion of its depth. Not to be harried by the moments that flash by nor changed by the ages that pass; to receive much, yet not increase, to receive little, yet not diminish; this is the Great Joy of the Eastern Sea.'

CHAPTER FIVE

THE SUDDEN STROKE

Wishing to entice the blind
The Buddha playfully let words escape from his golden mouth;
Heaven and earth are filled, ever since, with entangling briars.
—DAI-O KOHUSHI.

It is a strange fact that the majority of Westerners who have never concerned themselves with the Oriental doctrines should assume, when Eastern 'wisdom' or 'philosophy' is mentioned, that it is Buddhism that is under discussion. This is all the more surprising in that 'Hinayana' Buddhism, in itself a harsh, other-worldly and, to some extent, anti-social teaching, was propagated in the West, particularly towards the end of the last century, in a form that could hardly have been more bleak or less satisfying; when we add to this the gross misunderstanding of such terms as 'nirvana' (which was assumed to denote a total annihilation), it becomes even more difficult to see how such a travesty of wisdom could have won a relative popularity in the West, spreading its misconceptions far and wide, so that even to-day it is impossible for an educated European to approach Eastern ideas with an open mind.

How far so-called primitive Buddhism (called 'Hinayana', the Narrow Way, to distinguish it from 'Mahayana', the Great Way) is really diametrically opposed to the doctrines of Hinduism is still a highly controversial question, but modern research seems to suggest that the gulf, if gulf there is, is by no means as wide as the Orientalists of a few years ago supposed. 'I have seen', the Buddha said, 'the ancient Way, the Old Road that was taken by the formerly All-Awakened, and that is the path I follow'; and it seems legitimate to compare this Way with the 'ancient narrow path that stretches far away, whereby the contemplatives, knowers of Brahman, ascend, set free' of the Upanishads.

Western exegesis assumed far too readily that the Buddha's famous silence signified denial, and that, when he refused to discuss the nature of 'nirvana', this could only be because the state of 'nirvana' was a state of nothingness. In spite of his question, 'Were it not better if ye sought the Self', it was also assumed that his refusal to recognize any abiding self or 'ego' in the man who changes, dies and is reborn, from moment to moment, included a denial of the ultimate and changeless Self which is the principle of all that exists. And, above all, since only the best is good enough for the Western mind, it was assumed that the 'Hinayana' doctrine was the best and most authentic form of Buddhism, and the far more complete 'Mahayana' doctrine was virtually ignored.

In so far as the Buddha's teaching represented a protestant doctrine, its protest appears to have been levelled against popular superstition rather than against the orthodox teaching, although the latter was undoubtedly a prey to over-developed formalism in his time: the Brahmin priests allowed the mass of the people a considerable latitude of belief, indeed many of them probably entertained, themselves, views concerning such matters as 'transmigration', that were on a level with the popular misconceptions; but a tolerance akin to the Taoist desire not to pour scorn on 'what means life to the people' was always a powerful factor in Hinduism, and the Brahmins may well have felt that it was better for those who were unable to grasp the idea of the transcendent Self (that is 'the only transmigrant') to imagine that their own contingent selves were fated to survive and transmigrate, than that they should lose their faith and fall into the heresy of believing that nothing was eternal; superstition always reflects some aspect of the truth, however dimly, and so keeps the way open, whereas unbelief closes the door on the human spirit.

The Buddha, however, allowed no latitude, nor had he the slightest patience with the superstitions so dear to the popular heart: his doctrine was of an icy purity. Whereas Hinduism satisfies the needs both of those on the 'outward' path and those on the path of 'return', he spoke only to the wayfarer bound for home ('from which there is no coming back again'). There was in his message a sense of urgency, comparable to that of Bunyan's Christian as he flees from the destruction to come, and he commiserates with those 'whose Moment has passed' (who have not grasped the opportunity of Liberation). It was to the life of a monk or a wandering ascetic that he called his followers, and he had little to say to those who were not yet ready to abandon the world and follow him.

Even in the case of 'Hinayana' Buddhism, which has survived in Burma and Ceylon, this essentially monastic doctrine soon took on more colourful garments and found room for innumerable popular superstitions; and at the very time when Buddhism was perishing in India, it grew, on Chinese soil and under the influence of Taoism, into the splendid and even ornate structure of the 'Mahayana'. In the latter case, it must be confessed that most of the elements which the Buddha had so sternly cast out returned, invigorated by their period of exile; but this is no reason for condemning the Mahayana as inferior to the supposedly pure doctrine. We might reasonably say that it simply filled in the gaps left in the Pali canon (the scriptures of the Hinayana) and developed implications already inherent in the latter: it made something complete out of what had been little more than a framework, something corresponding to human needs as a whole.

The 'Mahayana' did not so much deify the Buddha as recognize in him a manifestation of the primordial 'All-Awakened' one; it did not so much spin a legend around his life as interpret that life symbolically. It spoke of the reality behind appearances as the 'Void' (sunyatá), meaning 'That' which is void of limitations, void of names and form; and it spoke of the Buddha himself as the 'Tathágata', which means 'That-become', or, in other words, 'He who has become That'. Far from refusing to discuss the condition of the being who has achieved Enlightenment, it described that state in ample—occasionally in lush—terms. 'This is the abode of those peerless ones who walk about everywhere without ever leaving a track behind', says the Prajnáparamitá Sutra, 'as their knowledge rests on absolute oneness. . . . In one particle of dust is seen the entire ocean of lands, beings and kalpas, numbering as many as all the particles of dust that are in existence, and this fusion takes place with no obstruction whatever'.

Above all, the Mahayana laid tremendous emphasis upon the Bodhisattva, the being who has deliberately refrained from coming to the final term of Enlightenment in order to help others on the Way, or who has taken an oath that he will not enter into 'nirvana' until everything that exists, every particle of dust even, has reached that term: a 'freeman', he submits of his own free will to certain limitations that he may continue to labour for the good of all beings: 'He does not retreat into the doing-nothing of Bhutakoki (the final term). He waits for it until his works are accomplished, although his deep insight penetrates even into the voidness of all things. His compassionate heart for all beings who are groping in the dark . . . and his "skilful means" which are generated from this all-embracing love and sustain him through the long and arduous course—these are the forces which determine Bodhisattvahood' (Prajnáparamitá Sutra).

The 'Mahayana', however, fell into that very formalism and over-elaboration which the Buddha had condemned in the Hindu doctrine, and there arose within it a movement of protest which demanded a return to the characteristic Buddhist simplicity. This movement was known as the 'Abrupt' school, since it stressed the abrupt and instantaneous character of the moment of Enlightenment and wished to dispense with the structure of ritual and metaphysics that had been built around this simple moment. In China it was called Ch'an and, crossing the narrow seas to Japan, it flowered as Zen Buddhism.

The comparison of Enlightenment or Liberation to a stroke of lightning is common to all the Oriental doctrines, and, in the West, St. Augustine tells in his *Confessions* how human reason 'in one tremendous stroke of vision arrived at That which Is'. In Islam, the Sufi is called the 'son of the Moment'; and the 'ancient narrow path' of the Upanishads is not a path into the future, still less into the past, but upwards through that undimensioned instant which divides past from future without having, itself, any duration; this is the way through the present and timeless Moment, and there is no other way but this. Where the teachings of Zen differ from the more orthodox doctrine is not in their recognition of the instantaneous and timeless nature of release or of any change of state, but in their impatience with the slow, step-by-step methods of approach to that Moment. To take a comparison from the field of medicine, the orthodox physician tries to cure his patient gradually, while the osteopath jerks the body back into order with a sharp and unexpected twist; the former method is that of the normal spiritual discipline, the latter is the method of Zen.

For the rest, the qualities peculiar to Zen are a matter of national temperament, rather than of doctrinal difference. Given a belief in Brahman, in Tao or in 'Suchness' (the Mahayanist term), the emphasis may legitimately be placed either on the transcendant or the immanent aspect of this reality. What is, in one land, an other-wordly doctrine, may appear in another as something very close to nature-worship; and Zen Buddhism is suffused with a profound sense of relationship with the natural world:

An old pine-tree preaches wisdom,
And a wild bird is crying out Truth.

This could hardly be further removed from the grim spirit of 'primitive' Buddhism. Yet there is at least one point upon which Zen undoubtedly returned to the original teaching; it turned aside from the metaphysical speculations of the 'Mahayana', just as the Buddha has turned aside from those of Brahmanism, and it played havoc with the forms of worship hallowed by long practice. A Zen teacher is discovered, while spending a night in a temple, feeding his fire with the wooden images of the Buddha. The Zen masters refer to each other as 'old rice bags'. 'Nirvana and Enlightenment', says one of them, 'are dead stumps to tie your donkey to!' The sacred scriptures are 'sheets of paper fit to wipe the dirt from your skin'. And the most ordinary things in human life are regarded as lying closest to the heart of reality:

How wondrously supernatural,
And how miraculous this!
I draw water and I carry fuel!

The Buddha's 'Noble Silence' is imitated. 'Silence! No barkling like a dog!' cried a Zen master to an argumentative disciple. It is a spirit comparable to that in which St. Augustine answered the question as to what God was doing before He created the world with the explanation, 'Preparing Hell for the over-curious!' or in which Meister Eckhardt said, 'Wouldst thou be perfect? Do not yelp about God!' Zen sets before man a single goal, Enlightenment; unbounded speculation and the building of intricate theologies are alike irrelevent. Theology weaves an elaborate net in which to trap the Divine; Zen tears the net to pieces and jumps on it.

The Zen masters are, as often as not, gnarled little men, always ready with a gutter-urchin gesture in the faces of the pompous, the self-righteous and the worldly. They are kindly, but they refuse to take others more seriously than they take themselves; indeed, 'seriousness' seems to them rather suspect, if not an actual obstruction in the way of Enlightenment. They are somewhat reminiscent of those peculiar Old Men of Edward Lear's limericks; this one, for example:

There was an Old Man who said, 'How
Shall I flee from this terrible cow?
I will sit on this stile
And continue to smile,
Which may soften the heart of that cow'.

The Zen masters accept the world in which they find themselves. If the 'Suchness' (or 'Buddha-nature') is in all things, it should not be necessary to grow wings in order to find it. There is no object in going ten thousand miles to reach that which lies at our feet. The task before them is not to discover the Real, for they already possess it, but to cut, with a single, well-aimed thrust, through the curtain which shuts out the light. 'Nirvana', they insist, is here and now; it is not to be found except in the present moment and the present task. 'The great Way is right before your eyes, but difficult to see'. And to search for Enlightenment is, it is said, 'like looking for an ox when you are riding on one'. In the words of a Zen Patriarch, Hui Neng, 'The only difference between a Buddha and an ordinary man is that one realizes it and the other does not'.

The condition of awareness is called 'Satori', and it consists, not in any mystical rapture, but in a lucid vision of things as they really are, that is, as aspects of the eternal Buddha-nature. But lucid vision is a function of the transformed personality, and without transformation there can be no vision. Satori is a realization at once of the Buddha-nature in the world and of the Buddha or divine being in man's own soul. It is impossible to see the world differently without becoming different in oneself.

Although every 'conversion', transformation or Enlightenment—there are many words for the one act—is regarded as being instantaneous, it may be preceded by numerous intimations. Flashes of Satori are, the Zen teachers acknowledge, common, long before that illumination of the whole man falls like a stroke of lightning. They are such flashes as must come to every man at some moment in his life, struck, quite unaccountably, from the most trivial or even ignoble experiences. Whereas for most of us they appear as something essentially 'out of this world', a passing intoxication unrelated to the normal and solid world that we know, they represent, for the Zen teachers, momentary perceptions of reality itself, of the only true 'normality', and our fashion of seeing the everyday world, far from being the only realistic one, is false and illusory, springing from a wrong attitude within ourselves, a rigidity of mind that distorts our vision. It is the purpose of Zen so to induce the true and lucid vision that it may be established as a permanent condition.

Buddhism, and Hinduism up to a certain point, teaches that the world we know is an illusion created by minds enslaved by their own error; Zen, however, goes a step further and completes the circle. To those who know nothing of Zen, it is said, mountains are just mountains, trees are just trees and men are just men. After one has studied Zen for a little, mountains are no longer mountains, trees are no longer trees and men are no longer men; their illusory nature is perceived. But to him who fully understands Zen, mountains are once again mountains, trees are once again trees, men are once again men. In other words, the objective world has to die a kind of death, that it may be resurrected in its true body. The old world, so stale beneath the incrustation of habit, is destroyed as an illusion; but, with Enlightenment, a new one comes into being; nothing has been lost, yet all is changed; the mountains are there, yet different; the trees, transformed; the men, reborn. And all this world, which had to die to us before we could see it in its true colours, is revealed even as it issues from the hand of God.

The world that must be forsaken is a world of bondage; the world of mountains, trees and men to which the follower of Zen returns is a world of freedom, not because man's body is any the less subject to the necessities of life, but because his spirit has attained supremacy and knows itself as free. Orthodox Buddhism occupies itself with the effort to escape from the wheel of birth and death and to attain 'supreme knowledge'; but the Zen adept sees that 'There is no birth-and-death from which one has to escape, nor is there any supreme knowledge after which one has to strive'. He has left such questions far behind him. There is no longer any call to escape from the prison-house of the world, for he no longer sees the world as a prison-house—that aspect of it was the creation of his own self-fettering mind—but as a revelation, in the form of what Blake called 'minute particulars', of an everlasting Truth.

Being free, he is not tempted to cling to anything; while enjoying the world, he depends upon nothing in it. 'Do not get yourself entangled with any object', says Lin-Chi, 'but stand above, pass on and be free!' 'What is Tao?' one master is asked; and he replies simply, 'Walk on!' Nothing is to be thought of as stable; no achievement is to be thought of as a resting-place: 'However repeatedly you are peeled off and thoroughly cleansed, never stay where you are'. And again, 'Do not linger about where the Buddha is; and as to where he is not, pass swiftly on!' The Divine, the Real, is eternal, but in human life it is manifest in the most transitory things, in the instant, the cry of a bird, the flash of lightning; a burst of laughter is carried away in the wind, swords catch the sunlight as their bearers pass over the brow of a hill, snow melts and blossom falls. What is most enduring in life and seems the firmest lies furthest from the Real, and to cling to it is to chain oneself in a dungeon far from the light.

Of all doctrines, Zen most clearly exemplifies the quality of lightness inherent in Spirit. Weight belongs to the earth, and it is earthly matters that are grim and earnest, steeped in that perpetual anxiety which every realistic morality has recognized as the root of all sin. Spirit, as Count Keyserling points out in his *South American Meditations*, is characterized by an extreme lack of all that the world understands by seriousness; it cannot be bound; it is eternally unreliable. 'Seen from Spirit', he writes, 'nothing is heavy; it takes all things lightly. . . . Thus, in the first place, spiritual man must impress man of the earth as wanting in seriousness. That is already true of the man of courage, for he puts his life to the stake; that is to say: he plays with his life. But the believer, above all, must appear most sadly deficient in seriousness to the man of heavy earthiness. Consciously, he stakes on what is uncertain. He trusts most rashly despite the opinions of the sententious and the objections of the grave'.

The connection between courage and spiritual faith is a profound one. Both courage and faith outrage the norms of the earth, scorning its practical and calculated values. If women have, in the past, been regarded as less courageous than men, it is because they are more intensely aware of the grim necessities of earthly life, and therefore less capable of the light-hearted play which is real courage—a courage distinctively human, for courage in the animal world never has this quality of play, but is always a state of possession by blinding passion.

What applies to courage, applies equally to faith; to 'seeing' faith, that is, rather than to blind animal faith. Moreover the state attributed by every religion to 'spiritual realization' is that of Joy. And Joy is essentially care-free. It is impossible to give up all concern for self without being released from all immediate care and anxiety. All care and all anxiety come from the sense of bondage, and the man of Spirit is free. His compassion—a quality attributed to him by Buddhism and Christianity alike—is free from that element of desperation which characterizes self-concern. His compassion may be full of sorrow, but never of despair, for he sees his fellow-men as they will not see themselves, that is, as free by nature and, in the world, the victims, not of a malignant fate, but of their own illusions. He desires their freedom, but he cannot share their bondage; for the illusion that has been dispelled is utterly destroyed.

This freedom is, from the earthly point of view, what St. Paul called the 'foolishness of Christ'. And it is significant that, in Europe, the religious man has frequently been represented as a half-wit, a kind of divine idiot, like Dostoievski's Prince Muishkin; 'pious' and 'fool' are two words that are easily coupled, and 'simple' has always had a double meaning. For the man for whom Spirit is the predominant reality cannot see what it so painfully clear to the man of the world, namely, that life is a very serious business; or at least, he sees its seriousness after quite another fashion and in reference to standards that seem, in relation to the practical world, totally irrelevant. The majority of humankind have always felt the Sermon on the Mount to be, not a counsel of perfection, but a counsel of folly. It is always 'folly' to trust in and to regulate one's life by something that can never be 'proved'. What could be more shocking to responsible opinion and good sense than to die joyfully, as though death were the smallest thing imaginable? To the Roman Emperor, watching a martyrdom, such behaviour must have appeared incredible folly. However much the world may talk of Spirit, it finds the power of Spirit a most upsetting phenomenon; unpredictable, subversive and impossible to bring to order.

This foolishness and lightness of heart is particularly characteristic of the Zen Masters. We have already seen what manner of men they are. There is no telling what they may not do next, what absurdity they may not perpetrate. Their teachings are paradoxical, their actions outrageous. Their manners are, in every sense of the word, shocking. And yet, in some strange fashion, they are closer to the natural world than are the worldlings who live in close bondage to it all their days. They live neither in the clouds nor in the depths, but in the world we know, amongst the hills and the fields.

An excellent illustration of an attitude to nature very similar to that of Zen Buddhism is offered by the story of the conversion of a certain Brother Lawrence, in Christian Europe, as told in a letter describing an interview with the holy man (quoted from *The Diagnosis of Man*, by Kenneth Walker): Brother Lawrence said 'that in the winter, seeing a tree stripped of its leaves, and considering that within a little time the leaves would be renewed, and after that the flowers and fruit appear, he received a high view of the Providence and Power of God, which has never since been effaced from his soul. That this view had set him perfectly loose from the world, and kindled in him such a love for God, that he could not tell whether it had increased in above forty years that he had lived since'.

There could scarcely be a better description of what is also the central experience of Zen, in spite of the totally different religious context. A Zen Master, weary of trying to describe Enlightenment to a disciple, takes the young man, who is still clamouring to be told the 'secret of Zen', for a walk. They pass a bush of wild laurel. The Master asks, 'Do you smell it?' 'Yes', answers the disciple. 'There', says the Master, 'I have nothing to hide from you!'

It is the aim of Zen, not to teach certain ideas about life, but to create a certain feeling for life; indeed, something much more than a feeling. A concrete demonstration of life itself is therefore much more effective than any subtle exposition. Upon one occasion, as a Master was taking his place to deliver a sermon to the assembled monks, a bird began to sing outside the monastery walls. The community listened in silence until the song was done; and then the Master rose to his feet, announced that the sermon had been preached, and departed.

Zen will not accept descriptions of the Real, or theories about it in place of Reality itself. And since the Real is manifest in everything that exists, it is considered wisest to allow the existent to demonstrate itself. The raising of a stick or a good clout on the ear is regarded by the Zen teachers as a better demonstration of life than any assertion about the ultimate nature of things. Attention is focused upon the Reality itself, and not upon our thoughts or feelings about Reality. Immediacy of experience is the aim of Zen. And to shock the disciple into such immediacy of experience is the purpose of Zen technique.

The Masters are adepts at administering the vital shock, physically if necessary. They believe that there is nothing better than a sharp jolting of the intellect and of all preconceived ways of thought to recall to a man the knowledge which he has lost, the Enlightenment which has been clouded over by the world. The powerful shield, formed by a lifetime's accumulation of mistaken habits of thought and of vision, has to be shattered before we can see the glory before our eyes or receive its image in our thoughts. The student who asks some earnest religious question receives the most startling and incongruous answer that his teacher can contrive. The blows fall thick and fast upon the head of the self-important 'searcher after Truth'; serious-mindedness is turned topsy-turvy, and pomposity is deflated.

Nor is any student of Zen allowed to overleap what lies

before his eyes. What use would the understanding of Buddhism be to him, if he did not understand the most tangible and immediate realities? A monk inquires about the nature of Truth; 'What is the Way?' he asks. 'What a fine mountain that is!' replies the Master. 'I am not asking you about the mountain, but about the Way!' says the monk crossly. 'As long as you cannot go beyond the mountain', the Master answers, 'you cannot reach the Way'. The Buddha-nature is not to be sought in the remote heavens, before it has been recognized in the objects around us. Upon another occasion, a Master gleefully leads his disciples into an involved argument regarding his identity, and when an exasperated monk finally asks, 'What are you then?' replies, 'I'm not a "what" either!'; perhaps, if the monk loses his temper, he will receive the lightning-flash of Satori and see his difficulties dissolve away. And when a Master asks a question, he wants the quick answer that leaps spontaneously to the tongue, before the mind, with its clever reasoning, has had time to interfere; one of them asks a monk something and snaps, 'Quick, quick, or thirty blows for you!'

But chief among the techniques for baffling the mind and arousing the intuitive powers is the 'Koan'. The 'Koan' is some totally illogical problem, to which, quite obviously there is no reasonable answer; and the monks of the Zen community must spend some hours of every day puzzling over the 'Koans' allotted to them, until their minds are exhausted and bemused with the struggle. However tired they may be, they are urged on to attack their 'Koans' with every faculty they possess. To roll the problem over and over, to pummel it and tear it to pieces, to examine it upside down and inside out, until the intellectual difficulties which it holds have, as it were, destroyed themselves by their own weight; until, in the calm that follows this battle, a new vision rises from the burnt-out ashes of the old and Satori is achieved. The monk struggling with his Koan is said to be like a mosquito trying to bite through a bar of iron; at the very moment of defeat, he forgets himself; he penetrates, and the work is done. After which, says the Zen

Master, 'Nothing is left to you but to burst out into a loud laugh!'

The meaning of this practice is sufficiently clear. The Koan is the image of life itself, which, in terms of reason, must always present a completely insoluble problem. But because we are always cheating and trying to solve human problems by some short cut—generally by an act of violence—we need to be reminded that such problems are not given us to solve, but to live through and to live out, until the problem itself is shattered and falls away. C. G. Jung has said that, in most cases, a neurosis cannot be cured; it can only be transcended. And the same applies to every problem, of which the Koan is a representation in miniature. The mind, struggling to find a solution, rushes from one extreme to the other; it takes counsel from a confusion of voices; 'Murder would solve it! Forgetting one side of the matter would simplify life! Escape! Escape!' But the only real solution is to admit that there is none, within the terms of the situation from which the problem arose, and to live through the consequences of that 'impasse'. Life presents a dilemma to which every final answer is the wrong one. Very well, say the teachers of Zen; then on with the dilemma!

There is one particular Koan which illustrates very well the problem with which Zen Buddhism itself has to deal. 'A man kept a goose in a bottle. It grew larger and larger until it could not get out of the bottle any more; he did not want to break the bottle, nor did he wish to hurt the goose. How would you get it out?' Here is the dilemma of the Buddhist, who must either free himself from the toils of the world or be crushed by them. There would appear to be two courses open to him, both of them suicidal. Either he can break his bonds forcibly and escape by violence, thus doing injury to the world; or he can submit to bondage, and so suffer slow strangulation and spiritual death. How does Zen deal with the matter? The disciple is set to attack the problem until Enlightenment breaks upon him and he becomes, through a transformation of his own spirit, free in the midst of the world; liberation, without severance.

But already explanation dismembers what has meaning only while whole. Between birth and death, human existence is a splitting of what is, in truth, whole and indivisible into frag ments which the mind keeps asunder, but which experience always re-unites. The moment—of action, of experience or of dream—is an indivisible whole; it is in the gaps between that the mind tears it apart in terms of subject and object, cause and effect. Living, we do not know ourselves; knowing ourselves, we are suspended between the interstices of life. Self-consciousness is the book we are allowed to read only during the suspension of life; that is the tragedy of self-consciousness. We think, 'This time I shall really see the god descend, catch and impress his image so that it belongs to me!' But the god comes, and we are blinded; when sight returns, the horizon is empty. We would catch ourselves, know ourselves in the moment of loving; but, so long as we watch, the moment does not come; and when it comes, sight is eclipsed.

This is one way of saying that the famous antithesis of subject and object does not exist in operation, but only in forethought and after-thought. Every actual experience is a little death, the extinction of self-consciousness. And it is this little death, which is the entering into the wholeness of the experience of the 'moment', that Zen emphasizes, drawing illustrations of it from the arts of fencing and wrestling. Jiu-jitsu is a practical application of Zen, being based entirely upon a union of attack and defence and upon the principle of allowing one's opponent to overthrow himself by his own force and weight—one yields so that he may fall. This has been compared to the principle whereby pliant branches bend beneath their burden of snow, instead of snapping through an effort to resist; bending, they let the snow slide to the ground, and then they spring back into place. As exemplified in Jiu-jitsu, it is yielding which achieves the victory that would have been impossible to force.

In the art of fencing, it is the principle of 'Immediacy' that is applied. 'When the hands are clapped', said a great Zen fencing-master, 'the sound issues without a moment's deliberation. The sound does not wait and think before it issues. There is no mediacy here, one movement follows another without being interrupted by one's conscious mind. . . . You just follow the movement of the sword in the hands of the enemy, leaving your mind free to make its own counter-movement without your interfering deliberation'. The bell's note does not wait and consider, after the bell is struck; and if the bell is true, the note rings true. It is just such spontaneity of reaction that Zen aims at inducing. The disciple, as we have seen, must answer his master as promptly as the bell-note answers the striking hammer. If he hesitates for so long as to take breath, the voice that issues from him will not be his own. Thought is not permitted to intervene between stimulus and reaction, question and answer. An almost unimaginable, an altogether forgotten spontaneity is demanded of the exponent of Zen. No second thoughts are allowed; not even first thoughts; only the most complete immediacy.

It was in painting, however, that Zen teaching found its most fruitful application. Its influence was very widespread and marvellously productive, but it is in the school of painting known as Sumiye that the spirit of Zen finds its most perfect expression. This Sumiye work is executed upon paper so thin that, if the brush hesitates for so long as a second, it tears; every stroke is final and irretrievable. 'The brush must run over the paper swiftly', says Suzuki, 'boldly, fully and irrevocably just like the work of creation when the universe came into being. As soon as a word comes from the mouth of the creator, it must be executed'. Not a line can be altered, touched-up or erased. Deliberation is impossible; if thought intervenes between inspiration and execution, the work is spoiled. What is beautiful, in the eyes of Zen, is what is inevitable, the free expression of Spirit casting its shadow on the earth; the painting is perfect only according to the extent to which the painter's hand and mind have done their work as passive instruments. The aim is not to trap Spirit and to pin it on to the paper, but in a few lines to show it as it moves, much as though a bird in flight had brushed the artist's paper with its wing. The artist's brush is an indivisible extension of his arm, and his arm simply follows the play of his spirit.

Thus Sumiye works are never static representations of nature; they are the reflection of movement. The tale is told that a horse came down from a Sumiye artist's picture and galloped away over the fields. If a bird is depicted, it seems on the very point of leaving the paper. Men, trees and rocks are shown in their essential evanescence. The Sumiye artist has no faith in 'objects' since everything in the world is in movement, if not in space, at least in time; everything is either forming or dissolving; everything is becoming. We may search for some handle embedded in this flux, offering a point of stability; we may create such handles for ourselves and grip them as though life itself depended upon a firm hold; but Zen calls upon its followers to abandon even the surest hold and to go out into the stream supported by faith alone.

The time comes when one must ask at what point in a man's life this 'lightness' which Zen teaches should be sought or can be attained. It is not a question that any Zen Master would consider worth answering; he would dismiss it as absurd, for there can be no 'should' in this matter and no planned timetable; Enlightenment comes when the man and those forces which conspire to make his destiny are ripe for its coming. It is not a flower to be plucked when we happen to feel the inclination; but it will lie in our way when we are ready for it.

It is doubtful, however, whether the Zen strictures against learning, study and spiritual training are meant to be quite as extreme as they appear to be. To restore the balance of truth, it is sometimes necessary to go to one extreme in order to combat another which has become firmly established, and the teaching which it was the task of Zen to attack was lost in a welter of book-learning, literal-mindedness and barren speculation; an excessive faith was put in mental acquisitions. What Zen asserts is not so much that knowledge should never be acquired as that, once acquired, it must be lost; a very different matter.

The accumulation of knowledge, the struggle towards a

rational understanding of the world, is the task of a lifetime. A tragic task, for every step forward is also a step back from the goal, and what is gained in concrete understanding of certain specific problems is lost from that awareness of the illimitable which alone offers any real reward. First we labour to amass facts and to forage in the wisdom of others, to learn whatever secrets may have been recorded. This is a necessary preliminary. And then we are called upon to cast away every atom of that knowledge. If we cling to it when the time of severance comes, we are less than the sorriest and least-instructed simpleton, and are committed to a prison of our own arduous building. Why, then, trouble with knowledge, if it must be renounced? Because, when it falls away from us, its seed, the final essence of all that we learned, lies somewhere hidden in a recess of our being. That seed is potent. There is something in us that is in the making; all that we pass through and all that we learn, though divested of the form under which we knew it and lost to memory, lies buried in that invisible seeding-ground and is incorporated in the blood and sinew of our being. But only on condition that we have surrendered it and no longer cling to any part of it; only on condition that it is no longer 'ours', to be exploited and put to use.

The final aim of all serious study is not to accumulate learning as an end in itself, but to see learning transformed into wisdom. But there is a gulf between the two; learning may be 'possessed'; wisdom may never be 'possessed'. Therefore the transformation entails the loss of all that 'belongs' to us. Learning is a filing-cabinet, which has its index, its known resources and its known limitations. Neither the resources nor the limitations of wisdom can be calculated; its index is not in our keeping; it has a will, even a life of its own; we cannot hold on to it, but can only pray to be touched by it, as by an instantaneous and divinely given insight. The agony of this transformation, then, lies in the fact that what was known and certain must be exchanged for something unknown and eternally uncertain to which no man has a claim 'by right'. A certain unwillingness to make this exchange is natural; one is not always ready to give up the 'bird in the hand'. Hence the Zen strictures against learning. The Zen Master is crying, 'Let go! Let go!' for he knows that there comes a moment when we must either let go or be dragged down into perpetual bondage by all that we have, with such pains, accumulated.

In this sense it would be true to say that Zen is only opposed to learning at the final stage, the moment of transformation. But in another sense, it must oppose learning at every stage, for learning may at any or at every moment obscure our vision and prevent our seeing what there is to be seen of truth, receiving what there is to be received of wisdom, here and now. The grim drive of the mind to discover the essentials of life usually leads directly to what is least essential; to the framework, the bare bones that derive meaning only from that which clothes them. What is of greatest value is often light as the butterfly's wing, and every system of thought sets out by excluding it. Permanence and eternity are opposites. The confusion of these two is the death of wisdom. Thought cleaves to what seems permanent, and it suffers the condemnation of all relative permanence. Flesh is closer to eternity than is bone; feeling is closer than is flesh; and the evanescent moments of delight and vision are closest of all.

What injustice!—the learned complain—that a drunkard, a laughing girl or a drowsy old man may, by grace, come closer to this mystery than all those philosophers who climb the ladder rung by rung and would, if they were made immortal, still be climbing at the end of time. It is the fundamental injustice (as the world understands the term) illustrated by the tale which Count Keyserling recounts of how the god Indra, travelling one day through a forest, came upon a penitent who, during long terms of meditation and self-castigation, had almost changed himself into a tree stump. 'How long must I yet practise that I may be free?' he asked the god sadly. 'Ten more years', said Indra. 'Ten whole years?' sighed the sage, and for his complaint, was at once precipitated into hell. Wandering on, Indra came upon another penitent. This one was of slight spirituality and hoped to attain salvation by dancing around a tree. He asked the god the same question; but he asked them cheerfully, in the midst of his dancing. 'It will take you a hundred thousand years', said Indra, smiling. The foolish penitent gave a skip and a hop: 'Only a hundred thousand years!' And no sooner had the shout of joy left his lips than he rocketed up to heaven, a liberated soul.

Seen from the point of view of earth and, above all, of human societies, which, by necessity, see all things in terms of order, as calculable and rationally related, Spirit is eternal caprice. A caprice as outrageous as was Christ's attitude to the adulteress in the eyes of the learned clerks of Israel. And every stroke of Spirit in the world precipitates the piling up of a thousand volumes devoted to 'explaining' it and confining this waywardness within a human order. It is the special quality of Zen that it rejoices in this very waywardness and puts its faith in what is most incalculable. No other teaching has so thoroughly avoided the temptation to explain Spirit in other terms than its own or to reconstruct human life within the terms of one of its aspects.

Nevertheless the freedom of Zen can never be attained prematurely. Each Koan has to be worked through to its bitter end, and freedom is the ultimate reward of whole-hearted wrestling with the problem. The road to freedom lies only through the most bitter experience of bondage and the most complete acceptance of that experience—the freedom lies concealed in the heart of the acceptance. There is no alternative to human life and all that it entails; but there exists that which may transform it.

This needs to be stressed in any study of Zen, for no ideal is more open to misunderstanding than that of 'lightness'. Every virtue or achievement of the spiritual life has a corresponding shadow; a shadow which frequently shares its name, and yet is far less its likeness than its opposite. 'Detachment' can mean the most perfect disinterested compassion and selfless devotion, or it can cover a multitude of sins. 'Introversion' can denote absorption in self or absorption in the spiritual principle of life. 'Unselfishness' can mean a real transcendence of self-interest, but it is also used to describe the condition in which self-interest is removed one degree further from the subject's own character, desires and personal achievements, so that, although anxiety for self has been overcome, it has been replaced by an equally harmful anxiety for some cause or for some other person, remaining as fruitful a source of evil as ever; the man who does wrong for the sake of his party or his nation or on behalf of his family is only at one remove from the complete egoist; what he gains in a relative 'unselfishness' is lost through the deadening of conscience which takes place when we believe ourselves to be acting altruistically.

That 'lightness' which is the finest achievement of Zen possesses this dual aspect. False 'lightness' is an escape; it arises when the fear of suffering has created a terrible insulation of the personality against every disturbing element, whether from within or without; it is the touch which brushes against the nettle for fear of grasping it. True 'lightness' is the abandonment of all mechanisms of insulation and of all the self-concern which makes such mechanisms necessary; it is the entrance into the transformed personality of a spirit which knows nothing of self-concern. Perfectly simple, it is in origin immensely complex; marvellously easy, it is prodigiously difficult of attainment. The word of a Zen Master, lightly spoken, deceptively simple, may be the crystallization of the labour of ages; and without labour, followed by the renunciation of the fruits of that labour, it is not to be understood.

Like the surgeon, whose years of arduous training go to direct a simple gesture of his knife, the Zen Master, when he raises his stick in answer to a question, acts from a wisdom not easily attained. The greater his proficiency, the simpler his gesture.

PART II

CHAPTER SIX

THE SOUND HEART: MAX PLOWMAN

It is significant that, if we search in the modern world for something that might be set over against the ancient traditional doctrines of the East, something to put on our side of the scales, we are almost bound to choose an individual or a handful of individuals. We cannot choose the Catholic Church, for that does not belong to the modern world, and this world, when consistent with itself, hates and fears the Church, well aware that, in spite of a few acts of appeasement carried out by certain of its representatives, the Church cannot be otherwise than at enmity with the aims and methods of our contemporary civilization. Nor can we choose Protestantism, for it is too nebulous, more a state of mind (or of emotion) than a doctrine, and its popular teaching has degenerated into mere moralizing and the propagation of pious hopes, without foundation either in human nature or in the dynamic of present-day society.

What, then, of modern academic philosophy? Here again there is nothing to answer our purpose; this philosophy, which Kant himself defined as a discipline for setting limits to the range of human knowledge, is, for the most part, little more than a game of words, propounding artificial problems and solving them artificially, or circling round the narrow cell to which physical science has confined it; when, occasionally, it breaks free, it does not go out to meet Reality, but dives into the lower waters of human feeling and impulse, where reside the phantasmagoria of the Unconscious. We cannot choose any of the fanatical political faiths, for these are inspired, to a greater or lesser extent, by a species of Satanism, and their fruits are either ruin or enslavement. We cannot set our material progress and the 'benefits of science' in the scales, for they are without weight when balanced against the knowledge of and participation in the divine mysteries, and must inevitably be short-lived when unaccompanied by such an awareness of man's 'true end' as would enable us to bring some order into the means at our disposal. It is certainly not to any of the products of our restless energy—explorations, discoveries, inventions—that we can point with real pride, for this very restlessness is the most damning symptom of our disease and provides the surest evidence that, since the sixteenth century, the energies of Western man have been denied their true goal and fulfilment.

Indeed, it has generally been recognized, although this is not always considered a matter for regret, that there is a close connection between 'genius' and frustration, particularly when the frustration takes the form of some physical or mental malady, and it is fairly automatically assumed nowadays that the more impressive forms of human achievement are substitutes, compensations for the failure to fulfil some simple instinctual aim, and that the 'higher' is always derived from the 'lower', the greater from the less. Substitutes these achievements certainly are, but not for mother-love or the pleasures of the bed; they are compensations for the failure to fulfil the normal, outwardly inconspicuous pattern of human life and for the loss of faith in and awareness of the truth; and failure is always failure, the substitute is never more than a substitute.

A cripple may become a great musician, but he is still a cripple and, at heart, would still prefer health to fame. If we lived in a healthier world, and were ourselves less in need of substitutes for the few things essential to the human spirit, we might well do without our works of genius. And if we wish to praise the West in this modern age, it cannot be for the cities we have built or the lands we have conquered as poultices for our sense of loss, or for the works of art created out of bitterness and frustration, since these things can never be more than 'second best', but only for the men who, in spite of their times, have remained sound at heart. This is what we have to put in the scales: nothing glorious, nothing stupendous, but the almost unchronicled history of the few who are hale and whole.

All who suffer from the same disease are much alike, but every healthy man is healthy after his own fashion. The choice of one particular example of human soundness in the midst of the contemporary environment must not be thought to imply that the man chosen is a fixed model to be imitated by others of a different constitution and different gifts; men cannot model themselves upon a man, for the single image of human perfection is, in the world of our experience, particularized into a diversity of images, corresponding to the diversity of gifts and potentialities amongst individual men and women. Nevertheless, the quality which we have called soundness of heart, the fundamental health and integrity which is the essential basis for the development, in a particular individual, of that seed of perfection which he carries within him, can only be considered in an individual form.

Max Plowman seems to have possessed to a very marked degree this quality of soundness, and he provides an interesting example from the point of view of this study; up to now, we have been considering the shortcomings of the modern world from the standpoint of alien cultures, but the moment has come to turn to a critic of this world who never left its confines, who was altogether its child and who shared many of its most cherished hopes and beliefs. Plowman stood alone; he was not in a position to thunder anathema from the secure foothold offered by some form of traditional faith; no church sheltered him and no ancient teaching provided his weapons. His religious faith—it might be more exact to say, his religious sense—however far he may unknowingly have been led in the direction of ideas that are universal and traditional, was individual.

He spoke of an experience after which 'The things which are seen are henceforth the shadow of the things unseen and one simply has no other life than the desire to bring that new life . . . out of its burning hiding-place—in short to BE what one IS, and not merely the shadow of a reflection'; and although he felt compelled to spend time and energy in attacking the anomalies which he saw all around him, he never ceased to wish that he might be free from the necessity for 'burying shadows in order to get into the sunlight'. He saw the problem of his times as that of 'How to restore to bereft human beings the core of life—a centre that will put the whole circumference into true ratio'; there could be no better or simpler statement of the aim of all traditional religious discipline, but Plowman was virtually unaware of his allies, and it is because of the singular concordance between the beliefs to which he came by a bitter personal struggle and the faith which, under diverse forms, was once universal, that he seems so well fitted to act as a link between the modern West and the doctrines which we have been considering.

Max Plowman was born in 1883. At the age of sixteen he left school and went into his father's brick business, remaining in that job for some ten or twelve years. He walked out when the conviction of the wrongness and inhumanity of capitalist industrialism overcame him, and turned journalist.

His letters of the period just before the war of 1914–18 and of the early war years contain the seeds of much that was to occupy his mind in full maturity. We find already a passionate faith in personal integrity and in the right of every man to follow the promptings of his own 'intimations', wheresoever they may lead. In 1913 he was complaining (in a letter) 'how false idealism can play the fool with immature sentiment'; that extraneous idealism which takes the place of faith and knowledge and proves such heady liquor to the young. 'Most people', he wrote, 'want to be true to themselves and to . . . the Right Thing . . . or civilized society or their ideal of themselves or their wives . . . and of course it plays the very devil'. There could be no divided allegiance. 'Life at its best creates standards which man cannot let go: towards them he is obliged to strive'. From these personal standards no outward circumstance must divert us; every man is called upon to give life and form to what lies within him, and Plowman saw the distinction that is made between self-expression and self-sacrifice as a false one; for both represent a transcendence of self in the spirit of love and creativeness which carries us beyond all selfish ends. And both stand above the niceties of the moral law, for it is, as he says, 'only when something in us is not finding its proper expression that we're concerned about right and wrong'.

We are everlastingly curious, but if curiosity is satisfied without a deepening of 'the capacity for realization' we reap only 'barren intellectual power'; we must not force people to admit conclusions for which their minds are not yet ripe. People must be left to find their true and unique way; 'If you willingly attract a person towards you, you have the same responsibility to that person as the sun has to a plant. The sun cannot stipulate how much the plant shall grow. . . .' The stages of life must be respected. Sincerity is a property of maturity; the young are 'like a highly sensitized plate with five senses each producing a thousand images upon it . . . an unformed person cannot be sincere in any deep sense'. It is the 'right direction' that matters. And the 'right direction', a law of movement, takes the place of the old static law, a strait-jacket forced upon all degrees of men. 'The only fidelity I will ever know now', wrote Plowman, 'is fidelity to the moment'; for we are always changing, whether in growth or regression, and 'one promise blackens all futurity'.

National life he described as the L.C.M. of personal life, and we could hardly expect it to be good when 'even the best of modern lives is so far removed from any attempt towards the Kingdom of Heaven'. The conditions of that life were destroying the very qualities in men that could alone redeem it; 'There will be a nemesis for every atom of work laid on men's shoulders which by its burden denies men the freedom of spiritual activity'. The development of the personal life was the touchstone of all else; if that life was cramped and distorted by the form of society—no matter how much material prosperity might be the immediate reward—that society must be sick unto death. And sick it was, for in 1914 war broke out.

In 1915 Plowman joined up. 'Someone has got to resist them', he wrote, 'Why not I!' and 'Who am I that I should say to another man, "You do my killing!" ' and again, 'I don't live in an ideal world, therefore there arises a time when non-resistance is criminal idiocy'. In the letters of this period there is a tone of self-justification that we catch at no other time in his life. His faith has been put to the test; he wonders if perhaps it has been found wanting; he is doing himself bitter outrage in killing at the command of outward authority, yet 'Who am I . . .?' Perhaps conscience, at such a time, is a luxury that cannot be indulged; wrong there, for conscience is no luxury and to ignore it is to take an axe to the very root of all good. Through the Battle of the Somme the inner conflict persists, growing more bitter. In 1917 Plowman was invalided home.

In the trenches and in battle a vision had come to him of the holiness and sweetness of life. From the simplicity of death a new simplicity of life arose. It is a vision that many soldiers see in hours of danger or privation—like the cry of the man out in the storm, 'Would God my wife were in my arms and I in bed again'—but lose after the first joy of home-coming. Plowman, however, retained it all his days, and in the essay he wrote while on leave, *The Right to Live*, he urged them to cling to that vision of what was essential in life as their most precious possession.

The essay is rather rhetorical, but ardent and sincere. The enslavement of man by man was, he wrote, humane compared with the enslavement of man by 'a vast inhuman machine'. We must free ourselves from 'the obsessions of a misused life', distinguish between the 'means to life and the purpose of life' and realize that 'power without wisdom is a curse'. We had gained a sterile power over the natural world, but our restless ingenuity would never bring us to wisdom or happiness, whatever wonders we might perform. Self-consciousness had given us the power either to deepen our harmony with the earth or to destroy it; and now power without wisdom had brought us to the limits of discord. We had denied the earth from which we sprang; we had denied the true law of our own natures, and our own natures had turned upon us, for we were born through love, nourished by love, bred in love, and when it ceased to be the law of our life we were given into the hands of a thousand devils.

Having written that confession of faith, Plowman took the logical next step. Some years previously he had 'renounced' the competitive capitalist system and now he 'renounced' what he regarded as its child, mechanized total war. In a written statement of his reasons for resigning his commission he said, 'I believe that if I now continued to act as a soldier I should be guilty of the greatest crime it is possible for a human being to commit'. The significant word is 'now'; it was only now that he had come to understand that he could have no part in modern war without betraying the faith that it was his life's work to proclaim. 'I no longer believe that war can end war', he continued; 'Virtue can never be imposed'. Each war makes the succeeding one more probable; we cannot complain if occasionally a man comes forward who would break the vicious circle. But complain we do, and the preparations for Plowman's court-martial went forward. Before any decision had been reached, the war was at an end.

Writing ten years later, he said, 'When I became a "conchy" it was with the knowledge that I was joining the fool's party'. His pacifism was not of the common brand of naïve optimism and wishful thinking. He had little patience with the bourgeois pacifist who had reaped the fruits of a competitive economic system and hope to have Peace thrown in as an extra bonus. 'Surely in any conscious person there comes a point of resistance to the existing order at which he finds himself unable to co-operate in it'; for him, that point had been reached.

A deceptive era of Peace had come to the world. It gave the way of life which makes wars inevitable the opportunity to increase its tempo. The vicious circle, or rather, the spiral was closing in, but at this point upon its circumference there was a brief respite.

In 1928 his young son, Tim became ill. Cerebro-spinal meningitis was diagnosed, and soon the doctors abandoned hope. He adored the boy, and he became convinced that if anything could save him it was the compelling power of his love. There began a long, bitter and finally triumphant struggle against the forces of death. 'Last Thursday the old fellow had a bad paroxysm. I put my arms round him and we fairly hung on to one another while Satan did his worst'. The eighteenth operation followed. Again the doctors assured him that there was no hope. For nine weeks altogether the struggle continued. The child recovered from the meningitis, and the doctors pronounced a 'miracle'. A few days later a cold developed; Plowman warned the doctors, but a cold was nothing to worry about. Pneumonia did its work swiftly in the exhausted body. Tim died.

Plowman believed that the strength of his love and of his faith had kept the child alive; and this came as a revelation that cast a kind of radiance over the remaining thirteen years of his life. In his letters of that time there is great pain, but also joy, deep and utterly confident, for the efficacy of love as an active power in the world had been proved to him beyond the shadow of a doubt. From then on much of what he wrote was a struggle to communicate the joy and the revelation that he had been granted. 'It's no joke being without him. You know what I mean—being without his tread on the step: his voice in the morning. But the old pet taught me all I shall ever know about life and death . . . and the invincible power of love'.

But how hard it was to communicate this knowledge! All except a few close friends avoided the topic of death for some time to come; death was a fact of which they had no wish to be reminded, and they took it for granted that his only wish was to forget and bring the child to a second death in himself. He wrote, about this time, 'It's a terrible thing to come back to this world after having looked in upon eternity. You open your mouth to speak and the words do not form themselves. You seem to be filled with divine communications, but no one understands the cypher. I have never been alone as I have been since Tim died. . . .'

And so the years passed. He was associated with Dick Sheppard in founding the Peace Pledge Union; he became its secretary. He edited the *Adelphi*; he wrote four books, some verse and a great number of letters; he struggled to persuade his Marxist friends that Marxism was not enough. There was no means in his country whereby a man of his kind could make his voice heard except in a small, ineffectual circle. When the second World War broke out he formed the Adelphi Centre in Landham (Essex), a small community living on the land; and there, in June of 1941, Max Plowman died.

The moment has now come to examine more closely the view of life which Plowman proclaimed in his letters and in his books of the period between the wars. A good starting-point is provided by Blake, for throughout his life the influence of Blake predominated over that of any other of his predecessors, and while he was editing the *Everyman* edition of Blake's works the bulk of his correspondence was devoted to the elucidation of the Prophetic Books and to discussions of textual difficulties.

The centre of Blake's world was occupied by the 'Fourfold Man', the man in whom the spirit, the head, the heart and the loins were harmoniously united; any dissociation of these functions and any attempt to live by one or two or even three of them alone brought disaster. In this fourfold man was consummated the Marriage of Heaven and Hell, Heaven representing the one clear light over all and Hell the dark world of passion and the senses. Divided, Heaven and Hell were equally barren, but from their union sprang joy. 'Oh that man would seek immortal moments! Oh that men would converse with God!' had been Blake's cry, but he had balanced it with—'Attraction and repulsion, reason and energy, love and hate are necessary to human existence'. And Plowman never doubted that human existence, even as a 'series of conflicts for the purpose of nobler synthesis', was good and sweet to enjoy. The image of the Divine was the whole man, not his emasculated effigy.

In that process of integration by which man becomes whole

or by which, in Jungian terminology, 'personality' is achieved there are three stages; the 'thesis' of Innocence, the 'antithesis' of Experience and the 'synthesis' of Imagination. Innocence is perfect in itself, but cannot be prolonged beyond its term; Experience is violent, possessive and at times nightmarish, and Imagination (not to be confused with fantasy) places the whole, the fourfold man over against the world as its co-creator with God. And, with the achievement of Imagination, the world is seen 'through, not with the eye' or, in other words, the lifeless images with which the senses present us are transformed and re-illumined by Vision. An object seen only 'with the eye' is without significance—men are seen merely as objects, obstructions to be moved out of our path when the occasion demands; seen 'through the eye', they are the Divine Image in human form.

These ideas, which run through all Blake's work, were central to Plowman's view of the world. 'The real problem', he said, 'is not whether the universe is coherent, but whether our experience in it is coherent'. And evil is not something to be fled from and feared, but a state of experience through which the soul must pass. Nothing is more fruitless than the attempt to 'leap-frog over experience'. Plowman gave his own interpretation of Blake's three stages of life:

Innocence = Instinctive life = Childhood
Experience = Self-conscious life = Adolescence
Imagination = Conscious life = Maturity.

The terms Childhood, Adolescence and Maturity must be interpreted freely; obviously, a man may remain all his days in the first or second of those stages.

We are led from self-consciousness to consciousness by love, in which our selfhood falls away and we are released to a full awareness of life and 'the other person', able to say, 'I live, nevertheless, not I!' Imagination (or Consciousness) is an inner synthesis of Vision and Experience. Joy is the fruit of this achievement, but happiness is, at the best, only a by-product. Happiness is a sign of physical and spiritual equilibrium; 'this may be maintained as perfectly on the level of the beast as on the level of the sage; but it is a condition which is inevitably disturbed by any effort towards development'. Happiness is a resting-place, never a goal.

It follows from this that good actions, like happiness, are a by-product. 'The conscious effort to do good is fundamentally immoral.' There is a strict division between those who believe in growth and those who believe the 'Evil has a separate existence to be combated'. Evil is 'Imperfect growth . . . the energy of life thwarted . . . a poor manifestation of life'; and to combat life, even in an imperfect manifestation, is a waste of time. 'We are overwhelmed', he wrote, 'with damned self-conscious posturings of ladies and gentlemen pretending they have received —or placing themselves in what they believe to be the correct attitude to receive—the outpourings of the Holy Ghost'. Life can be trusted; it is when we begin to 'draw back by taking thought for the morrow that we betray ourselves'. And 'Passion is the spring of wholeness and holiness'.

Plowman accepted the full implications of this view. And the chief implication may be expressed in the words of Christ (so inconvenient for the Christian who has come to comfortable terms with the world), 'Resist not Evil'. Only a man with the most utter and complete faith in a purpose behind life and in the potentialities of spiritual development present in every man could accept that. And we who cannot equal that faith have not the right to condemn it. 'You live by committing yourself to the Unknown,' Plowman wrote; and so long as we cling to the narrow bastion of selfhood we cannot do that; the Unknown is something to be feared, threatening our bastion, something against which we fight our endless, exhausting battle of self-defence and against which we guard ourselves by a mass of possessions.

There is neither wholeness nor faith when we are led to see 'with, not through the eye'; and this Plowman regards as the failing of modern science and psycho-analysis. 'To be able to observe and recognize the feelings of others with a pure objective recognition is to BE the Devil. Psychiatry is the twentieth-century witchcraft.' Analysts, lacking any idea of spiritual health (which cannot be defined in their terms), are driven to take 'the least offensive person as their ideal'; their reasoning is simple—lunatics are offensive, therefore the normal person must be inoffensive. 'Adjustment' is surely the sorriest ideal ever held up before mankind. They 'shove Eden before us and say we can get there by a simple process of subtraction, while Blake held up Jerusalem as our goal and said in effect that the way there was by addition'. They attempt to scrap everything that does not fit neatly into their narrow conception of man, and this process of paring will bring us at last to vacuity. 'The psycho-analyst's "normal man" . . . God defend us from all such castrated sterility!'

When we search for hope and joy in rational, scientific knowledge, 'As well might a man hope to beget a giant race out of the knowledge of female anatomy!' Knowledge is a part, a necessary part of wisdom, but knowledge to-day has become totally divorced from wisdom. Clearly, Plowman's polemic against the analysts did not imply any disregard for the unconscious forces in man, but simply a desire to see these forces through, not with the eye. 'How', he demanded, 'can those be free who have within them a power they can never wholly trust?' And those who 'think we can have free heads and slavish tails . . . believe in a "war of freedom"—the head fighting against the tail.' Our institutions are built upon the fear of instinctive life, and we receive intellectual but seldom affective education; emotionally, in fact, we often remain children long after we have become intellectually mature, and arrested development is synonymous with deformity—what has ceased to grow and develop decays, nothing can remain static. And it is infantile passions—deformed by our very fear of them—that lead us to disaster.

The scientific eye is, of course, infantile, and it attempts to keep the objects of its study in their stage of arrested development. This is particularly so when it turns its attention to sex, and in sexual matters we have exchanged 'for the solemnity of Puritanism the solemnity of science'; in neither is there any place for love or mirth. In fact, the scientific and so-called 'frank' attitude to sex is nothing but an attempt to sterilize it, an attempt bred of our fear and our refusal to accept and be humble before a Mystery (*The Mastery of Sex* was the title given to a recent book; a sign of the contemporary mania for mastering everything to hand). 'We're all sex-frightened', Plowman wrote, 'so we think of it only in terms of climax. . . . We don't know how to be expressive of intermediate stages of sex feeling because directly we are conscious of tenderness we know we are in the world of taboos', 'Our attitude to sex is rather a matter of bravado, "Who's afraid of the Big Bad Wolf!"' and our dance lyrics, caterwauled by innumerable crooners, are set to transform a Mystery which transcends beauty and ugliness into a cube of sugar or a pretty paper flower. A good full-blooded bawdy tale is a hymn in comparison. As with sex so with most of the other elements in human life.

All this 'scientism' belongs to that stage of development which Plowman calls self-consciousness. As an example of that stage he took Shakespeare's Hamlet, a man who had come too far to return to the simplicity of instinct but not far enough, until the play is done, to go forward into consciousness. Hamlet was trapped in that intermediate and impotent condition. He was a man 'so grievously hurt in a natural relationship that his instinctive life had been cleft from top to bottom', and those who have just emerged from the realm of pure instinct are too insecure on their newly fledged wings to face it squarely and repair the damage.

When Hamlet considers action, he cannot undertake it with the whole of himself and becomes 'nine parts actor taking his prompt from the Ghost'. The self-conscious man, neither harnessed to instinct nor wholly free, cannot act. And if he attempts to do so and denies the hesitations of dawning consciousness he takes the way of power and is condemned to the world of Macbeth, 'an insane slaughter house . . . the pole star of integrity lost'. Macbeth forces himself forward and brings forth Imagination in its monstrous embryonic stage; the energy of Imagination, once released, can never be called back, and when it is denied and disassociated from love it swings to the contrary pole and takes upon itself the images of fear.

Hamlet, however, refusing to take the fatal step, emerges at the last to true consciousness and cries: 'The readiness is all!' Those words were Plowman's text for the greater part of his work. Man cannot condemn the universe, for the part cannot arise and condemn the whole to which it belongs, but 'acceptance' is a word that, quite apart from its frequent misinterpretations, has too passive a sound for those who believe that man's role is a creative one. Plowman substituted for 'acceptance', 'forgiveness'. He maintained that we are in a sense re-born in every true act of forgiveness and that, without it, 'one just gets choked up with the foulness of oneself—breathing one's own air—living the life of perpetual self-justification'. We will so seldom admit guilt and have done with it, forgive ourselves, forgive the world and start afresh. And when it is we who are the injured party, or consider ourselves so, it is even harder to slough the burden of hatred, envy, righteous indignation and self-pity. 'We've got to give life the chance of acting freely towards us', Plowman wrote; we must not impede its rhythm by endless demands, complaints and expectations. Not to forgive is to be at war with ourselves, and it is we who are scorched by our persisting hatred.

Always, we are self-destroyers, and the spears we are for ever aiming at imagined enemies are plunged into our own hearts. We live as though in a perpetual state of siege, equally afraid of the mines beneath and the artillery without. Life is so 'cluttered up with self-protective rubbish and greedy self-seeking' that we move as clumsily as any medieval knight in full armour. And our state of 'preparedness' makes others prepare their defences against us (even animals attack those who are afraid and self-protecting). 'What the next man fears is my lust for possession,' and that lust for possession is bred of our desire to protect ourselves against him. The other man has every right to suspect our intentions, since fear of him makes us aggressive. 'But if my manner of life, and, far more, my whole spiritual address was such that he could have no such fear . . .'

then indeed a section of that vicious circle would have been broken.

'The way of spiritual progress', Plowman insisted, lay in a 'slow enduring growth—a gradual shedding—a gradual and growing ability to stand without props.' Instead of taking that way, we have devoted ourselves more and more completely to the construction of props; there is nothing over against us that we do not mistrust. Our conquest of the natural world was a part of this self-defensive campaign, and because our only thought is to 'use' nature and 'use' our possessions, we cannot love them. 'The idea of possessions only begins when love stops.' A child lives in its possessions and loves them just because it has no urgent need of them; our need has transformed ours into objects devoid of significance. 'Mechanization involves an abstraction from life, an abstraction made for the sake of utility'; the things around us should be regarded as 'appealing objects . . . threatening us with the sense of death unless they are continually dowered with our own life-energy.'

Here Plowman approached the Austrian poet, Rilke, who also maintained that the 'inanimate' is making a demand upon us, the demand to be 'redeemed' by being taken into our hearts and given a share of our life. And the question for Plowman was 'How much of the mechanized utility placed at our disposal by scientific discovery are we able to incorporate in our lives without damage to our distinctive human nature?' The question is fast ceasing to have any meaning, for it is now the 'mechanized utilities' that are incorporating us into their lives—or rather, into their death.

Who shall deliver us from the body of this death? 'Let a man say what he loves most and he becomes a self-determined entity,' wrote Plowman. He has, in fact, a 'right direction' and coheres into personality. 'In love you don't relinquish selfishness, you surpass it'; that fact was all-important to Plowman, for he had seen how fruitless were the antics of those who tried so hard to relinquish selfishness by the force of their wills. 'Life', he said, 'has got to be the perpetual exercise of the heart's affections or we atrophy the primary organ of life.' The heart's affections can only operate freely when fear is cast out; it is always fear that makes us cower back into ourselves. 'The vital principle of the world is love,' he insisted, 'and life is the activity of that vital principle in all its efforts to become perfectly expressive.' Love, at white heat, becomes Vision; and the force of Vision draws all the powers of man to it. Everything falls into place when that principle is firmly established in the heart, and all deliberate, self-conscious efforts towards integration are seen for what they are, the attempt to lift ourselves by our own boot-laces.

When we are so directed and empowered by love, the problems of conduct and morality fall away. 'Where the heart is fully persuaded, there's precious little sense of sacrifice.' And nothing is more dangerous than self-conscious self-sacrifice, with its burden of self-righteousness and its expectation of reward. This directing love is not a force generated within upon rare occasions, but a natural manifestation of the spirit, ready to flow outwards as soon as the obstructions of fear and self-protection are removed.

'My quarrel with my generation', he wrote, 'is that almost nobody has the guts to love anybody.' And it is not only that 'the effrontery of power has made nobility of life appear footling and civilized man is made ashamed of his immortal longings'; for the way of power and of compulsion has only come into being through our lack of faith in the efficacy of love. 'We ought to be anchored in simple human affection,' but now it is always a case of ' "LUV" or suspicious animosity'. The loosening of sexual taboos has had one curious result; it has made us suspicious and even a little fearful of any love that does not proceed directly from human coupling. The taboo on love or, as Ian Suttie calls it, 'the taboo on tenderness', has been intensified and to-day there is something embarrassing, even a little indecent about a profession of love for someone who is not bed-worthy. Suttie, the most brilliant of British psychiatrists and a man too little known in his own country, has a good deal to say about this 'taboo on tenderness'—a taboo so obviously present in the work of Freud—and traces it in the premature 'emotional weaning' of children and the contemptuous suppression of the natural manifestations of tenderness in the child. Certainly, it is a taboo deeply embedded in our present culture.

But Plowman was little concerned with taboos, and he used the word Love fearlessly; if his readers were embarrassed, that was their misfortune. Love, and the Vision to which it would finally bring us (when what Blake called the stage of Imagination was reached) resides only in the Individual; crowds, herds, nations and groups cannot approach it. 'Individual freedom is the basis of all other freedom and we can't build the house by pulling out the corner-stone', and 'I see the Individual as the everlasting term of reference'. Nothing that is of value can find expression in the world unless through individuals. And those who 'only exist in relation to other people . . . have not yet grown separate entities at all'. To shirk our individual development and our absolute responsibility for our own lives by an attempt to merge ourselves in the herd or the nation is a betrayal.

Perhaps the chief reason for the flight from the painful uniqueness of individual life is the fear of death, and many people defend themselves against this fear by a deliberate effort to trivialize death; they avoid thinking of it until it is upon them and then shuffle out under an anaesthetic. The evasion of the knowledge that, in an often quoted saying, 'Nature intends to kill us, and will succeed in the end', creates a blind spot in the heart; it represents, says Plowman, an attempt to achieve 'a loveless self-sufficiency'. 'To hold a trifling view of life for the sake of an easy exit by way of death' is not an uncommon expedient; and, by every act of denial, even the denial of majesty and terror to death, life is diminished. If death looks small, life will look smaller; and we are amongst the pygmies.

It is, according to Plowman, from awe of death, as well as from the moments of experience which are timeless, that the religious consciousness is built up, and its positive expression, he says, is in the acceptance of 'the burden of the incarnation of new value'. Wholeness and integrity imply the 'submission of the whole man to the purpose of life', a purpose beyond what we usually understand by 'Nature'. But full awareness of this purpose and, in fact, the religious consciousness belong properly to the third stage of the individual's development, that of Imagination. There is a mode of life suited to each stage: 'Action is lovely—in the child glorious: in the adult, less beautiful—in the middle-aged, unsightly—in the old, pitiable'. The crystallization of our 'intimations' into religion advances as outward activity diminishes. 'Our instinctive joy, experience may mar, but the joy that comes from imaginative insight is eternal'. Having been merged in the stream of experience, we emerge to find again, at a deeper level, the treasures that were washed away in that stream.

But merged we must be. We cannot skip over the stage of Experience; and premature non-attachment shows fear of 'the gold and black of joy and sorrow'. It remains true that 'the spirit has to humble itself in the incarnation of flesh to be expressive'; life is the attempt to 'embody joy' and 'to wish yourself out of the body while you are for a purpose confined to the body seems to me partial and wrong'. The sin, a sage of long ago explained upon being reproached for entering a brothel, lies not in entering in but in failing to emerge. The comparison may seem invidious (it is not Plowman's), but it is apt; to rest in the timeless divine and there forget the world is 'partial and wrong'. We have to learn not to divide Time and Eternity 'with a great divide—with a death', for 'the minutest particulars of personal feeling . . . are channels of immortal life'. To the depths of hell, all is impregnated with the divine; 'There's nothing to discard.'

We have to learn the hard lesson of accepting the shadow; 'As if the sun didn't compel the shadow! As if the strength of the shadow were not the clearest evidence of the sun's strength!'; of Shakespeare's tragedies he says, 'What a glare of sunlight they shield!' Evil is only profoundly terrifying when we fail to see it as shadow and mistake it for a world of darkness. We can only become fruitfully 'non-attached' through love; any other way represents 'a "categorical imperative" in the realm of the "spontaneous"'. We cannot comprehend evil except in that same spirit of love. 'God is known by the heart or not at all.'

And that 'knowing by the heart' grows in solitude. Without introspection, in the true sense of the word, man lives 'either in ignorance or in fear of himself and will transfer his ignorance or fear to the society to which he belongs'. Without introspection that is rightly directed the religious consciousness will not become expressive. Without it, the personal discovery of Value is impossible. And without a sense of Value 'the world becomes a house full of junk'. Value guides us, not to rejection, for nothing is to be rejected, but to a true assessment. An assessment whereby all things fall into place and the world becomes coherent. Knowledge, Plowman once more reminds us, is only potential value. Knowledge is one of those things that has to be assessed and set in its place, otherwise it comes to tyrannize over us.

But Value always tends to become static and formalized unless it is ceaselessly revivified from a personal centre. Formalized Value soon falls into decay, and the shreds that remain, suprisingly wiry in texture, compel the strangest absurdities. There is the happy story of a Scots lass who found her lover whistling on the Sabbath; 'Jock', she said, 'if I'd ha' thought ye'd whustle on the Sabbath day I'd never ha' let you do what you just done!' Forms 'wound and destroy the living patterns of our lives', and those patterns are 'made in heaven to be revealed on earth'. The process of the incarnation of Value does not lead to the creation of static and abiding laws. Upon every man falls the dread responsibility of re-creation.

From this faith and this uncompromising refusal to live upon the husks of other men's creations sprang Plowman's politics. 'The longer I live the more I see politics as "resultant" and NOT primary.' If a man has achieved integrity his political action springs naturally from his conscience; if not, then his politics are 'a brown-paper covering which he paints red or black or blue according to fashion'. Plowman could have no truck with political slogans or party labels. Once he had written, 'Terrible is my temptation to live from another's centre', but he never gave way to that temptation.

Individualism, he said, could only be transcended through imaginative love. When 'Socialism' was merely substituted for 'Individualism' the outcome was 'the surreptitious emergence of imperfectly sublimated individualism exhibiting itself in strange and perverse ways'. There was no short cut and, above all, no quick one. It is a lesson that the modern world has been very far from learning, although the illustrations of it have been sufficiently savage. Plowman's political faith was contained and fully expressed in his Pacifism.

The superficial discussion of opinions which spring from a whole view of life deeply embedded in the personality is absurd and fruitless. We see this borne out in discussions on sex between members of the older generation and this one, when the argument never touches the real point of difference, the fundamental divergence of outlook upon life. A common language is the prerequisite of all argument; those who differ on 'fundamentals' have no common language. In the case of Pacifism this is borne out even more clearly; and those who are blessed—or cursed—with a capacity for seeing both sides of the question are driven to despair by the futility of the usual arguments around the subject.

It is in part the difference between the man who lies on his belly in a field and the one who regards that field from a considerable height. To pretend that the one view is more 'true' than the other, in a general sense, is absurd. All we ask of a pacifist is that he should face and accept the full implications of his opinion, and this Plowman did. He would have no compromise and no capitulation to expediency; 'Every great decision in life has to be made in a man's soul as though it and truth existed alone in the world'. If we pay attention to expediency we can always find an excuse to hand for making the wrong decision and if the worst comes to the worst there are always people to assure us that the right one—or in fact any decision that is not forced upon us by circumstances—is 'selfish'. 'Adam had a poor excuse when he said, the woman tempted me; how much worse is the individual's excuse who says, the nation tempted me!' If it is our true conviction that we should fight, let us fight and glory in it; but not for any other reason under the sun.

Plowman's pacifism was 'based on a moral and religious absolute . . . the vindication of action which is not even called upon to know its consequences'. And if that appears a dangerous saying, we have only to remind ourselves that in fact we never can know the consequences that will proceed from our actions and it is only conceit that makes us think we do; certainly, they are never, in the long run, the expected consequences. In practice we have to make our decisions regardless of their unforeseeable outcome.

'Peace', said Plowman, 'is a condition of being and not a fact at all, as war is.' Real peace is a way of life in which the very grounds of war do not and cannot exist; anything else is a precarious sham. We can put an end to wars only by living 'like a human individual' in order that we may 'live communally'. 'But if a man lies to himself and behaves like a damn puppet at the command of social organizations, how the hell can he hope to sustain a human life?' He is condemned, then, to 'assume responsibility for everything—except himself'.

'War', he said, 'will grow more and more recurrent so long as people decline to regard it as a personal matter.' There is a need here 'for the conviction of sin in individuals'. We may believe it is necessary to fight and fight with courage, but we must not shirk the guilt that fighting, in however righteous a cause, involves. Killing by necessity or at the command of another is still killing and remains the individual's sole responsibility. There was a time when men thought it right to undergo some ritual of purification after battle; that time is past.

'The world is trying to get Peace on the cheap,' he wrote. When he 'renounced' war, he did not become a 'war-resister' ('Nice job combating a machine-gun!'). He renounced resistance to as well as in war, and saw his sole purpose as the creation of a way of life that would be a living illustration of the alternative both to war and to the civilization which produces it. He tried to break right out of the vicious circle—he was too honest to accept one segment of it and reject the other—for he saw as clearly as any man how our lives are caught up and held in these circles from which, until each individual becomes wholly self-determined and responsible, there seems no escape. 'All that I know', he wrote towards the end of his life, 'is that I've seen a great light. All I long for is to transmit that light.'

This longing was baulked by the conditions of his time. Plowman's tragedy lay in his impotence. A few men who have things of moment to say are gifted with the artistic powers which enable them to reach a wide audience; Plowman was not so gifted. When he talked with a few friends, we are told, his words held magic; when he wrote, he stumbled. What openings are there for a man of his calibre to make himself heard in our contemporary world? Power of one kind or another is the prerequisite for gaining a hearing.

This is the predicament of the modern intellectual—though Plowman was obviously much more than an intellectual—and it is the cause of that tragic cleavage between the intellectuals and 'ordinary people' which is so acute in our time. The intellectuals are read and listened to by other intellectuals, circling round head-to-tail; and outside that circle the world goes its way. If they are irresponsible and often trivial-minded it is for the very good reason that our society will not accord them any position of responsibility, and they remain lop-sided, ballooning in the clouds because they are not allowed to tie up anywhere.

Plowman had no means of playing the part for which he was so well suited. In America he could have hitched his wagon to a Soap-King's star. In England he could have addressed small gatherings of enthusiastic spinsters; given short, bowdlerized talks on the B.B.C., to which no one would have listened; but he could not give practical help to a world so sorely in need of it.

And so he remained a solitary figure, writing letters and talking with his friends. Ours, however, is a darkness in which even the candle under a bushel gives some comfort and some hope. And in gratitude we must do what little we can towards setting that candle upon a hill; that candle, and all others that reveal the presence of a wise man and a true one.

CHAPTER SEVEN

MASK AND MAN: L. H. MYERS

Life's energies and desires fascinate me—not as temptations but as mysteries.—(L.H.M.)

Plowman was a fundamentally simple man, whose life was more significant than his writing. In fact, his writing (most of it in the form of letters to his friends) was but a commentary on his living. We now have to consider a man of far more complex character; one who was divided against himself, and who achieved in his writing an integration and harmony that was lacking in his life.

A bitter critic of his times, L. H. Myers exemplified in his character—and illuminated in his writing—the dilemma of those times. Fascinated, perhaps even trapped, by 'Life's energies and desires', he was stretched out over the widening gulf between his life and his work until, one night in April of 1944, only four years after finishing his last novel, *The Pool of Vishnu*, which was a triumphant vindication of faith and serenity, he was driven by doubt, despair and the unfounded obsession that he had cancer, to take his own life.

If, as seems very possible, Myers is one day raised to the position he deserves to occupy in the hierarchy of modern literature, every effort will no doubt be made to solve the enigma of his life and character. Here and now, our concern is with his work; nevertheless, something must be said of the soil in which that work flowered. He was the son of F. W. H. Myers, founder of the Society for Psychical Research and the leading spiritualist of his day. As a small child he was accustomed to the presence in his home of mediums, seers and the initiates of various mysteries; at the age of six, during a seance, he was ordered under the table to hold the medium's feet, and, as he knelt there, paralysed with terror, the table rose a few inches from the floor; falling back into place one of the legs caught his finger, and the scar remained to the end of his life.

He never, in later life, expressed any particular 'faith' in spiritualism, but the effects of such an environment upon a young child are not hard to imagine, and he retained always a sense of strange forces and demonic presences at work in the world. And he knew, as perhaps few sane people do, the meaning of 'absolute fear': 'I tell you', says one of the characters in *The Pool of Vishnu*, 'there is Terror beyond the Terrible. . . . The things to be feared are limited, but Fear is without limits . . . the Hell into which you sink alone. It is the solitary dark—where all courage, and all love, and all hope, are dead. They are of reality, but Fear is of unreality—which has no bounds, no law'.

The second formative element in Myers' early life was of a different nature, and yet became connected in his mind with the first. At the age of fifteen, when he was staying in a Swiss hotel with his parents, he was seduced by a girl of seventeen. He was of an age when sex and magic can easily become confused in a boy's mind, for there is a natural similarity between forbidden pleasures and hidden mysteries; it does not seem extravagant to attribute the strange atmosphere, half-erotic, half-magical which pervades certain passages in his work to the linking of those two elements of his early experience.

The revelation of sex had brought him to a precocious awareness of the personal life of the adult world. When, at the age of eighteen, he lost his father and was compelled to shoulder the sole responsibility for disentangling his confused affairs, he received a revelation of its public life, of the ways of lawyers and bankers, and of the power of money. The power of sex and the power of money! These were the secret rulers of our lives —even of the elegant life of Edwardian society, with which he soon became familiar.

In his early twenties the breakdown of his health led to a visit of two years to Colorado (where, returning at the age of twenty-seven, he married), and the impact upon an English-bred spirit of that strange and lovely land was a lasting one; it finds its echo in the descriptions of the Indian desert in *The Near and the Far*. It was also about this time that he went through an experience of the kind usually called 'mystical'.

The final shaping influence of Myers' early life was what the Victorians called 'High Society', in which his extraordinary charm and good looks—in combination with a private fortune—assured him considerable success. No man ever knew his adversary more intimately than this fierce opponent of the values for which that society stood. He remained, however, to the end of his life, attached to many of the tastes bred in his early days, and was responsible for founding Boulestin's Restaurant in London.

Myers was forty-one when he published his first novel (*The Orissers*, upon which he had been working for over ten years); his fourth and last book (*The Near and the Far*, which had appeared first in three separate parts and, in the present edition, includes *The Pool of Vishnu*) appeared when he was just short of sixty; and he had given, compressed into those few works, all that he had to give. The completion of *The Pool of Vishnu* (the final part of *The Near and the Far*) represented, in a sense, the end of his life; it almost seemed as though he had not left himself with the strength to go on living. 'I think your suggestion that I put serenity into the book', he wrote in a letter, 'instead of finding it in my own life is shrewd and, in fact, right'. He had deliberately turned his face to the wall; 'I have no wish to live. . . . During this period I've been in a backwater and withdrawing from life. . . . I, as a conscious being, bury my past and forget it'. There was little flame left for the veronal to quench.

The enigma of Myers' character is balanced by that of his literary reputation. No novelist of comparable distinction has been so little known to the general public. Yet few writers have been more kindly treated by the reviewers; *The Orissers* was greeted, upon its publication in 1922, with a flood of eulogy;

one reviewer compared it to *Moby Dick*, another to *Wuthering Heights*; a third pointed out that, if Myers had published separately the 'casual aphorisms scattered throughout the story' he would have established a reputation as 'a thinker of startling subtlety and originality'. *The Near and the Far* met with even warmer praise; an eminent critic and novelist wrote of it, 'The book seemed to touch every aspect, to sound every depth of human experience. After all had been said so perfectly and so finally, what use was there in my ever taking up my pen again?' In spite of this, Myers' work is almost unknown outside the small circle of his enthusiastic admirers.

That *The Orissers* should have been forgotten is understandable. No great novel ever had so many faults; no faulty novel ever achieved such greatness. It is a clumsy masterpiece, long-winded, involved, digressive; philosophical dissertations alternate with melodrama; the style is stilted and, at times, quite atrocious ('The Devil take you! said he. Not a word did the other reply'). But the neglect of *The Near and the Far* is more difficult to explain; by the time he wrote it, Myers had learnt his craft and achieved a style remarkable for its lucidity. *The Orissers* is clothed in a kind of jungle darkness, but *The Near and the Far*, although it contains scenes of darkness and horror, is surrounded with the atmosphere of fairyland, as one may see from this description, on the first page, of the desert at evening: 'There it lay, a playground for the winds, a floor for the light of evening to flow along, the home of mirage and coloured airs.'

It is, however, true—and this may suggest a partial explanation of the mystery—that the reader who has been accustomed to keeping books, and particularly novels, in separate compartments (the Psychological Novel, the Historical Novel, the Adventure Story, and so on) may feel that *The Near and the Far* is 'neither fish, flesh nor fowl'. The story is set in India in the time of Akbar (a contemporary of Queen Elizabeth's), since Myers wished, in his own words, 'to carry the reader out of our familiar world into one where I could—without doing violence to his sense of reality—give prominence to certain aspects of human life'. A few of the great number of people who have a special liking for historical novels may have been led to it for this reason, and they must inevitably have been disappointed; the equally great number whose pet aversion is the historical novel may have been put off by the mistaken notion that the book belongs to this class of fiction. Again, some may have turned to it from an interest in the customs and manners of sixteenth-century India, and been outraged by the liberties which Myers takes with the Indian background; others, who have no such interest, may have felt that a book about faraway people in a far-off country held nothing for them. Those in search of a philosophical novel may have been put off by the stories of political and amorous intrigue; others, in need of a good story, may have shunned a book that they were told was 'philosophical'. In each case, if the reader had gone beyond his first glance, he might have been delighted by the manner in which the various strands are woven together and the way in which the philosophy illuminates the story and the story illustrates the philosophy; but in such matters the first impression counts for a great deal.

There are some who may have found the dreamlike quality, the deep-sea enchantment of the book, contrary to their taste. Of *The Near and the Far* we might say what Otto Fischer wrote of certain Chinese landscape paintings: 'despite their perpetual agitation, they seem as remotely distant and as profoundly calm as though they drew secret breath at the bottom of the sea'. Even the vilest characters in the story have the bright colouring of rainbow-hued tropical fish, and although all the characters are from our age—and their problems are our problems—the story has been distilled from a mind of such uncommon fineness and from a sensibility so intensely alive to the mysteries of human existence that even the most ordinary incidents are invested with an almost unearthly brilliance which lifts them out of the realm of our normal experience.

Finally, it may appear to some that the problems with which Myers was preoccupied, both in *The Orissers* and *The Near and the Far*, are not the essential problems of life in our time; that he wasted himself in attacking an aristocratic society which, by the time of his death, had virtually ceased to exist. But the fundamental vice which he was concerned to expose and which he chose to analyse under the forms of snobbishness and social competitiveness is a universal quality of human nature, as is the driving fear behind it. It was with this fear and with the various masks which it compels men to adopt that Myers was concerned in all that he wrote.

'Man', he wrote in *The Orissers*, 'assumes a character and, having done so, can let the character part play itself'. By so doing, he cuts himself off, not only from the powers above, but also from other men, for only persons can enter into true communion with each other; masks cannot.

The central character of *The Near and the Far* is the young Prince Jali, son of the Rajah of a small principality. After a sheltered childhood, Jali is taken to the Imperial Durbar in Agra and encounters, for the first time, the great world. He is from the first fascinated by 'the essential secrecy of the human mind'; he begins to perceive that the behaviour of the people around him is no more than play-acting and that their lives are ruled by secret drives and fears which are never openly mentioned. The people of the Agra Palace, he realizes, express themselves as 'types'; they present 'stock-in-trade figures' between whom only stock-in-trade intercourse is possible, and the camouflage of type satisfies their instinct for secrecy. The 'false coin of appearances' is easy to pass from hand to hand, whereas the spiritual element which resides at the centre of the person is, by its very nature, elusive and intangible; what is required for the purposes of social intercourse is a firm, clearly marked surface personality that may be summed up at a glance. To Jali it seems that people have to choose 'between SEEING and BEING'; in so far as they limit themselves and, as it were, contract their vision, they become 'opaque, solid, comfortable to themselves and others'. But this solidarity, which Jali mistakes for true BEING, is in fact the mask behind which the true personal life, touched, as it always is, with the universality of spirit, dwindles away to a shadow. The blossoming of the character comes about only through the impoverishment of the person.

At a much later stage in the story, the wise Guru, who expresses the faith to which Myers came, in his work if not in his life, states the same principle with calm assurance: 'Many people are satisfied to communicate with one another merely as members of a type, but the personal spirit in you craves for something more. You must not hold it aloof from other persons as persons—for to do that is to hold it aloof from spirit as a whole.' It is only by making a breach in the masks which shield us from one another that we can break out into 'meeting'; and, for Myers, the medium in which that meeting takes place is the medium of the timeless spirit.

Jali himself, after his first experience in the Agra Palace, tries a number of masks in the hope of finding one that suits him and so protecting the nakedness of his spirit. He becomes a precocious rake, taking the Palace women by storm, and believes for a short time that he had both discovered the secret of the lives around him and assuaged his own sense of isolation. His story is in fact the tale of the masks which he assumes and discards. His uncle (one of the old ruling class who, deprived of his responsibilities by the new dispensation, gives himself up to amorous adventure and political intrigue) advises him, before he sets out for Agra, to do as the world does; 'Not to be afraid of this world you must belong to it. . . . In a nightmare, the way to escape a pursuing tiger is to turn oneself into one'; and it is not until he meets the Guru that Jali learns to do without this tiger-mask that falsifies human nature, leading men to live lives of perpetual pretence and to commit crimes natural to the mask but not to themselves.

Fear and a secret enmity between man and man in the natural life are the cause of masking, and the mask fulfils the function of the crustacean's shell; this is why true meeting and true communion can only take place through something which transcends the natural life. Enmity is inherent in nature and is only temporarily overcome by a coincidence of appetites which draws individuals together for pleasure or protection; it is because our life is of the spirit as well as of nature that love and friendship can triumph over hostility and endure in spite of the ebb and flow of feeling and passion.

Myers, as we have seen chose to consider fear and enmity in a particular context, and he was specially concerned with the intensification of these evil drives under a competitive economic system, but it would not be difficult to transpose what he had to say to other forms of society. In *The Near and the Far* he describes a society woman who is the slave of her own false standards: 'With every movement, every intonation, and—as far as possible—with every thought and emotion, she was applying tiny brush-strokes to a never finished portrait of herself.' He shows how her judgment of people is vitiated by what is in fact a cheap and trivial sense of values and analyses her obsession with the cult of 'first-rate-ness'; she pays tribute, 'now to the lovely honesty of a child like Savitri, now to the successful caddishness of Narayan, now to the goodness of the Guru, and now to the high birth of a villainous Sesodia. All these she measures by the same yardstick'. But it would be a fatal mistake to suppose that these faults belong exclusively to any particular class of society. 'The most powerful of appetites', as young Jali learns, 'is the craving for consideration'.

Myers saw snobbery (a fault as common in greengrocers' wives as in princesses), not as a superficial vanity, but as the symptom of a deep-rooted evil; and no man could have been more intensely aware of the entanglement of such hidden drives as this with the sexual instinct. It would perhaps be true to say that, while he never regarded sexuality itself as in any sense evil, he was peculiarly sensitive to the overlapping of the sexual instinct in other spheres of the human personality and he believed that sexuality is frequently distorted into the forms of evil. Nicholas in *The Orissers*, is made to say that the harlot is less wholly bound up in sex than the 'respectable' woman and that it is only when sexuality is 'tricked out by art in robes of Romance' that it 'penetrates into every department of the mind and . . . attempts to make subservient to its ends every activity of man'. The respectable woman, who simply wants 'a home and family', is the instrument of sex to a far greater extent than the girl of pleasure, and it is the former who, even though unconsciously, is the mortal enemy of spiritual freedom. It was partly to the rule of women in modern society that Myers attributed snobbery (in its widest sense) and the falsity of social relationships.

The rule of women, undeniable, for example, in the United States, has taken a curious form. Enough is known of the ancient matriarchal societies to suggest that the 'natural' woman (so far as one can generalize about so improbable a creature) is the very opposite of the American 'ideal of Womanhood'; she is cruel, amoral and totally unscrupulous. It almost seems as though the women who have gained the upper hand in the United States, far from imposing feminine standards upon society, have imitated and grossly exaggerated ideals that are of masculine origin. 'Miss America'—and, above all, 'Mrs. America', in her club—is the American male's fantasy of woman come to life with almost nightmarish exactitude. Just what we are to understand by the 'rule of women' is, therefore, a more complicated question than it might at first appear, and it may be that, when women gain the dominant role in a formerly patriarchal society, they hatch out and rear into monstrous growth many of the vices latent in that society.

Myers, in any case, was concerned with particular examples of this feminine domination. When women rule over society, says Nicholas in *The Orissers*, fashion rules; and fashion is 'change without progression, activity without achievement'. The intellect moves forward towards creation, but the feminine spirit, through 'fashion', diverts it into circular motion. At heart, says Nicholas, women desire to keep men from roving by keeping them in emotional bondage. But since Myers generally saw the forces which motivate human beings as exterior (residing in nature, rather than in the person), he regarded this bondage as one in which the woman was as much enslaved as the man. He might have said, with Blake,' If only the men would do their duty, the women would be such wonders!' and there are feminine characters in his novels who wait, almost unconsciously, for a man to liberate them from themselves. Woman is not happy in her 'mission of enslavement'; in *The Near and the Far* a young Rajput noble is driven by his mother and his wife to sacrifice his life in a war in which he has no real concern, but his widow is afterwards consumed by a sense of guilt, realizing, if only dimly, that she has sacrificed him to the emptiest of ideals.

It is in Myers' attitude to sex and to the women whose life is ruled by it that we see most clearly the influence of his childhood experience; he realized, as did very few of his generation, that there are demonic energies at work in the world, and he was the only English novelist to analyse the manner in which these energies, searching, as it were, for a handle by which to raise themselves into the world of action, may fasten upon the sexual instinct and employ it as their instrument (he was, of course, equally aware of the way in which the lust for power may be similarly employed). It seems fairly probable that the strictures of early Christianity against sex were based, not upon an absurd squeamishness and Manichaean dualism, but upon a perception of the fact that man, on the side of his sexual instinct, lies dangerously open to those regions of darkness which extend both within and around him, and whether we prefer to regard the demons who inhabit these regions as, in the jargon of modern psychology, agencies of the Unconscious, or as disembodied energies which threaten the fragile structure of human order and sanity, is relatively unimportant.

When, therefore, Myers comes to consider the problem of evil, he relates it very closely to the problem of sex. It has been said, no doubt with reason, that he was one of the very few modern novelists to show himself more interested in good than in evil, and he is certainly almost unique in having drawn the character of a saint in a manner that is completely convincing; but his passionate concern for human goodness is the measure of his interest in evil. Throughout his work he makes an implicit distinction between what, for convenience, we may call natural evil and spiritual evil. In *The Orissers* he was primarily concerned with the former. This novel is the story of a battle between two families, representing two utterly opposed kinds of human being, for the inheritance of a country house, and it is fought over the body of the dying monster, John Mayne, who has pursued power regardless of the cost in human suffering, but has been destroyed in his attempt to conquer a woman of the Orissers, who represents for him all those spiritual values which he cannot, for all his power, seize and possess. John Mayne is a blind Titan; and his evil has remained, as it were, unconscious until he makes contact with the Orissers and the light of spiritual awareness falls, however dimly, on the wild beast in his heart; it is this contact and this dim awareness that rob him of his strength, which rested upon his comparative innocence and the single-mindedness of his pursuit of power.

But it is in Madeline, his niece, that natural evil is most clearly expressed (she is the 'respectable' woman denounced by Nicholas); she is cunning, virtuous and self-dramatizing; her whole life is a kind of tortuous ruse, the purpose of which she herself does not perceive, for she regards herself as the epitome of 'healthy-mindedness' and serves the dark power of her own femininity in sublime unawareness. John Mayne, watching his niece on horseback, rejoices in the sense she gives him of 'life's willingness to dispense with spiritual significance'; her body, even when his own is shattered and on the verge of dissolution, seems to him 'a brutal exposition of the self-sufficing-ness of the flesh'; it represents 'vitality without the spark'; and in him the physical vigour of unregenerate nature fights a losing battle against the in-break of spiritual awareness. Another member of the household, also watching Madeline, reflects that her faults, which he has tried to regard as trivial feminine weaknesses, represent 'something big and powerful . . . the source of her strength'.

The Orissers is a chaotic novel, and in it the good is mainly shadowed forth in forms of violence and revolt. Cosmo Orisser, the central character of the earlier part of the book, is a man so possessed by rage as to stand on the borders of insanity: in his way of life he is a debauchee, a being of uncouth violence, vindictive and embittered. His rage is a protest against the complacency and sham idealism, the meanness and hypocrisy of the world. He is consumed by his vision of what might be; a way of life compared with which our own is unbearably squalid; and by his 'extravagant standards of sincerity', none can escape the charge of hypocrisy. It was in this character, one may suspect, that Myers projected his idea of himself when he was outwardly the playboy of smart society. But by the time he came to write *The Near and the Far* he had come to a far calmer and much more balanced vision of the world, and natural evil had fallen into place. In the character of Gunevati, which seems at times to dominate the later book, he achieved a triumph.

It is a measure of the skill with which Myers portrays the girl that we are aware of her at one and the same moment as a cheap little trollop and as a creature of mystery, the servant of demonic powers which hold all the glitter and the fascination of the abyss. In herself she is little more than a child, and when she becomes involved in the intrigues over the question of the Emperor's successor, she is utterly pathetic; yet she is also the focus of all those secret powers of darkness which underlie the world of will and consciousness, and Jali, whom she seduces, realizes that 'while she stood for so little in herself, she represented so much in the world'. Hers is a mode of existence into which consciousness cannot descend without horror, and Jali, one sultry afternoon in her room, 'felt the Present expand, and stagnate, and reflect everlastingness; but there was no foretaste of beatitude in this experience; it was rather an initiation into a state of living death'. Just as the Sage's wisdom is a condition 'beyond good and evil', so hers is a state prior to this distinction; she is evil and yet innocent, hardly more responsible for her actions than a beast.

It is when Gunevati encounters spiritual evil that she is destroyed. She lives for a time with Jali's teacher, a wise and humane old Brahmin named Gokal, who has become infatuated with her; she tries to poison him and then takes refuge in the 'Pleasance of the Arts', where the Emperor's son, Prince Daniyal, holds his court. She, upon whom the influence of a wise and in many ways saintly man had made no impression, falls completely under the spell of the sham intellectualism of the 'Pleasance'. She falls in love with the Prince, regarding his homosexuality as a delicious naughtiness and a badge of intellectual distinction; she, who has participated in ritual killings and orgies, is shocked and charmed by his trivial sins, his pettiness and meanness. Jali, seeing her at this time, realizes that she is doomed; 'She had neither the heart nor the mind nor the will to escape her fate. Her perversity and triviality were as stubborn and fateful as any of the virtues of wise and saintly men'. At the Prince's command she is thrown to a mad elephant and trampled to death.

Yet even her death is fraught with significance. A strange vision falls upon Jali and the old Brahmin Gokal, who are living near the 'Pleasance'; Gokal describes it later to Jali's father: ' . . . this same face of nature shivered and trembled as might its own reflection upon the surface of the lake. I tell you, Amar, everything wavered as if it were threatened with the loss of its flimsy surface actuality'; and Jali, remembering long afterwards how the girl's seemingly humble death had been heralded by such mighty portents, wonders if 'perhaps the whole mechanism of generations and events was only the apparatus by which some value of which we had hardly any inkling was being brought into actuality'.

Jali himself falls for a short time under the spell of the 'Pleasance' and does his best to persuade himself that the place is really 'a small gem-like thought in an unthinking world', but he cannot quite believe that artificiality is the sole canon of art, that opinion, taste and value are no more than a woman's fashions in clothes, and that a new and glorious philosophy of life may be obtained simply by turning the old one topsy-turvy. As he begins to uncover the secrets of the 'Pleasance', he comes to see it as something not merely contemptible, but menacing; beneath the brilliant façade run currents of ugliness and cruelty.

In the personality of the Prince, 'the posturer has swallowed up the man'; there is really no human person left in him, he is all mask. He exemplifies that trivial-mindedness which Myers regarded as the cardinal sin. 'If', says Gokal in *The Near and the Far*, 'triviality takes an important place in the world, if it is the chief barrier between man and God, then triviality is important. No corruption is more easily spread than that of trivial-mindedness'. This state of mind is one ruled by an inverted sense of values, in which all that is of true significance is ignored and all that is trivial is exalted. It was Myers' belief that this trivial-mindedness, which he regarded as the distinctive quality of many modern intellectuals, is a source of incalculable evil in the world; he was, perhaps, primarily a moralist, and to perceive this we must realize that what he condemned were not the harsh or abominable sins of natural man, however cruel, but this outrage upon God and man whereby the trivial-minded deprive the world of meaning, mock and caricature all goodness and nobility of soul, and deny the values inherent in human existence, not from overmastering passion, but upon a whim.

Humanism, which comes so easily to set man—or Art, or the State—in the place of God, seemed to Myers to fall into this very sin. He had castigated it through the mouth of Nicholas Orisser. In *The Near and the Far* he uses Jali's father, the Rajah Amar, as his instrument and sets him arguing with an English humanist named Smith, who is travelling in India. It is significant that, in the case of Smith as in that of the Prince, the spiritual inversion is accompanied by inversion of the sexual instinct, but, unlike the Prince, Smith is sincere and conscientious and takes himself very seriously as an apostle of reason and enlightenment. He talks vaguely, but with enthusiasm, of 'Goodness, Truth and Beauty'; it seems to Amar that by Goodness he means only 'virtuous behaviour', by Truth 'the pursuit of certain comparatively unimportant kinds of knowledge', and by Beauty 'works of art'. His agnosticism seems to Amar to lead to a neurotic fear of intolerance, cruelty and physical pain, and to a monstrous over-valuation of the inessentials of human life: his refusal to recognize the existence of a 'spiritual sense', which is 'the faculty of spiritual discrimination', 'the valuator of those other modes of valuing', vitiates his judgment of people and of human life itself.

During a journey which the two men make together, Smith is horrified by the murder of a man who had mocked an Arab, the captain of the Chief Priest's bodyguard, at his prayers. This Arab, Fazul, demonstrates by his very existence the inadequacy of Smith's conception of human nature. For the Arab, 'as a chieftain going forth to war from the barbaric splendour of a Moorish palace, or as a sneak-thief in a slum, is unmoved either by rational altruism or rational self-interest'. Smith, with his faith in good-will and tolerance as the cures for all the world's ills, cannot comprehend the unequalled and fanatical faith in God which springs up in the splendid aridity of the desert; indeed he opposes to that God-directed fanaticism his own fanatical scepticism, for there is always a certain intensity of envy and hatred in the unbeliever's attitude to the believer. Amar, although himself a Buddhist, unconcerned with the personal aspect of deity, respects the primitive faith of Fazul and perceives in Smith a rather distasteful pettiness of mind and spirit.

In the character of Rajah Amar, Myers moved a step forward towards his conception of what constitutes human goodness. Amar has great nobility of character and absolute integrity, but he has chosen the road of asceticism and suppressed many of his natural instincts before the time is ripe. His strength is not the supple strength of the true holy man, but a brittle and unbending quality. He has not, his brother-in-law tells him, come to terms with the feminine in himself—'and of that we all partake'. Ignoring certain forces within himself, he underrates their significance in the world around him; his friends try to persuade him that the Prince is something more than a frivolous playboy—is, in fact, evil, and propagates evil—but he drifts into alliance with the Prince's chief supporter. Through the central section of the book, which is chiefly concerned with Amar, there is a mounting sense of tension as, sick in body and beset with worldly problems, he struggles to make the final preparation for his retirement from the world.

At heart, he detests the Prince, but will not admit the fact to himself; he has adopted the false mask of invulnerability, and the forces of the earth beat more and more fiercely against the armour of his indifference.

He calls to pay his respects to the Prince, who taunts him on the subject of his wife's infidelity, and his will snaps; he draws his sword, and is struck down by the bodyguard. He recovers from the blow to find that he is blind; after many weeks of spiritual agony, during which all that he had built up during the years of self-discipline seems lost to him, he finds peace and stumbles out one night into the desert to join a band of pilgrims bound for a monastery in Ceylon. Seated by a camp fire, a blind old man in rags, conversing easily with these new companions who are unaware of his identity and whose faces he will never see, he reflects that 'a spirit, after its nonage, should be so greatly at ease with itself . . . so secure in its own home, that, coming forth to meet others, it is radiant with a childlike unself-consciousness, friendly and unafraid'. So Amar has learned to do without his mask.

Rather the same lesson is suggested by the story of the Brahmin Gokal's infatuation for Gunevati. The old man, after a life devoted to study and meditation, regrets all the illusions he has not pursued, all the follies he has not committed; and in his grotesque and slavish adoration of this low-caste girl who is the priestess of a forbidden and obscene cult, he pays for his past denial of life. Betrayed and humiliated, he passes, like Amar, through a long period of illness; to him also all seems lost, as he sits weeping over the cloths and trinkets that the girl has left behind in her flight. But he recovers, purified and made humble by his experience; like Amar, he achieves freedom.

In a short novel, *Strange Glory*, Myers dealt with the same theme more fully; Wentworth, a wise and holy man who lives in the swamp forest of Louisiana, has a past that might have qualified him for a place in *The Orissers*; he has made three fortunes and two disastrous marriages, killed his second wife's lover and served a long term of imprisonment.

But the storms of his life are recollected in the most perfect tranquillity; an almost unearthly peace pervades the story. Wentworth has retired to the forest, not from fear of the world, but because modern life seems to him to smother the natural communion of men and women and to destroy their awareness of connection with the springs of life. 'When I look into the past', he says, 'I see a procession of people all in fancy-dress—the human spirit taken in by its own various make-believes'. Once again, the good man is the man without a mask. Just as he has retired from the world when the time was ripe, so timeliness seems to have governed his life; when asked why he married his second wife, a Creole girl whom he had seen for a moment standing in a doorway, he answers quite simply, 'I was ripe for something like that!' The fact that his marriage led to the murder and to his imprisonment is unimportant, for it led also to this life in the forest, a life of richness and of true communion. There are only a few things in life, Myers believed, that must be put first; the rest have to find their place in the rear as best they can.

To cling only to essentials appears often as a kind of simple-mindedness. When one of the characters in *Strange Glory* sets out to ask Wentworth's advice, she reflects that he is too naïve to understand the complexities of her life and is certain to over-simplify the situation. Yet it is the nature of such complexities to be made up, to a great extent, of inessentials, and it is inevitable that the wise man should cut through them in a way that may seem harsh and inconsiderate. Returning from her visit, she complains that 'His touch, never light, had been particularly clumsy now and then'; clumsy because he swept aside the web of inessentials and struck at the heart of the problem. Not all sensibilities are worthy of consideration; not all are of equal value (in his later years, Myers regarded 'good taste' as one of the most baneful influences in modern society, and rejoiced in tales of outrage upon social decency), and there are moments when people need to be told that their tears are self-indulgent, their anger childish, and that the things they consider important and treat with respect are trash.

The character of Wentworth is an advance sketch for that of the Guru in *The Pool of Vishnu* (the last section of *The Near and the Far*). And the character of the Guru represents the final fufilment of Myers' work; there could have been no question of his writing another novel after the completion of *The Pool of Vishnu*. It would not be possible to distinguish, in the novels, the elements taken from the Oriental doctrines, of which he had a fairly wide knowledge, from those which were of essentially personal origin or for which he was indebted to the work of C. G. Jung; Myers was not at any time concerned to give an exposition of the Vedanta or, for that matter, of Buddhism, and where the influence of these doctrines in his work is clearly indicated it was an influence working more or less unconsciously. When, however, fairly late in life, he read *I and Thou* by the Jewish religious philosopher Martin Buber and found in it a crystallization of many of the ideas which had been maturing over a period of years in his own mind, these earlier influences fell into the background; he shaped the character of the Guru in the light of Buber's teaching and, conceivably, shaped it more firmly than he would have done had he relied solely upon his own personal convictions.

In the Guru's philosophy, the criticism of modern life which had been a constant element throughout Myers' work is married—and very successfully married—to Buber's mysticism. False relationships are once again analysed, but there is now a greater emphasis upon the positive alternative to such masked converse, the true communion of those who meet, not as members of a type or of a class, but as persons, face to face, linked together through the Centre, the 'Mystery' which far transcends our life and yet lies all about us; a communion which lasts but a few moments, yet fructifies in the arid wastes of a life far from the Centre and closed to the 'Mystery'.

'My theories', says the Guru, 'amount to nothing more than that every man has the right to be treated as a person—and not merely as a member of a category or a class'; and he puts these 'theories' into action, even in his relationship with the Emperor. In argument with the Chief Priest of the Emperor's new cult, he makes a more resounding confession of faith; 'Spirit, which must stream through the individual man, if he is to preserve a sane and living soul, must stream through society as well. When the stream tarries, the body politic stiffens into a prison house; forms and institutions become manacles, and the State turns into a monstrous slave-driver. Demoniac forces have taken control. With the leaders there is only a semblance of leadership. . . . Your priests too will pretend to enclose the spirit in churches. But these churches will be empty. Spirit is waiting in the market-place—waiting for the re-awakened and re-awakening man'.

It is in the soundness of the personal life that the Guru sees this spirit fruitfully at work. And when he has to help a young girl who is trying to make the bitter choice between, on the one hand, her duties to her father, to the State which he rules with her aid and to the Emperor, and, on the other, her love for a young Rajah who must abdicate if he marries her, the Guru does not hesitate in the advice he gives; he is convinced that the renunciation of her love for reasons of duty and expediency can lead only to the deterioration of her character; he warns her that those who make a renunciation of this kind make others suffer for it in the long run, and that if she gives way to her father, who is making use of every trick known to possessive love, she will be indulging him as one might a spoilt child; and he adds, 'I am suspicious of duty because it has come to be associated with rules of conduct which have a social rather than a spiritual sanction'. He asks her, in short, to abandon the false relationship of mutual domination between her father and herself, to abdicate from the role of the magnanimous princess upon whom the court officials fawn and whom the peasants—while keeping their distance—adore, and to enter upon the hard road of equal and complete relationship with the man she loves. And the Guru's advice is accepted.

At the close of the novel the Guru, now mortally ill, sits talking with Jali by the pool of Vishnu. He speaks again of the lack of candour in human relations and of how each man crouches behind his defences. 'Children cling to their childishness, aristocrats to the accepted notion of the aristocratic nature, soldiers to the accepted notion of soldierliness, and so on—all for the sake of the advantages they gain from being incomplete human beings'. Most people, he continues, live 'upon a plane of existence which is hardly personal at all'; they identify themselves almost entirely with the figure they present to the world; but spirit resides only in true persons, and the man who surrenders to his own mask lives a shallow life without any real contact either with his fellows or with the 'Mystery' which is over against him. The personal is alone truly universal: 'the man who speaks out of his own personal depths speaks for all men. . . .'

How far, Jali asks, may one compromise? Compromise is permissible, the Guru answers, but never adulteration: 'Intention must never be adulterated. A terrible purity of intention is demanded of man'.

Evening falls by the pool, and now the author puts Martin Buber's words into the Guru's mouth: 'This is the heart of the mystery. . . . Although we know that we are spirit, and that all spirit is one, yet by an unalterable rhythm of our being we swing out from the world of communion into the world of separated things'.

'How to hold fast?' Jali asks; 'How—in the world of separation—to hold fast?'

'One must cling to the memory. One must remember and one must act. The knowledge gained in communion, and ripened in solitude, must pour its life into the world. . . . Thus only will you and the world about you live'.

CHAPTER EIGHT

MONK AT LARGE: ALDOUS HUXLEY

In dealing with matters which lie outside our normal field of experience we tend very easily to confuse—if not to regard as identical—things which, in spite of appearances, have little or nothing in common with each other. This is the case, for example, when we consider the question of asceticism and of the ascetic's attitude to the natural human instincts; we forget that asceticism is nothing but a discipline devised for a particular purpose and directed to certain precise ends, and that there is nothing more spiritual or holy about it, taken in itself, than there is about an athlete's special training; and we confuse it with Puritanism (a doctrine, or rather an attitude, that is unbalanced, and therefore heretical, in whatever religious context it may be found) and with that emotional—one might even say neurotic—revolt against the needs of the body and against the very conditions of human life which is the form generally taken by Puritanism in our time. Such an attitude as this is as far removed from that of the genuine ascetic as is the attitude of a crank who will eat only certain types of food from that of the athlete who finds it necessary to follow a certain diet.

In earlier times, however, provision was made both for the man who had deliberately chosen to put aside certain of the sweets of human life in order to follow a hard but rewarding vocation and for his weaker brethren who, on account either of some fault in their emotional make-up or perhaps of certain events in their early life, could not, with a clear conscience, either desire or relish the pleasures of the senses. To-day, those whom an inbred squeamishness might once have led to a quiet life in the cloister are denied that refuge, and the whole tenor of the modern world persuades them that they must at all costs 'live', 'experience', 'get the most out of life'. Eating without relish, they are easily sickened and, forcing themselves to live a life for which they are not emotionally equipped, they are soon embittered. Pleasure they may have—the pleasure of doing outrage to their own native fastidiousness—but it is always deeply imbued with a sense of guilt, and it ends in disgust. It is interesting, in this context, to note how many people obsessed by sex and given up to a career of frantic promiscuity are, and have been since adolescence, horrified by the very existence of their own sexual instincts and by the antics which they force their bodies to perform.

Closely connected with this attitude, although not always identical with it, is that of the man who attempts to enclose himself in a false self-sufficiency and who, hating to surrender his body (and, in fact, surrendering it only in appearance), would refuse in the very same spirit to surrender his soul to God; the man whose resentment of the conditions of human life is a symptom of a far deeper resentment directed, not only against the alien powers within himself, but even against the divine power. Chastity may be a virtue; it may also be a sign of Luciferian pretensions.

These considerations have their relevance to our principal theme, for the Eastern doctrines have suffered a good deal in Western eyes from the adherence to them of people who looked only for a justification of their own hatred of life, and the most eminent, certainly the most widely known, protagonist of these doctrines to-day is a man who has seemed to exemplify in his work the attitude of a modern 'monk at large'. The publication of Huxley's book, *The Perennial Philosophy*, must have doubled, in the course of a few weeks, the number of people in England and the United States who have some slight interest in the Oriental doctrines, and if we are to show why this book has, on the whole, given a dangerously misleading impression of the traditional religious and metaphysical teaching we must trace in detail the path by which Huxley came to adhere to this teaching.

In tracing this development through five of his novels, we must give full weight to his criticism of modern life as such—a criticism sharpened and at times distorted by his attitude to human life as a whole—yet valid, none the less. But it is essential to distinguish, beneath the surface of wit and elegance, such sound criticism of what is specifically modern and abnormal from the Puritanical rejection of conditions inherent in our existence, with which it is interwoven. To make such a distinction is by no means easy, for Huxley has something of a magician's talents; he casts a spell from which it is difficult to escape, and his wit (that unkind wit, which is at the furthest possible extreme from the merry wit of such a writer as Linklater) and his merciless observation of squalid pleasures, shoddy motives and petty vanities exert a kind of fascination over many of his readers, while they remain dimly aware that they are being presented with half-truths that are exciting to the nerves in a way that the whole truth is not; more often than not the excitement is that of playing 'peeping Tom'.

It is partly the sheer effectiveness of half-truths which makes *Point Counter Point* such a fascinating, yet such an unsatisfactory novel. The story opens with the ending of a love-affair doomed from its very inception by bogus idealism and sentimentality. Already Huxley is sealing up a bolt-hole; the novel is chiefly concerned with carnality, but he is reminding us that the alternative does not lie in 'Love' after the manner of Mrs. Browning. We are assured, as we shall be again and again, that the wages of sin are death; or worse, dust without the explosive illumination of death. Yet here, at the very beginning, is something that reads almost like a comment upon the pages that follow; 'When truth is nothing but the truth, it's unnatural, it's an abstraction that resembles nothing in the real world,' says Philip Quarles who may, with due caution, be equated with the author. There are many passages in the novel that strike us as particularly 'true' representations of life, but with the kind of truth that camera and dictaphone give us. And the satire is not so much the savage, personal irony of Swift as the naughty delight of a small boy who has caught his elders with their trousers down. Quarles is accused by his wife of communicating only 'by wireless across the Atlantic'; he builds a screen of words between himself and the world, just as Burlap builds one of bogus emotionalism, old Bidlake of exclusive sensuality, Lucy of cold and self-protecting greed, Spandrell of cynicism, Lord Edward of scientific knowledge and Webley of action. Each has his defence-mechanism which has become rigid and automatic in operation, cutting him off from all but one small section of human experience.

Of Quarles we are told that 'In the ordinary world of daily human contacts he was curiously like a foreigner'; yet a foreigner without the traditions and security of his own land behind him. Huxley writes of a life that he feels instinctively is foreign and, in fact, barbarous, but he has as yet no standpoint of his own from which to judge it or by means of which to demonstrate an alternative. He is still officially a sceptic; he is not in a position to assert that human life as he sees it, a life of animality thinly covered by bogus values and pretentious idealism, is wrong in comparison with another way that would be right. He still believes that the body is the only reality of which he can be certain, and he has not yet wholly accepted the verdict of his own feeling, which is that the body is vile. There are, indeed, moments when the influence of his friend, D. H. Lawrence, is obviously at work; such a sentence as this might have been written by Lawrence himself, 'He loved her as a fossil child of the 'sixties might love—timidly and very apologetically; apologizing for his ardours, apologizing for his body . . .' And Lucy's 'sin' when she sleeps with Walter lies in the fact that she will not allow him or herself to rest in the almost holy peace of satiety, feeling it to be 'intrinsically rather absurd'. The model for Rampion, the one character who never suffers the lash of the author's ridicule, was obviously D.H.L. 'Barbarism is being lop-sided,' says Rampion; 'You can be a barbarian of the intellect.' At this stage Huxley seems aware of his own lop-sidedness.

The false spirituality of Burlap is nauseating. In the Rogue's Gallery of *Point Counter Point*, Burlap is the Rogue-in-chief. Yet why is he treated so mercilessly? Why are his small pretences and insincerities caricatured with such ferocity? Perhaps because a Burlap who lived sincerely would offer an alternative to a life to which, Huxley will soon try to prove, there is no alternative but flight. Burlap might have offered the alternative of spirituality worked into the fabric of life, of love at home with sensuality; so Burlap must be shown as wholly contemptible. We find again and again that the type of person who might destroy Huxley's thesis by pointing a way between naked sensuality and complete denial of the body is caricatured. Old Bidlake is such another; he has at least enjoyed the good things of life in a happy and straightforward manner, without self-reproach or the titivations of nausea; but the happy sensualist is not to be left in peace; he is convicted of selfish greed, and he, like other characters in the novel, is afraid of any depth of feeling and tries to erase from his memory his second wife, for whom he had cared deeply; he is tortured by the fear of death—he has used the animal body, but is terrified when it catches up with him. A Bidlake who had not tried to get something for nothing, who had accepted the conditions of life as the price of his enjoyment of it, would have deprived the novel of some of its force.

Spandrell, the Comic Opera cynic with his deliberate self-conscious wickedness, seems, in comparison with Bidlake, to be on the side of the angels; for Spandrell's wickedness is set up as a judgment upon the nature of life, a revenge upon the life-force for sending his mother to bed with the lecherous major. While debauching factory girls and breaking their spirits in order, as it were, to deface the image of God in the human person, he preaches a pseudo-asceticism and blazes the trail for what will soon emerge as 'Huxleyan mysticism'. His sensuality, which he is at great pains not to enjoy, is a kind of self-flagellation; and, at the end, he finds proof of the existence of God in the abstract melody of a Beethoven quartet. A suitable companion-piece to Spandrell is Lucy, no more healthily sensual than he; a woman such as 'Rosie' in Maugham's *Cakes and Ale* could never live in a Huxleyan atmosphere. Like Mrs. Thwale in *Time Must Have a Stop*, Lucy uses people for her pleasure, in contempt and cold blood, and she too hates the body upon which she depends for her agreeable sensations. Her motto, 'Living modernly's living quickly', might have come straight out of *Brave New World*.

The seeds of *Brave New World* were sown in 1926 when Huxley wrote the *Los Angeles Rhapsody* about the City of Dreadful Joy. Here already, in Los Angeles during the Boom period, he had found the Good Time Gospel fully developed; 'The joy of always being busy, of having no time to think . . . of dancing to the noise of savage music . . . the joy of cuddling provocatively bold and pretty flappers . . . of being always in a crowd, never alone'. Here also was the bogus religiosity; 'Dr. Leon Tucker with his Musical Messengers in a great Bible Conference . . . organ chimes, giant Marimbaphone . . .' and 'Thousands and thousands of flappers . . . so curiously uniform, unindividual and blank'. This is a pre-view of the Brave New World of peace and plenty, and, reflecting upon the present (*Point Counter Point*) and the future (*Brave New World*) we are tempted to pervert the Hindu aphorism and cry, 'This is vile. That is vile. Take vile from vile and vile remains'.

Brave New World is perhaps Huxley's most notable achievement. Such a warning desperately needed to be sounded; and he sounded it so loudly and stridently that there are people who remember the book as they remember some recurrent childish nightmare, the stories of snakes when they were small, of war when they were a little older. Yet there are some who comprehended the satire as little as an inhabitant of the New World might do, and who took it for a glowing picture of a wholly desirable Utopia. It was Huxley's task to demonstrate quite mercilessly the logical conclusion to the majority of contemporary ideals and ideologies; the fact that, in spite of the book being suffused with the author's hatred of the world he is depicting (a hatred, one must confess, not unmixed with relish), certain people should have found in it the projection of their own day-dreams, is the measure of his success.

Social Stability is the watchword of the Brave New World and biological engineering its method; the ideal is 'adjustment', that adjustment which is also the ideal of so many present-day psychiatrists; for with adjustment comes happiness of a kind, and with happiness comes stability. Indeed, happiness and not pleasure is the bed-rock of that society; for pleasure carries within it the Dionysian principle, is by nature intense and leaves in its wake unrest. In the Brave New World intensity and unrest are abolished; the authorities 'object to anything intense or long-drawn'. Liberty, they assure us, is generally 'Liberty to be inefficient and miserable'. The prophets of efficiency and happiness are without doubt on the side of the robot society; so also are the advocates of 'satisfaction' (that will-o'-the-wisps pursued by so many self-styled 'realists'), for 'Feeling lurks in that interval of time between desire and consummation' (a half-truth, but one which has a certain validity); 'Shorten that interval, break down all those unnecessary barriers'.

And the purpose of life in the Brave New World? 'Wheels must turn steadily, and cannot turn untended.' Man is finally reduced to being no more than an adjunct of the machine; in fact he has ceased to exist as man. And because the machines need attention, the chief virtue in those who tend them is the 'sense of social solidarity', that social sense so highly rated even to-day in our semi-mechanized civilization. In the Brave New World, 'Everyone belongs to everyone else'.

All that is intense or personal is potential dynamite under the body politic. When one of the characters (Bernard) gropes for a self that is separate from the herd, he is mocked by the gramophone within Lenina, 'Never put off till to-morrow the fun you can have to-day'. And when the two of them hover over the sea, facing 'the rushing emptiness of the night . . . the pale face of the moon among the hastening clouds', Lenina cries, 'It's horrible!' and switches on the radio. The Controller, himself free from the conditioned illusions that keep the rest safe and happy, perpetuates the system whilst half aware of its fatuity, like the Grand Inquisitor in Dostoievski's Legend. Talking to the Savage (the outsider, who is the closest possible equivalent to a man of our own time), he points out that, whenever in the past the masses have seized power, comfort and happiness have been the only recognized values; as Controller, he is doing no more than give the people what they want.

Until at last the Savage claims the right, the inalienable human right to be unhappy. 'Not to mention the right to grow old', he is reminded, 'and ugly and impotent; the right to have syphilis and cancer; the right to have too little to eat; the right to be lousy'. 'I claim them all!' the Savage answers. The Controller shrugs his shoulders; 'You're welcome'. But the Savage has made the very claim that our world lacks always and everywhere the courage to make; we, indeed, abandon, one after another, the conditions which can alone form the basis for a truly human life, in return for the most trivial material advantages, acting, again and again, like those islanders who clamoured to exchange their pearls for a trader's worthless trash.

Such a world as Huxley has imagined, if it did come into being, could endure for no more than a few years, for the only source of stability in a civilization lies in a spiritual principle which is eternal and unchanging, and no civilization which ignores this principle can hope to have any solid foundation; but this fact does not make his picture any the less true as a projection of the fantasies of innumerable individuals in the contemporary world. The fantasy is, however, peculiarly nightmarish because, as Huxley has depicted it, it seems to exclude all hope; there is in it no seed of regeneration, just as there has been no seed of goodness or of triumph in his picture of contemporary life. Up till now, Huxley's role has been almost exclusively that of the detached critic of certain ways of life; but in *Eyeless in Gaza*, the novel which follows *Brave New World*, he takes a cautious step forward; he begins to suspect, and he will soon become convinced, that he is in possession of an alternative to the way of life which he has satirized so savagely, and he faces the task of demonstrating this alternative in his work. Up to this point it has been possible to regard his novels as justifiable satires upon one kind of misdirected life, but now the assumption seems to be made that this single aspect of life represents the essential character of all human life as such, and it is upon this assumption that the new doctrine of salvation is based.

What is in fact the real nature of the 'slavery' with which *Eyeless in Gaza* is concerned? The obvious answer would be 'slavery to passion', yet a moment's reflection will remind us that uncommonly little passion enters into Huxley's world; and, upon reading the novel, we discover that the flaw in almost all the characters, as in those of *Point Counter Point*, is not passion but the reverse—the fear of intensity or depth of feeling, the refusal ever to surrender the small private citadel of the self. A perverted 'non-attachment' is Anthony Beavis's chief sin; yet now we find that Huxley's road to salvation is the road of 'non-attachment' and withdrawal.

The transition from an altogether false immunity in the face of human passion to what Huxley is convinced is a true and sound immunity has been a little too swift, a little too much in the nature of a conjuring trick. An author's inner conflicts are frequently projected in his work, so that in it he may be for ever attacking his own weaknesses; yet if that should apply in the case of Huxley and if he has himself suffered from the first and perverted form of 'non-attachment', then we may justifiably ask whether the neurosis (for such it must be called), after being driven from one vantage point, may not have reappeared at another. We may question the value of a faith that springs from such dubious roots; and question again whether the second form of non-attachment may not be as perverted as the first. In so doing, we need not oppose Huxley's assertion that wisdom begins with liberation from self-will, but ask only if he may not have misinterpreted the meaning of liberation; whether he may not be, as one of the characters in a later novel says of Bentham, 'So nearly right; but so enormously wrong'.

In the early part of *Eyeless in Gaza* we are given a picture of goodness in the person of Brian. But Brian is not whole, and cannot be holy; and significantly enough his flaw or neurosis takes the form of a morbid horror of physical love and of his own sexual desires (this presumably on account of an attachment to his mother. Shades of Spandrell!). In Brian we find a convincing character, but one who cannot be good in the perfection of an undeformed nature: in Miller, the saintly mouthpiece for the author's dawning faith, we have no doubt an undeformed nature, but as a character he carries curiously little conviction. He expresses the 'right views'; we are told that he is living in accordance with them; but we are unimpressed. Brian dies through a puerile essay in wickedness on the part of Anthony Beavis, who has made love to his fiancée in order to win a trivial bet. The moral law has entered Huxley's world in full majesty; the evil ramifications into the future of even the smallest sin are, we are assured, infinite. And yet Anthony Beavis's approach to the good life, many years later, is not unconnected with this early sin (just as Sebastian's salvation, in *Time Must Have a Stop*, stems directly from his betrayal of Bruno Rontini). Is it so strange that the emotionally deformed Brian should have to die that Anthony may emerge whole?

The crucial moment in the lives of the two principal characters, Anthony and Helen, comes on a roof-top in the South of France. Helen, we should note, suffers from a morbid fastidiousness, together with a desire to titivate and play upon her own disgust (as when she stole the kidney, 'oozy with unspeakable slime', from a butcher's shop). The scene on the roof is idyllic—summer by the Mediterranean; two sunburnt bodies, naked together; the private tempest and the succeeding calm; the drone of an aeroplane overhead; and then comes the catastrophe. From that innocently blue sky a small dog falls and is reduced to pulp on the roof, spattering the two bodies with blood.

How differently various authors would have treated this incident. For Lawrence, no doubt, it would have been an assertion of the kinship of blood. For Thomas Mann . . . but in this case we know the answer; in *The Magic Mountain* Hans Castorp, lost in the snow, dreams of a perfect land of Harmony and Perfected Humanity, cries, 'Oh lovely, lovely! How joyous and winning they are . . .' and is then shown the dark horror which is complementary to this joy; two witch-like women are dismembering a child among the flaming braziers. For Huxley, however, the incident is comparable to the Buddha's meeting with the old man, the sick man and the corpse. Anthony starts on the road to 'non-attachment'; Helen has fled.

Anthony dreams of a sticky, rubbery substance, sickeningly filling his mouth; in *Brave New World* the Savage had been sick, explaining, 'I've eaten civilization!' It is not civilization that sickens Anthony but the dual nature of life itself. He meets Staithes, who combines Communism with a desire to make people fully 'conscious of their own and other people's disgustingness'. There is universal nausea, increased by Anthony's meeting with a mistress of long ago, now an obscene, drug-sodden hag. Flight is the only course. 'What we're all looking for', he is told, towards the end of the novel, 'is some way of getting beyond our own vomit'. 'Separation is evil . . .' he meditates; impossible 'the actualization of goodness by creatures who, if they were not evil would not exist'; we shall soon be told that this is the Oriental view of life; that is as it may be, but it is certainly the view of certain Protestant theologians.

Here Huxley seems to have reached a dead-end in his development. The next novel, *After Many a Summer*, merely increases the intensity of horror; the gulf between life as we know it—or rather as Huxley sees it, thrust ever deeper into degradation—and the perception of eternity has been expanded even further. The novel opens with a descriptive passage reminiscent of *Brave New World*; this is California, the California of the Los Angeles Rhapsody and, incidentally, Huxley's chosen domicile. Here is the Beverley Pantheon, The Personality Cemetery, with its motto, 'Death is swallowed up in victory'; 'The victory', Huxley explains, 'no longer of the spirit but of the body, the well-fed body, for ever youthful, immortally athletic, indefatigably sexy'.

Into this world comes Jeremy Pordage, surely the meanest of God's creatures and an example of a degeneracy at least as deadly as that of Huxley's California, only less blatant. He is trivial-minded upon every level, writes essays that are 'sacrilege in lavender' and, when at home (under the domination of his aged mother) enjoys once a fortnight 'an hour and a half of infinite squalor with Mae or Doris in a flat in Maida Vale', this squalor and the 'erotic routine' being 'the apotheosis of refinement, the logical conclusion of good taste'.

If Pordage is a small, pale monstrosity, Jo Stoyte and Dr. Obispo are fully grown monsters. When the baboons in the Castle begin to copulate, Virginia clasps her hands and cries, 'Aren't they human!' The comparison is not, in this case, very flattering to the baboons. We are spared nothing; during the description of Stoyte's ageing body as seen through Obispo's eyes, we are compelled to imagine this same body going through the 'erotic routine' with Virginia, but at times the horror verges on hysteria and so loses its force.

A large part of the novel is comment and exposition, in the form of several monologues by Mr. Propter, supposedly a Buddhist (though little inclined to imitate the Buddha's 'noble silence'). Pordage meets Propter: 'Well I'm damned', says Pordage; 'We mostly are', answers Propter, with a severity more Calvinist than Buddhist. Finding himself in such a nightmarish world—a world, Huxley insists, by no means exclusively modern, in proof of which he gives us the notebooks of the 'Fifth Earl', who was much addicted to 'posthumously cuckolding' his friends on the very beds on which they had died—Propter's verdict is hardly surprising; 'If you carry your analysis far enough, you'll find that Time is Evil. . . . Time and craving, two aspects of the same thing'. But how thoroughly—one might even say with what blatant dishonesty—Huxley has weighted the scales in order to obtain this verdict.

Here the straight line of Huxley's development ended. It seemed doubtful whether another novel could follow upon this orgy of rejection and 'nay-saying', and *Grey Eminence*, the biography of a mystic who made the fatal mistake of stepping into the world of action, did not resolve this doubt. Meanwhile, however, it was known that Huxley was practising some form of spiritual discipline and guiding his footsteps in accordance with the Highest Common Denominator of all the 'great Faiths' —a doctrine that must be high indeed. It seemed possible that, in casting aside the obvious attachments to sensuality and so forth, he might free himself from the more subtle attachments of nausea and horror which had been the mainspring of his satire. Standing at a distance from the world, he might now see human life with a new compassion and a new depth, melting at last into tenderness towards the sins of mankind. Then came *Time Must Have a Stop*.

The new novel was praised by the reviewers as a return to Huxley's old, scintillating manner. In a novelist of such experience, skill and technique were bound, if given their chance, to turn out a book worth reading. And this book is immensely entertaining, immensely skilful—sufficient excellence, no doubt, in another, less prophetic author. But it does not call for artistic assessment; it is not primarily, in aim or method, a work of art, but a sermon and a clinical study. We are shown, more clearly than ever before, the merciless operation of cause and effect in the moral sphere; we are called upon to take up our staffs and come away from this stew of corruption before it sucks us down.

Here all the answers are dusty, particularly for Sebastian, whose adolescent day-dreams of 'incandescent copulation' with 'Mrs. Esdale' come to earth in a humiliating fiasco with a tart. And the lascivious Mrs. Thwale, whom he next encounters, is uncommonly like a Gargoyle set up to frighten children: 'At the memory of those extremes of pleasure and shamelessness and self-abandon she smiled a little to herself'; her art is done on lavatory paper, her studio is the W.C.; from 'between the curtains of her spiritual private box' she watches and operates upon the outside world (in this case Sebastian), practising '. . . that almost surgical research of the essential shamelessness . . . the delicate gluttony of those soft lips'. A true Huxleyan, she enters the darkness with a torch which casts a sinister glow upon the forms there; 'A maniac struggling in the musty darkness with another maniac. . . . Twin cannibals in Bedlam'. These passages are written with a curious and slightly unpleasant relish; it is as though a Puritan divine, preaching against the sins of the flesh, were to make his denunciations all the more juicy while peeping up under the skirts of his congregation. And what love of God, one feels bound to ask, could grow from such hatred of the world?

A selfish, greedy and over self-conscious young woman who cannot rid herself of the obsession that the pleasures of the bed are hideous is made into a monster, or at least casts upon the walls a monstrous shadow when Huxley's radiant 'Ground' shines forth. A pleasure-loving man, Eustace Barnak, is consigned to self-damnation. Eustace is tempted by a little tart who promises to spank him; he is consigned to eternities of cold and agonizing lust after death. His 'large, loose lips' are given to closing 'damply and lovingly' on the 'six-inch coffee-coloured nipples' of cigars; plagued by his pleasant vices, he lies on the lavatory floor suffocating in cigar smoke. Tempted, after death, by the warm and inviting womb of an art-dealer's wife, he condemns himself to a fresh incarnation.

The experiences through which Eustace passes after death, suggested by the Tibetan 'Bardo Thodol', are described in a very persuasive piece of writing. He sees his life's experiences as 'mere clots and disintegrations, mere absences of light, mere untransparent privations'. He is compelled to agree with Mrs. Thwale that the essence of human life is shamelessness; shamelessness of bed and board, of slobbered cigars and little tarts with hairbrushes. And the world, when he revisits it through a medium, is still behaving badly; Mrs. Thwale is tracing obscene words on the palm of Sebastian's hand.

But what of the constructive elements in the book, the assertion of faith? Bruno Rontini, particularly when placed beside the uncommonly effective villains of the piece, does not carry conviction, and he figures less in the novel than does Mr. Propter in *After Many a Summer*; yet if ever a book needed to be built round the character of a saintly man, this one does. The fact that Huxley found it necessary to add an Epilogue in which he sets forth what he regards as the essential requirements for the 'good life' suggests that he knew very well he had failed in the novel. There is much in the Epilogue that, taken in isolation, is wise; 'One was guilty by being content to remain a spiritual embryo, undeveloped, undelivered, unilluminated'; few would question that. There is much that Huxley has said before; Lyric poetry is 'Just ow! or oo-ooh! or nyum-nyum! or damn! or darling! or I'm a pig!—suitably transliterated'; another half-truth. But the holy counsels of the Epilogue seem a little pathetic—and altogether ineffectual—following, as they do, hard upon the triumph of the World, the Flesh and the Devil in the novel.

The whole spirit of Huxley's work is Western through and through: the predominance of his concern for morality; his obsession with the ideas of guilt and sin; his exaggeration of the antithesis between 'spirit' and 'matter'; his ambivalent and tortuous attitude towards sexuality; his desire to impose a single rule upon all men and to measure all by the same yard-stick; all these are essentially Western characteristics—they belong to certain decadent forms of Christianity, and not to any Eastern doctrine (nor, for that matter, are they found in Meister Eckhardt, the Christian mystic for whom Huxley appears to have the greatest admiration). For the Oriental, 'The last achievement of all thought is', as Coomaraswamy says, 'a recognition of the identity of spirit and matter. . . . There is then no sacred or profane, spiritual or sensual, but everything that lives is pure and void. This very world of birth and death is also the great Abyss'. This would, of course, be grossly misleading if we were to leave out the word 'last' or if we were to forget the tremendous discipline which is the necessary preliminary to this 'recognition' and which places it at the opposite pole from the vague and sentimental pantheism of certain Westerners, but nevertheless the fact that such a recognition lies at the back of all the Oriental doctrines saves them from that dualism into which Protestant Christianity so easily falls (and from which Catholicism has not, in practice, been altogether free).

It is therefore extremely unfortunate that Huxley should have attributed his own attitude of mind—the attitude which we have seen set forth in the novels—to Buddhism and the Vedanta. And when he goes so far as to attribute it to what he calls the Perennial Philosophy and what others have described as the Universal Tradition it is really time to call a halt and examine with a critical eye the interpretation which he puts upon this philosophy or Tradition. To see why, although this Tradition allows of innumerable different applications and, in a sense, interpretations, Huxley's exposition is misleading, we must consider the distinction which René Guénon makes between 'synthesis' and 'syncretism'.

Syncretism Guénon defines as the 'juxtaposition of elements of diverse origin, assembled "from the outside" . . . without any principle of a more profound order to unify them . . . such a conglomeration cannot really constitute a doctrine, any more than a pile of stones can constitute a building'; synthesis, on the other hand, 'starts from the principles, that is to say from that which is innermost; it goes, one might say, from the centre to the circumference. . . .' Now Guénon believes, as Huxley claims to do, that the truth which is the kernel of every 'orthodox' doctrine is one and the same; the doctrines, however, differ considerably as applications of this truth to the human situation. They are different means to a single end; what Guénon calls 'synthesis' recognizes them as such, from the point of view of that end, without in any way confusing them, whereas 'syncretism' makes a vain effort to collect and assemble into a kind of super-doctrine the 'best' elements from these separate doctrines.

A simple illustration may be used to emphasize the distinction; there may exist several different cures, all equally effective in dealing with a particular disease (although no doubt one will be more suited than the others to the condition of a particular patient), and the object of all these curative methods is one and the same; nevertheless, no patient in his right mind will ask to be treated by all these methods at once. So Guénon treats each traditional doctrine as an integrated structure, as a way to be followed step by step, whilst reminding us that one particular doctrine may be clarified by the comparison of certain of its elements with the corresponding elements of another; but since it is most of all in their practical applications, and therefore in the rules of morality laid down for their adherents, that these doctrines differ (such rules being comparable to the regimen laid down by the doctor for his patient), he would never dream of trying to construct from mutually incompatible elements a 'universal moral law'.

It is precisely as a moralist that Huxley has approached both the Oriental doctrines and Christianity, and, in his book, *The Perennial Philosophy*, he has undertaken a labour of selection and rejection which no man on earth is entitled to undertake. He approves of Jalalu 'din Rumi and quotes him; but he cannot stomach the Moslem doctrine of the 'Jehad'. He approves of Shankara, but has no use for what is sometimes called 'popular' Hinduism. He approves of Meister Eckhardt, but is highly suspicious of St. Augustine. The quotations which he makes are always interesting; the observations that he makes upon them are often apt, even when couched in a jaw-breaking scientific jargon; but the final impression which the book gives is that Huxley has filched from various doctrines, without any regard for their context, those elements which seem to support his own attitude to life.

To the last and in spite of every effort to escape, Huxley has remained a rationalist and a scientist, bound to that 'modernism' which, in his youth, he so brilliantly exemplified and which, in his prime, he so bitterly attacked. It is a curious paradox that, for all his longing to escape from imprisonment in the 'self' and for all his contempt for 'personality' as such, everything he has touched has taken on the particular and distinctive flavour with which the reader of his novels is thoroughly familiar. But the moment has come to consider two men who have approached the traditional doctrines in a very different spirit.

CHAPTER NINE

TWO TRADITIONALISTS

From the Stone Age until now, quelle dégringolade!
—JOHN LODGE

As a writer, René Guénon defies classification. The gulf which separates his work from that of his contemporaries cannot be bridged by any formula of compromise; so contrary to the whole trend of European thought since the Renaissance are the doctrines which he expounds—and so strange are these doctrines to the contemporary mentality—that, were he anything less than a consummate master of lucid argument and forceful exposition, his work would certainly be unknown to all but a small, private circle of admirers. Nor is the intrinsic strangeness of his teaching the only difficulty which his readers must encounter; he is not only a man completely convinced that he is in full possession of the truth (a fact which gives his writing a tone, easily mistaken for arrogance, which is not to be found in the work either of modern sceptics or of modern 'believers'), but he is also a mathematician and a Frenchman, and in him the blade of French intellectuality is tempered to a razor-sharp edge. An Italian critic has defined the characteristics of his style as 'clarity and rigour'; his clarity is of an icy brilliance, and his rigour allows no concession to sentimentality or human weakness. Guénon is not concerned with the reactions of his readers; if they do not share his certitude, so much the worse for them; if they allow themselves to be put off by his uncompromising manner, the loss is theirs; he states the truth, they may take it or leave it as they choose.

TWO TRADITIONALISTS

It is questionable whether anyone with the normal tastes and intellectual background of our day can approach Guénon's work for the first time without a sense of revulsion; yet so tremendous is the achievement embodied in this work, and so essential is it that we should be made acquainted with the teaching of which he is the greatest living exponent, that those who allow themselves to be governed by this initial reaction and do not return to the attack are indeed the poorer for it. Whether or not we are drawn to agree with his doctrine, we cannot fail to be astonished by the power and universality of this intellect, ranging, as it does, over the whole field of wisdom, human and divine, and by the magnificent symmetry of the body of work which it (the impersonal pronoun is appropriate) has built up during a quarter of a century. If we placed Guénon's first book, published in 1921, beside his most recent one (1947), we should find it impossible to guess, from the contents, which came first, nor should we suspect that more than a year separated the two, for we are accustomed to writers whose thought 'develops', and here there is no question of development in the accepted sense of the word. The sixteen books which he has published might well be the consecutive chapters of a single vast work, planned in detail before it was undertaken, and executed according to plan. Not only is there a wonderful coherence between the different chapters of each separate book, but the same coherence binds the whole series, as the bricks of a single edifice; and never for a moment does the tone of triumphant certainty falter.

It may be almost illegitimate to speak of Guénon as the 'author' of these books, so savagely would he denounce the imputation that any idea expressed in them is 'his own'; it might be more correct to say that there exist a number of orthodox expositions of the traditional wisdom of humanity which, for convenience, bear the signature 'René Guénon'. Who the man who bears this name may be, and what may be the form of traditional doctrine which he outwardly practises, are matters of no consequence; in reply to a foolish critic who wrote of his having 'passed' from Hinduism to Islam, he wrote (and the phrasing is typical), 'We have never "passed" from one thing to another, as all our writings abundantly prove; and we have no need to "seek the truth", since we *know* (and we must insist upon this word) that it exists equally in all traditions. . . .'

Since Guénon's books are now in the course of being published in England (four have so far appeared: *East and West*, *The Crisis of the Modern World*, *Introduction to the Study of the Hindu Doctrines*, and *Man and His Becoming according to the Vedanta*) it seems as well to mention the superficial difficulties which his work presents, particularly from the point of view of the English or American reader; having mentioned them, we may brush them aside as irrelevant, and turn our attention to a far more effective stumbling-block, one which stands in the way of many people who might otherwise approach Guénon's work with an open mind.

Guénon's theme is the primordial and universal Tradition which, he maintains, was the fountain from which the great religions (of the present, as of antiquity) and the metaphysical doctrines which they contain, as well as the myths and rituals of 'primitive' peoples, originally flowed. The language of this Tradition was and, in the main, still is the universal language of symbolism; and it is impossible to expound it without making use of the ancient symbols which, even to-day, are still found throughout the world and which, according to the psychologist Jung, appear again and again in the dreams and fantasies of Westerners who, in their ordinary lives, are totally unacquainted with them. Unfortunately, for the last hundred years or more in the West, these sacred symbols have been left entirely in the hands of what can only be called the 'lunatic fringe' of society. The educated Westerner who has met the symbolism of, for example, the 'seven rays of the spiritual Sun', the 'four rivers of the terrestial Paradise' or the 'World Wheel', has met it only in the context of bogus occultism, spiritualism and every kind of irrational and eccentric nonsense, and he is very naturally suspicious of all such symbols.

The traditional symbolism has been, for so long a period,

the happy hunting ground of cranks that it takes a man of Guénon's intellectual power and integrity even to begin to clear away the false accretions, and to rescue one of the most precious of human possessions from the mire. He found it necessary, when he set out upon his life's work, to devote two lengthy volumes to the task of renovation, denouncing, in the first (*Le Théosophisme, histoire d'une pseudo-religion*), Theosophy, and, in the second (*L'Erreur spirite*), Spiritualism. Only so could he prepare the way for a true interpretation of doctrines and symbols which have been twisted into monstrous and fantastic shapes by the misguided enthusiasm of the 'occultists'.

Symbolism, says Guénon, 'constitutes a much less narrowly limited means of expression than ordinary language; suggesting as it does far more than it expresses, it provides the support that is best adapted to possibilities of conception that lie beyond the power of words'; quite apart, however, from the unfortunate associations which many of the most ancient and universal symbols have for us, the vast majority of Westerners are to-day singularly incapable of thinking in terms of symbols (or of true analogies), partly because our education and the general intellectual trend of our times have conditioned our minds to work in quite another way, and partly because many people have little idea of what the word 'symbol' itself means and even confuse symbols with 'conventional signs'. Now a symbol may be defined, in a general sense, as a reality of one order which corresponds to (and so participates in) a reality of another, higher order; a true symbolism is therefore inherent in the nature of things, and the use of a particular symbol to denote a particular reality of the divine or 'principial' order is in no way a matter of choice. When, for example, we say that such and such an object symbolizes a particular divine aspect, we mean, not that a number of human individuals once agreed to use this object to denote the aspect in question (in the sense of an algebraic equation: 'X' = 10), but that the object is a direct, although limited, expression of the divine aspect and that, using it as a tangible support of contemplation, we may reach awareness of its supernatural prototype. We have, therefore, to avoid two common errors; firstly that of mistaking the symbol for the thing symbolized, as when we call those who recognize the sun as a symbol of the divine power 'sun-worshippers' ('No object of sense', said Dante, 'is more worthy to be made a type of God than the sun'); secondly, that of supposing that there is no real and objective relation between the symbol and that which it shadows forth.

It will be necessary to return to this all-important subject, but enough has been said for the moment to indicate Guénon's attitude to the symbols in which the ancient Tradition is expressed. But what is this Tradition, and what evidence is there that it ever existed? Guénon himself does not consider that the matter admits of any argument; and this is certainly not the place to enter upon such a controversy. It is, however, worth noticing that anthropologists have been at great pains to find an explanation for the existence, in different parts of the world and amongst races that are not known to have had any relations with each other, of identical symbols, employed in an identical manner, of rites, the meaning of which appears to have been forgotten by the people who practise them, and of certain elements in the beliefs of 'primitive' peoples which suggest a far higher 'cultural level' than that at which these peoples are now living.

Two explanations have been advanced, in order to bring these facts into line with the modern evolutionary obsession; certain writers, amongst whom W. J. Perry is perhaps the best known, have maintained that these myths and symbols were derived originally from Egypt and that Egyptian culture once spread through the world leaving behind, when it receded, these vestiges; the theory does not bear very close examination, and it is not widely held, but its exponents have, quite un wittingly, piled up a wealth of evidence for the existence of a universal human tradition (see, in this connection, *The Primordial Ocean* by W. J. Perry). The second explanation is based upon the theory that, since human beings are much alike the world over, since their brains are similarly formed and, under primitive conditions, their experience of life does not differ very widely from one part of the world to another, identical ideas as to the origin of the world and the nature of the Universe arise quite independently. The theory does not explain why human minds should so obviously fail to work uniformly, the moment the bonds of tradition are weakened, nor does it account for the precision with which the ancient symbols are used; like so many facile pseudo-scientific solutions, it raises more questions than it answers.

Guénon, in any case, has no interest in persuading anyone to agree against their will to his assertions. He believes that there exists a universal Tradition, revealed to humanity—indeed, inherent in the human mind—at the beginning of the present cycle of time, but partially lost to the present race of men; but his primary concern is less with the detailed forms of this Tradition and the history of their decline than with its kernel, the pure and changeless knowledge which, although more difficult of attainment now than in the days of the world's youth, is still accessible to man through the channels provided by traditional doctrine. He points out that, since what he calls metaphysical knowledge is a permanent and changeless certitude, there can be no place in this realm for discussion or argument. 'It is very difficult', he writes, 'to make our contemporaries see that there are things which, by their very nature, cannot be discussed. Modern man, instead of raising himself to the truth, tries to drag truth down to his own level. It is always possible to hold discussions within the realm of individual opinion, as this does not go beyond the rational order, and it is easy to find more or less valid arguments on both sides of a question when there is no appeal to any higher principle'. But as soon as our concern is with the perception of first principles and with the awareness of the universal truth which is one and the same for every man who truly knows it, there is nothing that can be discussed in human terms, and all controversy is left far behind.

We have already seen, in connection with the Hindu doctrines, that man is traditionally believed to possess—or rather, to have access to—a power of direct, intuitive knowledge which is free from the accidents and limitations of the individual nature and which carries with it an immediate certainty provided by no other kind of knowledge. In the modern world, we tend to think in terms of 'intellectual progress', by which we mean a progress in the ideas which men formulate with regard to the nature of things; but, from the point of view of traditional knowledge, there can be no progress, except in so far as particular individuals advance from ignorance to reflected or rational knowledge, and from reason to direct, intuitive knowledge. The final term of this advance (which Guénon calls 'metaphysical knowledge', since it lies beyond the sphere of nature) cannot be defined, for it is, in essence, 'knowledge of the Universal', and definition would limit what is in fact unlimited; nor is it in any way dependent upon rational 'proofs'; 'When one knows with a more than mathematical certainty that things cannot be otherwise than they are, one becomes as a matter of course disdainful of experiment, because the verifying of a particular fact never proves anything more or anything different than the mere existence of that particular fact'.

In metaphysics, there can be no question of 'discoveries' of any kind. All that is capable of being known has been known by certain persons at any and every period; but their knowledge could not be handed on as a mathematical formula is handed on; it could only be shared with those who were prepared to follow in their footsteps and imitate their labours. But it is also true that all that can be expressed of this essentially inexpressible knowledge has found expression, time and again, in diverse forms; since the truth itself is beyond every expression that can be found for it, it follows that there is no such thing as the perfect formulation; all are necessarily inadequate (the particular cannot fully express the nature of the universal), and all, if taken too literally (as though a signpost were taken to mark the end of the journey), lead to error. Every formula that is true within its limits and that is adapted to the time and the occasion will serve as a 'support' of contemplation, an aid towards the understanding of that which can be enclosed in no formula, symbol or philosophical system; and it is only over such formulas and over possible defects in exposition that the occasion for controversy can arise.

Everything relating to the order of metaphysical knowledge, lying, as it does, beyond the contingencies and limitations of our minds and imaginations, opens up a truly boundless horizon. 'The things in question', says Guénon, in a rare burst of enthusiasm, 'are the most tremendous that exist, and compared with them everything else is mere child's play'. It is only by analogy that we can speak here of knowledge, for this is a total awareness in relation to which all the superlatives that the experience of life will provide are inadequate; in it, to know and to be, to enjoy and to possess, are one, and the man who has participated in this awareness can no more question the truth than he can doubt the shining of the sun when he stands in its glare.

'The truth is one', writes Guénon, 'and imposes itself alike upon all those who know it provided, of course, that they actually do know it with certainty. . . . In this domain one is outside and above the particular points of view; the differences never lie in anything but the more or less outward forms'. But Tradition, at once the repository of this knowledge and the regimen for its attainment, admits all the aspects in which the single truth is reflected in our world; 'it does not set itself against any legitimate adaptation . . . it opens up possibilities to the intelligence which, like truth itself, are unlimited'. Those who are qualified to speak in the name of a traditional doctrine have no need to engage in polemics; they have only to expound the doctrine to the best of their ability, for such as can understand it, and to 'denounce error' when it arises (Guénon points out that, whereas practical tolerance, as applied to individuals, is an excellent virtue, theoretic tolerance, which claims the same rights for all beliefs, can only spring from a rooted scepticism). Their function is not to compromise the doctrine by taking part in strife, but to pronounce the judgment that they have the right to pronounce. Knowledge, says Guénon, enlightens action, without partaking of its vicissitudes; the spiritual guides the temporal without mingling with it, and thus everything remains in its right order. So, at least, it should be: but to-day—'the profane presume to discuss what is sacred, and to contest its character and even its existence; the inferior judges the superior, ignorance sets bounds to wisdom, error prevails over truth, the human supersedes the divine, earth overtops heaven, the individual sets the measure to all things and claims to dictate to the Universe laws drawn entirely from his own relative and fallible reason'.

It should by now be clear why Guénon does not offer 'evidence' for the assertions he makes. The perpetual demand for proof and evidence arises in a world which, at heart, doubts the existence of any ultimate truth, and certainly questions whether any man has ever known such a truth. But for the man who cannot doubt his own certainty, the demand for proof is essentially a frivolous demand; he does not suffer from the illusion that he may, in some miraculous way, transfer his knowledge and understanding to another by defeating him in argument; he knows that the most he can hope to do for his fellows is to show them the way by which, through the grace of God and by their own unfaltering effort, they may come to the place where he stands and see what he sees. 'It is truly strange', remarks Guénon, 'that people demand proofs of this knowledge instead of seeking to become themselves aware of it by undertaking the necessary labour'.

Here, beyond doubt, St. Augustine's 'Believe in order that you may know!' is the essential advice. No man can set out to reach a place in the existence of which he does not really believe and have a reasonable hope of arriving there; belief, in itself, may not take him very far, but it will make his journey possible and set his feet in the right direction. The spectacle, so common to-day, of the sceptic sitting tight and asking to be convinced by rational argument is a curious one; as well might a bird sit on a branch and ask for proof that he can fly, instead of spreading his wings.

But to question the practical effectiveness of rational argument is not to deride reason. All true knowledge (of which reason is a form) participates, to a greater or lesser extent, in the nature of that supreme knowledge which we have been considering; but the value of indirect knowledge is only relative in comparison with the value of that which penetrates directly into the nature of things. Reason can only function truly in the light either of faith or of the supreme knowledge itself—in the darkness it cannot find its way—but the relative subservience of its role does not detract from its nobility, for in the order of human reason is reflected something of the divine order and harmony. The play of reason, writes Titus Burckhardt, one of Guénon's collaborators, in an article on Islamic Art, 'loin de limiter l'âme muselmane, lui fera au contraire pressentir des possibilités illimitées d'ou jaillissent toutes les sources de la nostalgie et du ravissement'. The great gulf which separates the supra-rational from the irrational (and, according to Guénon, intellectual intuition from intuition of the sensible order) is the measure of reason's domain; between the perfect order of heaven and the chaos of the dark waters extends this human order, the kingdom of reason, but reason is no more self-sufficient than is the human order itself; both can exist and fulfil their function only if they submit to that which is above them.

But from reason to rationalism (from reason as the servant of divine wisdom to reason snapping at its own tail) is a far cry, and Guénon sees a close connection between modern rationalism and modern sentimentality, regarding them as two sides of the same coin; 'To denounce sentimentalism is not to deny sentiment any more than to denounce rationalism amounts to denying reason; sentimentalism and rationalism are both nothing more than the results of exaggerations and intrusions, although the modern West sees them as the two items of an alternative from which she cannot escape'. It is only because the modern mind faces almost exclusively outwards, towards the world of the senses, that sentiment seems inward and subjective to it. In fact, not only the senses, but also reason and emotion are relatively exterior things compared with the spirit which is at the centre of the individuality, and the psychologist's introspection itself grasps nothing but phenomena or, in other words, the outward and superficial modifications of the being.

Guénon is equally scornful of another distinction dear to modern philosophers, that between those who base their doctrines upon reason and those who lay the emphasis upon intuition (of the sensible order), vitality, instinct, or the 'life force'. Both reason and 'life' are, he insists, conditions peculiar to the sensible world, and 'the modern West, but for exceptional cases, takes the sensible world as the sole object of knowledge—whether she prefers to attach herself to the one or the other of this world's conditions, or whether she studies it from this or that point of view, scouring it in no matter what direction, the domain in which her mind works continues none the less to be the same always'. The so-called antagonistic theories are far more nearly equivalent than their respective partisans will admit, and neither the mechanistic theory of the rationalists nor the 'life-philosophy' of the vitalists can escape, even for a moment, from the limited sphere of 'becoming' in which we at present find ourselves.

Both these doctrines, on the occasions when they admit the existence of something beyond the sphere of sensible reality, lead to the substitution of religiosity for religion and to a belief in a vague 'spirituality' which is in fact nothing more than a sentimental aspiration. Guénon, in any case, considers that religion degenerates inevitably into religiosity, the moment the doctrinal or metaphysical element in it is allowed to fall into the background; not unnaturally, he regards the distinction between metaphysics and religion as equivalent to that between the ways of 'jnana' and of 'bhakti' in the Hindu doctrine, and just as the 'way of love' runs very easily to error and extravagance when it lacks the stiffening offered by an orthodox traditional doctrine, so religion, divorced from dogma, falls a prey to every kind of personal fantasy and neurotic sentimentality.

But if Guénon regards the way of worship, the way of personal devotion to a personal God, as, in a sense, subordinate to that way which leads through intellectual understanding to the total awareness of the supreme Principle, which is prior even to Being (as the Godhead is prior to God), this does not mean that he in any way decries religion; he denies nothing that, in its own sphere and so far as it goes, leads man effectively towards his last true end, indeed he regards religion as the only way that is fully adapted to human nature as we find it in the vast majority in this age.

It is because few if any modern activities lead, in the slightest degree, towards that end, that he is so bitter in his condemnation of the modern world, and it is because, in a traditional society, all things are ordered, in theory if not always in effective fact, to a supernatural end (as well as to a natural one) that he regards the framework of tradition as the only one in which human life can fulfil its function in the universal order. As an example of the typical fruitlessness of our activities, he cites the passion for research, taken as an end in itself, regardless of whether it terminates in any solution. Forgetting the 'Seek and ye shall find' of the Gospels, the modern Westerner seems to seek merely for the sake of seeking; he is almost afraid of finding anything real and final, for he gives the name of 'death' to whatever constitutes a definite finality and the name of 'life' to what is really no more than aimless agitation. 'This unhealthy taste for research', says Guénon, 'real "mental restlessness" without end and without issue, shows itself at its plainest in modern philosophy'.

He blames the ancient Greeks and what he calls the 'classical prejudice' for many of the fundamental faults of the modern world. He remarks that 'it almost seems as if the Greeks, at a moment when they were about to disappear from history, wished to avenge themselves for their own incomprehension by imposing on a whole section of mankind the limitations of their own mental horizon'. He blames them for the substitution of the rational for the truly intellectual and of science and philosophy for metaphysics; he points out that, in their civilization, rites and symbols inherited from an ancient and forgotten tradition rapidly lost their exact meaning, and that the imagination of a predominantly artistic people, freely expressing itself through the individual fancies of its poets, covered these symbols with an almost impenetrable veil, until the ancient metaphysical myths had degenerated into mere allegories.

The modern world has, of course, gone much further than did the ancient Greeks in the denial even of the possibility of a real knowledge which transcends the narrow limits of the individual mentality. 'To turn an intellectual infirmity into a barrier which no one may pass—that is something the like of which was never seen or heard before'. And agnosticism, a confession of ignorance masquerading as a confession of faith, is, at least in the form in which we know it, a specifically modern phenomenon; agnostics and sceptics acknowledge their ignorance 'only on condition that no one has the right to know what they themselves do not', and the passion for equality and uniformity, together with an envious hatred of all that savours of 'privilege', gives to modern scepticism a peculiarly vicious edge.

The fact that the ignorant should be able to set themselves up to condemn knowledge and that the unbeliever should resent faith indicates clearly that our modern civilization, whether in the spheres of philosophy, politics, art or science, is a civilization without principles. 'It is', says Guénon, 'as if an organism with its head cut off were to go on living a life at the same time intense and disordered. . . . With the suppression of pure intellectuality, each special and contingent domain is looked on as independent; one infringes on the other, and everything is mingled and confused. . . . Natural relations are turned upside down and what should be subordinate proclaims itself autonomous mentally as well as socially; all hierarchy is done away with, in the name of that hallucination, equality; and as equality is, after all, impossible in actual fact, false hierarchies are created, in which anything, no matter what, is given the highest rank, whether it be science, industry, morals, politics or finance, for want of the one thing which can and must normally assume the supremacy, that is, once again, for want of true principles'.

The notion that principles can be evolved from a study of events or of sensible phenomena, or that they may be created by our reasoning power, is, according to Guénon, a pathetic fallacy; synthesis can never be the product of analysis, and the accumulation of facts of one order can never lead us to the knowledge of realities of another order; the so-called syntheses of modern science are purely hypothetical, whereas a true synthesis, starting, as it does, from principles intuitively known, partakes of their certainty. Science can never lead to certainty, and its position in the general scheme of things is, traditionally, a very subordinate one; when, however, science breaks free from the principles by which it was formerly ruled and tries to function independently, it can do no more than observe events and draw up laws of probability. It is because these laws of probability and the conclusions drawn from them with the aid of human reason are generally mistaken for valid statements of the real nature of things that we have what Guénon calls the 'gigantic collective hallucination by which a whole section of humanity has come to take the vainest fantasies for incontestable realities'.

'Never', he says, 'until the present epoch had the study of the sensible world been regarded as self-sufficient; never would the science of this ephemeral and changing multiplicity have been judged truly worthy of the name of knowledge. . . . According to the ancient conception . . . a science was less esteemed for itself than for the degree in which it expressed after its own fashion and represented within a certain order of things a reflection of the higher immutable truth of which everything of any reality necessarily partakes; and as the features of this truth were incarnated, as it were, in the idea of tradition, all science appeared as an extension of the traditional doctrine itself, as one of its applications, secondary and contingent no doubt . . . but still a veritable knowledge none the less, since it kept a link with that supreme knowledge which belongs to the order of pure intellect'.

So Guénon claims that the modern sciences are 'degenerate vestiges' of the ancient traditional ones, indeed that the former are constructed from the ruins of the latter with the materials that had been rejected and left to the ignorant and the 'profane'. Thus, to take only one example, modern chemistry has its origins in the inability of certain men to understand or to penetrate the symbols of the alchemists and in their misconception of the true nature and purpose of alchemy; thinking that no more than material operations were in question, they launched out upon experiments which could have had no possible interest for the true alchemist. Similarly, astrology, the ancient science in which the apparent movements of the heavenly bodies were taken as symbols, on the one hand of man's spiritual development, on the other of realities beyond the world of the senses, degenerated into astronomy, which concerns itself only with the structure of the universe (not with its meaning), while a perversion of true astrology lingered on in the form of the so-called 'art of divination'.

If such an attitude as this seems almost incredible in the modern world, it is because the concentration of all our energies upon discovering the mechanism by which contingent events are brought about has resulted, amongst other things, in a distortion of human experience. The ancient sciences used our human experience of the world about us as a solid foundation upon which to set the ladder of wisdom, and the fact that this experience does not altogether correspond to the physical reality of things as it is revealed by the telescope or any other scientific instrument does not make it any the less real in its own order. We see the sun rise out of the eastern sea, pursue its course across the sky and set in the west, and this experience provides the basis for an effective system of symbols. The knowledge that, in 'fact' (that is to say, from the point of view of some abstract being who is able to survey the solar system from a point in outer space), the earth spins round the sun adds nothing to this symbolism and is, in the main, irrelevant.

There is no reason, of course, why the Copernican system should not provide an equally fruitful symbolism, but the fact remains that the ancient tradition is, as it were, drafted in terms of actual, 'pre-scientific' experience. The human mind, as we find it, is deeply embedded in the normal experience of a being who can have but a 'man's eye view' of the heavens, and when this mind attempts to achieve a kind of angelic detachment, to hover above the earth and see things 'objectively', it may learn something of the physical mechanism of the universe, but it will discover nothing of its significance; to grasp significance—and truly to rise above the subjectivity of normal experience—we have to make use of a power which is above the mind, and we advance, not by distending to a monstrous extent the power of our senses (as the telescope distends the power of the eye), but by leaving the senses where they belong and using their fallible evidence as a stepping-stone to that which the mightiest telescope will never discover.

'Allah', says the Quoran, 'disdaineth not to coin the similitude even of a gnat'. There is no event, no phenomenon of any kind, that may not be employed as a valid symbol of the divine realities, for there is, according to traditional teaching, a perfect correspondence between all the orders of reality; the support by which we raise ourselves above the limitations of our particular level of existence may be no more than a grain of sand—no more, perhaps, than a momentary effect of sunlight on a girl's hair—but, so long as we know how to use it, it will take our weight. In practice, however, men must live in a fairly stable world if their experience is to offer them a really firm support, and they must be agreed, although innumerable different pictures of this world may be 'true' in a certain sense, upon accepting one particular picture as the framework in which their earthly life is set. In the modern world, under the influence of science, our picture of the physical universe changes almost from day to day, and, upon such quicksands, we find no support. It does not in the least matter what this table, this chair, may in 'fact' be made of (and the knowledge of their actual structure will serve only to multiply, through applied science, on the one hand our physical needs and on the other our means of destruction in war); all that matters is that chair and table should fulfil their proper function as supports and that we should be free to consider, not the hypothetical atoms of which they are said to be made, but the ultimate principles of the world of which they are a part.

It has been necessary to harp on this matter, but unless it is recognized that the ancient, 'pre-scientific' view of the world was not simply an illusion, bred of ignorance, but a point of view perfectly valid within its own order, there can be no understanding of the traditional doctrines. Until our minds are led back from the wastes of outer space—or of 'inter-atomic space'—to the vital centre of human experience (in which neither nebulae nor atoms have any place) we shall not find the way to true, effective, and transforming knowledge. The Kingdom of Heaven is not to be found in the neighbourhood of Orion.

If Guénon looks to the East for a rectification of human knowledge, it is because, in the words of one of his translators, the West is in the position of the 'foolish virgins who, through the wandering of their attention in other directions, had allowed their lamps to go out; in order to rekindle the sacred fire, which in its essence is always the same wherever it may be burning, they must have recourse to the lamps still kept alight by their wiser companions'.

To turn from Guénon's monumental work to the scattered essays in which Coomaraswamy has treated various aspects and applications of traditional doctrine is to descend to a far kindlier climate, while remaining in the same country (a country so wide that everyone may find there the region that suits them). The icy glitter is replaced by a warmer glow, the attitude of calm disdain towards all things modern by a more human indignation.

Ananda Kentish Coomaraswamy was the son of an eminent Ceylonese lawyer, the first Hindu to be called to the Bar in London; his mother was an Englishwoman. He was brought up and educated in England, and received the degree of Doctor of Science from the University of London; he worked for a time as director of Mineralogical Survey in Ceylon, and went, in 1917, to the United States, where he became a research fellow in Oriental art at the Boston Museum of Fine Arts and, later, curator of that museum; he died in Boston, at the age of seventy in September of 1947. Had he been a less modest man, he might well have reversed Pandit Nehru's famous confession of being 'a queer mixture of East and West, out of place everywhere, at home nowhere' and claimed, with every justification, to be out of place nowhere, at home everywhere; no one could have been better fitted, by birth and by training, to bridge in his own person the gulf between East and West.

Coomaraswamy's work does not present such formidable difficulties as those which the Western reader finds in Guénon's books. No one familiar with the work of the late Eric Gill will find anything strange in Coomaraswamy's approach to the problems of the modern world, and Gill, in his *Autobiography*, wrote a decidedly effusive panegyric of Coomaraswamy. His method of writing, however, is one that makes considerable demands upon the reader; sometimes the printed page is a mosaic of quotations, in which Sanskrit and Pali (the language of the Hinayana Buddhist canon) jostle with Greek and Latin, French, German, and Italian; and the English language itself is here used with a precision which, in these days when words are employed so loosely, seems to belong more to the region of mathematics than to that of prose; Coomaraswamy splits up certain words which have lost their meaning through long misuse, with a hyphen between the two parts, to show their true derivation (so, 'in-genious' and 'con-form'). Further, and this is a stumbling-block not to be underrated in an age when reading is regarded mainly as a relaxation and an aid to slumber, each of his essays or articles is followed by several pages of notes, in extremely small print, and many of his most important reflections are compressed into these notes.

Although, in such books as *A New Approach to the Vedas* and *Elements of Buddhist Iconography*, he interprets certain aspects of the Oriental doctrines with great learning and subtlety (Coomaraswamy had a curious tendency to give his books rather forbidding titles; the most interesting collection of his essays is in a volume called *Figures of Speech and Figures of Thought*), the main theme of all his work was the traditional philosophy of art, to-day chiefly associated with the East, but prominent both in

Plato and in the doctrines of the Christian philosophers of the Middle Ages. But since the division which we make between life and art (and, in particular, between the 'fine' and the 'applied' arts) is strange to the traditional teaching, Coomaraswamy, even when discussing the complexities of Buddhist iconography, is writing about human life in its most practical sense. For human life is human labour, and human labour is art (labour without art is no longer human). It is chiefly on account of his greater interest in the conditions of life of the men and women around him that Coomaraswamy's work seems more straightforward than Guénon's, rather than on account of any difference of belief between the two men.

It was upon the saying of St. Thomas that 'Art is the imitation of Nature in her manner of operation' that Coomaraswamy based his exposition of the 'traditional or "normal" view of art', making it clear that the 'Nature' which St. Thomas meant the artist to imitate is not the created nature that forms our immediate environment, but creative Nature, that 'Nature' which is one of the names of God and 'to find which', in the words of Meister Eckhardt, 'all her forms must be shattered'. He points out that it is the basis of Plato's criticism of naturalistic poets and painters that they know nothing of the reality but only the appearance of things, 'for which their vision is over keen'; their imitations are not of the divine originals, but only copies of copies.

If this doctrine is ignored and forgotten to-day, it is because we have lost the habit of contemplation and, in any case, no longer believe in a reality, supersensual and invisible, to which contemplation would raise us and in which abide the principles that are to be imitated in our lives and in our work. Convinced that no one knows the final truth about anything, we only know what we like (or what, in accordance with the vagaries of 'taste', we approve of), and we 'desire a freedom to do and think what we like more than a freedom from error'. Our educational systems are chaotic because we are not agreed for what to educate, and we make an ideal of 'self-expression' because we no longer know what else there may be to express.

The traditional doctrines are in agreement as to what is to be imitated, what expressed; 'Lo, make all things in accordance with the pattern that was shown thee upon the Mount' is the Biblical formula, and 'It is in imitation of the divine forms that any human form is invented here' is the Hindu one; so Plato says, 'The city can never otherwise be happy unless it is designed by those painters who follow a divine original'.

In his imitation of a 'divine pattern', the artist is undertaking an activity parallel to and strictly comparable with the creative activity of God; from the traditional point of view, the world itself, 'together with all things done or made in a manner conforming to the cosmic pattern', is a valid source of information, because it shows forth in its own substance realities of a higher order. It follows that all dualism is foreign to this teaching, and that, as Coomaraswamy says, 'an access to reality cannot be had by making a choice between matter and spirit considered as unlike in all respects, but rather by seeing in things material and sensible a formal likeness to spiritual prototypes of which the senses can give no direct report'. So it is that 'man knows immortal things by the mortal' and that the divine silence is known through the divine utterance.

If the objects of the senses reveal (although, from another point of view, they may be said to veil) an ultimate significance, then the chief function of human art must be to express, as clearly and as precisely as may be possible, a meaning which transcends the sphere of our ordinary, practical life. So art is said to be an 'intellectual virtue'; and Coomaraswamy quotes, on more than one occasion, the words of Walter Andrae, 'To make the primordial truth intelligible, to make the unheard audible, to enunciate the primordial word, such is the task of art, or it is not art'. The work of art is, in essence, a reminder—it recalls to our minds that which we have forgotten while occupied in the business of the world, and this experience, whereby our forgetfulness is beaten back, is called, in the Buddhist canon, 'Samvega', that is, shock; it is the sudden shock of at least a momentary escape from the limitations in which are are normally confined, a momentary reminiscence of 'who' we really are (' "That" art thou!'), and it is said by the Buddhists to lead to the 'full-awakening aspect of delight'. This shock is compared to that felt by a horse struck by a whip; and it is assumed, as Coomaraswamy points out, that, like the good horse, we are more or less trained, and hence that more than a merely physical shock is felt; the blow has a meaning for us—it instructs us and it reminds us.

Aestheticism, with all the modern philosophies of art which hang upon the word, knows nothing of this doctrine; it has to do only with a titillation of the senses and the enjoyment of emotional excitement for its own sake; 'Aesthetic experience', says Coomaraswamy, 'is of the skin you love to touch, or the fruit you love to taste', but 'Art is an intellectual, not a physical virtue; beauty has to do with knowledge and goodness, of which it is precisely the attractive aspect; and since it is by beauty that we are attracted to a work, its beauty is evidently a means to an end . . . the purpose of art is always one of effective communication'. The doctrine of 'Art for art's sake' is but another example of the terrible isolation of modern life, in which every activity is cut off from its source and its significance, to be confined in a narrow, private compartment.

Hand in hand with 'Art for art's sake' goes 'Industry without art'. In place of a life of which unity is the ruling principle, we lead a disintegrated existence in which many things that can only function properly in unison have fallen apart into a sterile separation. None of the 'primitive' peoples, whose cultures 'we affect to despise and propose to amend', has dispensed with art; everything made by man, from the Stone Age onwards, under whatever conditions of hardship and poverty, has been made by art to serve a double purpose, at once utilitarian and spiritual; we alone, for all our vast resources, make a division of art, one sort barely utilitarian, the other luxurious, and have quite overlooked what was once the highest function of art, to express and to communicate ideas.

There was a time when it would have been unthinkable that anything, whether natural or artificial, should have a use and not also a meaning; the man of that time (and the 'primitive' to-day) 'could not have understood our distinction of sacred from profane or of spiritual from material values; he did not live by bread alone. It had not occurred to him that there could be such a thing as an industry without art, or the practise of any art that was not at the same time a rite, a going on with what had been done by God in the beginning'. And when, to-day, we collect his weapons or his household articles and find them marked with what we mis-call magical signs, we remain blind to the fact that these symbols are not a simple 'ornamentation' of the object, but an essential part of it, but for which it would not be worthy of human use. Man has a twofold nature, and the things he uses, if they are to be truly useful, must serve both his natures, just as his actions, if they are to be truly human, must express both his natures.

It is worth noting that Guénon, in his study of the world's decadence (*Le Règne de la Quantité et Les Signes des Temps*), devotes a chapter to 'The Degeneration of Coinage' and shows how, once, every coin had a double use; it was both a quantitative unit of value and the vehicle of a certain spiritual significance (expressed by the symbols engraved upon it), so that trade between different peoples was never merely an exchange of goods (we know too well how fertile a source of discord such trade is), but also a means of communicating certain spiritual values. And Guénon points out that, in a traditional culture, every object, while perfectly fitted for the use for which it is intended, could at any moment, all the more because it was in real use (instead of being treated as a 'work of art') serve as a 'support' for meditation binding the individual to his source in a conscious awareness of unity.

The idea of all human labour as art and, indeed, as ritual, is bound up with the doctrine of vocation, upon which we have already touched when considering the 'sva-dharma' or 'own rule' which is inherent in every individual nature; and it is perhaps in this question of vocation that we see most clearly the gulf which separates our contemporary disorder from the traditional human order. 'Man devoted to his own vocation', says the Gita, 'finds perfection.... That man whose prayer and praise of God are in the doing of his own work perfects himself'. To understand what is meant by this (and to avoid the error of supposing that there is some peculiar virtue in simply doing well whatever 'job' may come to hand) we must realize that, in a traditional society, the various crafts have each and all of them a symbolic meaning, that the exercise of the craft is, for those who are aware of that meaning, a sacred ritual, and that the very instruments employed are directly related to particular aspects of the divine activity (a whole volume might be written upon the significance of the plough or of the stone-mason's chisel).

In such a society, therefore, the craftsman who fulfils his vocation is not only doing the work which best accords with his fundamental nature, but he is also, in every moment of labour, conforming to a spiritual discipline which is likewise adapted to his specific needs and capabilities. The fact that his talents might, in some other kind of work, earn him more, bring him greater leisure or higher repute, is irrelevant; for it is only by this work, which is his vocation, that he can accomplish his own individual destiny.

In his apprenticeship and initiation the craftsman learns what he needs to know—all, in fact, that is relevant to his vocation. It may well be quite unnecessary for him to read or write; it is only in an industrial society, in which vocation ceases to have any meaning and in which the making of things is no longer an art and a ritual but mere coolie-labour, that literacy becomes important; and to-day we are beginning to learn just how quickly a 'primitive' people degenerate when they become literate. Coomaraswamy quotes Professor G. L. Kittredge to the effect that 'When a nation begins to read . . . what was once the possession of the folk as a whole, becomes the heritage of the illiterate only, and soon, unless it is gathered up by the antiquary, vanishes altogether'; he also draws attention to Tom Harrisson's comments on the natives of the New Hebrides; 'Without writing, memory is perfect, tradition exact. The growing child is taught all that is known. . . . Intangible things co-operate in every effort of making, from conception to canoe-building. . . . The natives easily learn to write after white impact. They regard it as a curious and useless performance. They say, "Cannot a man remember and speak?" '

It was Plato's opinion that 'This invention will produce forgetfulness in the minds of those who learn to use it'. Amongst the 'primitive' peoples who have learned to read, the great treasury of myth and fable, the tales that, by their symbolism, provide a ladder to heaven, and all the wisdom, both spiritual and canny, are swiftly forgotten, and the people become as ignorant as any 'literate' Westerner. It is surely time that even the most fervent advocates of universal literacy realized to what use this doubtful gift is put by the vast majority.

Coomaraswamy defines the chief characteristics of the modern world as 'disorder, uncertainty, sentimentality and despair'; it is, he says, a 'world of impoverished reality', in which we go on living as if life were an end in itself and had no meaning. 'Our boasted standard of living is qualitatively beneath contempt. And we have destroyed the vocational and artistic foundations of whatever traditional cultures our touch has infected. We enjoy 'drainage without architecture', while sentimentally admiring "architecture without drainage" '. And when we appropriate and pretend to admire works of art belonging to a traditional culture, our attitude is that of a small child who, unaware of its proper use, plays with a knife because it shines and is pleasant to touch; we use as pretty or bizarre ornaments things that were made for the purpose of expressing a precise meaning. Our ignorance of the few things that matter is as prodigious as our knowledge of trivialities; in the words of W. M. Urban, 'at no other time have men been so knowing and yet so unaware, so burdened with purposes and so purposeless, so disillusioned and so completely the victims of illusion'.

While the vast majority of our people are condemned to a labour which may justly be called 'unfit for free men', not to achieve any valid end, but to produce utilities which are not truly useful and of which men have no need until an artificial one is created (so that, with every rise in the minimum standard of living which seems essential to us, our lives become more burdened) and while the mass-produced trash from our factories is spread far and wide in the world, both art and the spiritual values which art should express have become luxuries divorced from normal life, daily labour; they have become those 'higher things of life', pale and anaemic, which the 'educated' chain-belt worker is asked to appreciate in his leisure hours. What Coomaraswamy calls our 'exaggerated standards of living and equally depreciated standards of life' have robbed even the privileged few 'of all poise, of the power to walk or to dress or to marry wisely, or to desire children or lovers, or to believe in any power not legally exteriorized'.

Obviously, a vocational society is not, in our sense, a democratic one, nor does it offer what we are pleased to call 'equality of opportunity'. Coomaraswamy defines the political alternatives of the modern world in these terms: 'A democracy is a government of all by a majority of proletarians: a soviet a government by a small group of proletarians; and a dictatorship a government by a single proletarian'; it must be understood that, by 'proletarian', he means any individual who has no place in any of the social orders into which a vocational society is divided; 'In the traditional and unanimous society there is a government by a hereditary aristocracy, the function of which is to maintain an existing order, based on eternal principles, rather than to impose the views or arbitrary will of any party or interest'. In such a society, 'the life of the community as a whole and of the individual whatever his special function may be, conforms to recognized patterns, of which no one questions the validity; the criminal is much rather the man who does not know how to behave, than a man who is unwilling to behave'. It is the aim of the various forms of proletarian government, on the other hand, to achieve a rigid and inflexible uniformity, and all the forces of education are directed to this end, whereas, in a 'primitive' society, education is not compulsory, but inevitable, just because the past is there 'present, experienced and felt as an effective part of daily life, not just taught by schoolmasters'.

We rightly make a distinction between, for example, the

alcoholic, who, on the whole harms only himself, and the drug addict who frequently takes pleasure in persuading others to share his addiction; for purposes of comparison, it is to the second class, that of the addict who propagates his vice, that the Western world belongs. The people upon whom we have forced the gift of our civilization have either died out or degenerated, even if the case of that South-West African tribe which, under German rule, committed tribal suicide in a generation by terminating every pregnancy by abortion, is an extreme one. Amongst the many examples of the baleful influence of Western civilization upon a 'primitive' people which Coomaraswamy quotes (generally from the works of academic anthropologists who have no axe to grind), we might select the Australian aborigines, of whom D. F. Thompson observes that their mythology 'supports the belief in a supernatural visitation that comes upon those who disregard or disobey the law of the old men'. 'When', he says, 'this belief in the old men and their power—which, under tribal conditions, I have never known to be abused—dies, or declines, as it does with civilization, chaos and racial death follow immediately.'

The spectacle of the devastation which we have wrought throughout the world—not the physical destruction, for that is relatively unimportant and relatively soon mended, but the destruction of the life-spirit of so many peoples—must breed, in those who see it with unprejudiced eyes, a justified anger against the modern world and all its works. If such a writer as Coomaraswamy seems at times to be overcome by his own indignation, we can hardly blame him; for to destroy faith and significance, to take from a particular race or tribe the spirit which, in their daily lives, they incarnate and foster, is precisely the function of the Devil. Yet when some small measure of what we have done to others is done to us, we enjoy an orgy of self-pity.

'The bases of modern civilization are', says Coomaraswamy, 'to such an extent rotten to the core that it has been forgotten even by the learned that man ever attempted to live otherwise than by "bread alone" '; and 'bread alone' is, in fact, what we offer to the 'primitive', in place of his sacred lore and ritual. Coomaraswamy insists that what seems to us irrational in the life of 'savages', and may be 'unpractical, since it renders them unfit to compete with our material force', represents the vestiges of a primordial state of metaphysical understanding; and that if the 'savage' himself, generally speaking, no longer comprehends his own 'divine inheritance', this ignorance on his part is no more shameful than ours, who do not recognize the intrinsic nature of his lore. 'We do not say that the modern "savage" exemplifies the "primordial state" itself, but that his beliefs, and the whole content of his folklore, bear witness to such a state.'

This 'savage' still retains the outlines of a full and unified life. 'How dare we forget', asks Coomaraswamy, 'that we are dealing with peoples "whose intellectual interests are the same from the top of the social structure to the bottom", and for whom our unfortunate distinctions of religious from secular learning, fine from applied art, and significance from use have not yet been made?'

It was Coomaraswamy's life-work to expound the doctrines upon which, in the past, and even to some extent to-day, a unified and truly human life has been based. 'All of his "myriad-minded" concentration', wrote R. A. Parker, 'together with an almost fabulous self-discipline and purposive "drive", have been yoked together to demonstrate the single voice of human aspiration. It is we, the contemporaries, with our genius for fission and division, who are lost . . .' unless, of course, we are prepared, even at this late hour, to see our error and to submit, in all humility, to the ancient and for too long forgotten rule.

CHAPTER TEN

CONCLUSION

At the risk of seeming to imitate Guénon's so-called arrogance, I have made no attempt to soften or to gloss over the contrasts between, on the one hand, the traditional doctrines, the traditional view of life, and, on the other, those views and beliefs which have, for the most part, seized upon men's minds since the Renaissance; it would not be difficult to select certain particular aspects of the ancient doctrines (as has, indeed, been done, time and again, in the case of Hinduism) and dress them up in such a way as to make them perfectly acceptible to the sentimental and rationalistic prejudices of the modern world, but such a labour of forgery and falsification is altogether profitless. There is no reason for concealing—there is every reason to emphasize—the fact that the whole of that view of the world and of the nature of things which is called traditional, and of which the Oriental doctrines offer a contemporary example, is absolutely opposed to the most fundamental beliefs, ideals and assumptions of the Western world as we find it to-day, and indeed that this world might be quite simply defined as 'anti-traditional', provided we use the word 'tradition' in Guénon's sense and do not confuse it with customs, habits and conventions which are of comparatively recent origin. It is impossible to pass by gradual stages from the modern view of life to the traditional one, for the gulf between them cannot be bridged; it can only be leapt across. There exists, however, an organization still active in the West which may, with some justification, be called traditional; the Roman Catholic Church.

CONCLUSION

Jacques Maritain, the eminent Catholic philosopher, uses almost the very words that Guénon has used again and again to define the basic malady of our world. 'The disease afflicting the modern world', says Maritain, in his book on St. Thomas Aquinas, 'is in the first place a disease of the mind; it began in the mind, it has now attacked the roots of the mind'. More sentimental, more superficial critics will claim that our trouble lies in the moral sphere or is due to the loss of 'faith'; but the Catholic recognizes, in the light of his doctrine, that it is a perversion of the mind, a loss of true knowledge and even of the belief in the possibility of true knowledge, that is the basis of our contemporary disorder; man, as man, is characterized, according to the Hindu doctrine, by the mental faculty and, according to Catholicism, by reason, and when error creeps into this, the specifically human sphere, its ramifications spread throughout the whole of human life. By every reasonable standard, the heretic, no matter how saintly, how virtuous, his character may be, is more dangerous than the blackest of villains, the most monstrous of evil-doers.

But what of that part of the traditional view of things which seems most unacceptable to the modern mind? Guénon writes of the final stage in the world's degeneration, immediately preceding the divine intervention whereby the order of heaven is restored and paradise regained, as the reign of Antichrist, that simian parody of the Messiah; the Catholic philosopher, in the book quoted above, says, 'As history draws nearer to Antichrist and suffers in all its visible structure transformations preparing the way for the advent of Antichrist, so also it draws nearer to Him Whom Antichrist precedes. . .' And although it may be difficult to reconcile the Catholic claim that Jesus Christ was unique, his birth as God-Man an event without parallel in universal history, with a doctrine which regards him as one of several divine manifestations in human form and as appearing in an age of growing decadence for the purpose of, as it were, slowing down the inevitable process of decay, yet certain remarks quoted from Pére Allo's book on the Apocalypse suggest that the divergence is not quite as wide as it might seem;

'. . . the earthly phase of the Kingdom of God, the phase of the conquests of the Gospel is sufficiently coincident with the last and most desperate efforts of Satan to prevent the coming of that Kingdom'.

Speaking of the intellectual chaos from which springs every kind of disorder in the practical sphere of action, Maritain suggests that the work of the negative forces is to-day so far advanced that only an 'inexorably rigorous philosophy' can get the better of it, a philosophy so comprehensive (so truly Catholic, in fact) that it can include in its territory all the diverse spheres in which the human mind moves. 'So it comes about', he writes, 'that what is most apt to our needs is precisely the absolutism of truth, what is most opportune and "practical" is doctrinal radicalism, but a radicalism devoid of all narrowness and brutality, all partiality and fanaticism, and suspended therefore from the only true Absolute, from the transcendence of primary Truth, whence all things proceed to being'. Maritain, of course, believes that the doctrine of St. Thomas is alone capable of filling this role, that it alone is sufficiently 'rigorous', sufficiently 'radical' to offer a cure for the errors of modern thought, and yet so comprehensive that it can find room for every aspect of the multiform truth.

A Catholic critic of Guénon's, Walter Shewring, wrote, 'he stands for the primacy of pure metaphysics over all other forms of knowledge, and presents himself as the exponent of a major tradition of thought, predominantly Eastern, but shared in the Middle Ages by the scholastics of the West . . . clearly Guénon's position is not that of Christian orthodoxy, but many, perhaps most, of his theses are, in fact, better in accord with authentic Thomist doctrine than are many opinions of devout but ill-instructed Christians'. Guénon himself regards Catholicism (and who says Catholic says Thomist) as the main, if not the only hope for the West; but, on the other hand, neither Guénon nor any man who believes in the existence of a universal Tradition, of pre-Christian origin, of which all other traditional doctrines, however widely they may appear to differ on the surface, are particular and therefore limited adaptations, can give complete primacy to one such adaptation, even though it may be the one best suited to the temperament of a particular race. And this is an attitude that no good Catholic can tolerate.

Many Catholics would no doubt denounce Guénon as a Gnostic (this term has sometimes been used with a freedom and a lack of precision which almost suggests the propaganda methods of contemporary politics), and there are many to whom the methods of the traditional doctrines of the East seem to represent an impious attempt on the part of the finite human mind to 'play at being pure spirit'. This is not the place to enter upon a very difficult and complicated controversy, but it does seem that this Catholic prejudice is based largely upon certain misconceptions of the meaning of terms employed by Hindu and Buddhist alike—and, in particular, upon a failure to grasp the distinction made by the Hindus between the terms 'manas' and 'buddhi'. It is never suggested in the Hindu doctrines that the human mind, as such, can ever become 'pure spirit' or, indeed, become anything other than what it is; nor is it ever suggested that man, as such, can become God. Between the Hindu concept of 'buddhi', the light of a knowledge which is not confined within the limitations of the human mind, and the Catholic concept of 'grace', there does not seem to be so wide a divergence as might at first appear.

A further distinction which, it seems possible, may have been too often exaggerated is that between the 'Supreme Identity' of the Oriental doctrines and the 'beatific vision' of Christianity. In his book, *Prayer and Poetry*, the Abbé Bremond writes, 'All men have the same supernatural end, the beatific vision. A pagan of the days before Christ, or of our own if saved . . . has the same essential recompense as the canonized saints. From which it follows that all the help God gives us has for its supreme end to lead us to the beatific vision'. Now in a region so far beyond the power and range of human words, and in speaking of matters to which the terms used in our ordinary human discourse can be applied only by analogy, can we really make so firm a distinction between 'vision' and 'being'? And can we really regard as totally incompatible two doctrines, one of which states that the true end of every being is to be rapt in the vision of God (which implies a total forgetfulness of self and an all-absorbing awareness of God alone), and the other that our end, however long and through whatever spheres our migration may lead, is to be reunited, in perfect awareness, to 'That' which is the source of all things?

The Catholic theologian would no doubt maintain that, although there are certain obvious points upon which Hinduism (to take one example) is in agreement with Catholic doctrine, a real correspondence between Hinduism and Catholicism can only be established by distorting the former and completely overlooking the 'spirit' of the latter. This compels us to ask what is the 'true form' of any particular doctrine, and how is it to be established. Are we to take a kind of Gallup Poll and say that Hinduism is quite simply whatever the majority of Hindus believe; or is there, in the case of every great doctrine, a 'true form' which would remain unaltered even if the whole body of believers had departed from it? If we hold to the former opinion, then we leave the field of doctrine and religion wide open to the illusions of the masses and the phantasies of the individual, and very soon a situation arises in which the doctrinal framework is shattered and we can only say, as in the case of contemporary Protestantism, that 'Some believe this, some that; and there are a few points upon which the majority still agree'. In such a case there is indeed no 'true form' of the doctrine, for there is no doctrine left; only a network of sentimental aspirations and moral conventions.

If, on the other hand, we believe that each of the great doctrines represents a special adaptation of one single and eternal Tradition, revealed in its different aspects at different times and under varying circumstances, then there indeed exists an orthodoxy to depart from which is heresy. And if we study the great heresies of the past, as of the present, in the light of this belief, we shall find that the majority of them are just as heretical from a Hindu, Buddhist or Moslem point of view as from that of

Christianity. Heresy can be absolute; and there are certain recurrent errors which adopt very similar forms the world over, which represent everywhere the same kind of perversion and lead to the same kind of catastrophe. There is not only a perennial philosophy; there are perennial heresies.

Maritain points out that we fall into error 'because we are incapable of comprehending simultaneously apparently opposite truths which are in reality complementary. 'Exclusion' is thus the cause of heresy. . . .' Even a fairly superficial examination of heresy will show us that, in almost every case, it affirms nothing new, but confines itself to denying certain elements in the orthodox doctrine against which it has arisen; in compensation for this denial, it has to over-emphasize certain other elements, so that it is always characterized by a lack of proportion; indeed, it might be possible to define orthodoxy as 'sound proportion'. Just because a heresy exists only by virtue of denying something (as the word 'Protestant' so clearly indicates) its denials are always fanatical, sometimes hysterical; if it did not keep on denying, it would have no further excuse for existing. And the lower reaches of heresy (such as 'liberal Protestantism') are only divided by a narrow margin from complete scepticism, which is, after all, the logical conclusion of 'denial'.

But if this is so, then how are we to distinguish between an orthodox doctrine which, in so far as it is an adaptation of the truth to the needs of a particular race or a particular period of history, must of necessity ignore some aspects of that truth and give primacy to others (as, for example, Christianity gives primacy to the personal aspect of the divine), from heresy, which has simply taken the work of selection and exclusion a step further? Only, perhaps, by insisting upon the distinction between to 'ignore' and to 'deny'; orthodoxy ignores certain aspects of the truth, because it must provide a practical 'Way' of spiritual development, suited to people who are in possession of only a part of that total human nature which man is said to have possessed before the 'Fall', and a 'Way' is only marked out by selecting a particular direction and concentrating upon it, to the exclusion of all the other equally possible directions;

heresy, on the other hand, denies the existence of everything outside its own narrow sphere.

Now the work of selection, whereby an orthodox doctrine—or a true offshoot of such a doctrine—comes into being can be undertaken only by a man or by men who are in possession of the total truth and who are able, therefore, to keep the right proportions in their adaptations of it; in the case of heresy, however, the selection is made by people who do not understand the profound reasons for the existence, within the orthodox doctrine, of elements which seem out of keeping with the 'spirit' of Christianity (or of Islam, as the case may be), although these are in fact the very elements which save the doctrine from an exclusive one-sidedness. And so we are back at the definition of orthodoxy as 'proportion'.

According to the 'traditionalists', one effect of the world's gradual descent from unity to the utmost dispersion in multiplicity is that the section of the total and complete human nature which any individual man can call his own becomes, with the passage of time, increasingly narrow; in consequence of this, the various orthodox doctrines tend to become increasingly partial, to draw further and further from the single primordial Tradition and to diverge more and more widely from each other. This need not be a matter for regret, so long as the spiritual leaders of these various doctrines remain themselves aware of a wider, more universal truth and know that the teaching which it is their business to guard and to interpret is by no means the one and only valid presentation of that truth. But when the leaders themselves fall a prey to that partial-mindedness which necessarily characterizes the mass of 'believers', then orthodoxy itself becomes tainted with that sin of 'exclusion' which, as Maritain has pointed out, is the chief cause of heresy.

It would be presumptuous to speculate upon the present situation within the Catholic Church; but it may be legitimate to point out that Christianity seems, from the first, to have been particularly exposed to the dangers of one-sidedness; in its early, bitter struggle against certain rival doctrines, it learned to regard with harsh intolerance everything that savoured of 'paganism', and the very fact that it has placed the chief emphasis upon personal love for Jesus Christ has exposed it to further dangers—for although, in the saints, this love has risen far above the vagaries and the exclusiveness of human emotion, being, in their case, raised to a higher power, yet in the ordinary devoted Christian the fire of love has often burnt with a smoky flame. Whoever suggests that there are other ways than the Christian whereby man may come to his 'last true end' seems to deny Christ, and that, to his lovers, is an unforgivable sin.

There are some who would attach a special significance to the Christian attitude to sex, an attitude which, in spite of all that may be said about the sacrament of marriage, is by no means free from fear, contempt and outright rejection; nothing could be more foreign to Christianity—and nothing arouses more horror in the ordinary Christian—than the sacred uses to which Hinduism puts human sexuality. But when a religion hands over a wide section of human life to the Devil, it is always possible that the Devil may accept the gift; sexuality, exiled from the sphere of the sacred and condemned as evil, all too easily becomes evil; and it may be that Christianity has not been altogether guiltless in that work of reducing the sacred sphere to one small, constricted part of life, which has culminated in the modern 'profane' world to which the very idea of a real sanctification of human actions is foreign. One is compelled to ask whether the destruction of Christendom, a destruction brought about from within, may not have been due, in part, to those forces which Christianity had driven into exile; whether, in fact, Catholic Christianity, unlike either Hinduism or the Moslem faith, may not have carried within itself the seeds of its own destruction.

It may be unwise to raise these questions without following them up more fully; but, while their further development would lead away from the theme of this study, it has been essential at least to raise them, for the time seems near when the Western world may be ranged in two camps, the Catholic and the Marxist, and, in any case, it would be preposterous to ignore

Catholicism when considering the possibilities of a return, on the part of the West, to a traditional view of life. Marxism represents, in a certain sense, the logical culmination of the anti-traditional and so, in a narrower sense, anti-Catholic movement of the modern world; and Catholicism, whatever its failings, is alone in the West in possessing the latent resources with which to meet the Marxist onslaught. The opposition offered to Marxism by liberals, social democrats and other 'moderates' has its basis in sentiment; it is none the less sincere, none the less worthy of respect, for this, but the fact remains that the roots of Marxism go much deeper than the level of sentiment and draw strength from a real spiritual perversion. And while it may be said that the Marxists will always have to reckon with the tenacity of those who fight for their freedom and for their very lives, it is essential to remember that Marxism attacks the mind of man before it lays hands upon his body, and that the bravest of men, the sturdiest of fighters for freedom, may, in a very short space of time, be so perverted in his mind that his courage is turned to devilish purposes and his 'love of freedom' serves the ends of tyranny.

Those to-day—and that means the majority of Westerners—whose 'convictions' are based upon a certainty of what they 'like' and 'dislike' and upon a strong 'feeling' that certain things are right, certain others wrong, give a dangerously misleading impression of soundness and stability; there can be no stability in the emotional order, so long as it is unsupported by anything of a deeper, less mutable nature, and the day comes when these people 'change their minds', by which they mean that their feelings have, at the command of agencies over which they have no control and of which, indeed, they are for the most part quite unaware, changed their direction. It is disturbing to find how many of those who appear adamant in their hatred of Marxism hold, in fact, a view of life and of the nature of things which would provide a perfect foundation for the Marxist philosophy. The anti-Traditional or, as one may legitimately say, the 'heretical' movement of the modern world, making use, for its own purposes, of many of man's noblest and most generous aspirations, flows onwards; only a traditional doctrine, only some form of 'orthodoxy', can provide the necessary counter-force to check this movement.

But the return of our civilization to a way of life framed in some traditional setting would necessarily imply the return of the spiritual authority to its rightful place in the social scheme. The spiritual authority of Christendom was vested in the Catholic Church, and there exists to-day no vestige of any other organization that could fill this role in the Western world. René Guénon analyses the growing disorder of human society in terms of the gradual usurpation of power by less and less stable elements in the community; very simply his argument is this: stability can only be maintained in human society for as long as the temporal power acknowledges its subordination to the spiritual authority and carries out, in the field of action and of administration, the orders of that authority. The time comes, however, when the kingly or aristocratic power proclaims, first its equality with, and then its independence of the spiritual authority; in so doing, it makes inevitable its own destruction, for it was but a delegated power and it remained stable and secure only for so long as it was legitimate. The process of usurpation, once started, must continue, and temporal power passes from royalty to the *bourgeoisie*; finally it falls into the hands of the workers.

Now according to Guénon, and history would seem to bear out his contention, human society becomes increasingly unstable and falls further and further from those immutable principles to which it was once anchored, as the process of usurpation continues; the pace of the descent and disintegration increases, so that the *bourgeoisie* hold power for a shorter period than did the rebel aristocracy, and the workers will hold it for a shorter period still. The question then arises as to whether a real return to a sound social order, subject, once again, to the spiritual authority, is possible, or whether society is to pass into the next stage of decadence, and the 'egalitarian' period—which hardly endures more than a moment—is to be followed by the creation of a false and inverted hierarchy, in which the lowest elements of society take total power into their hands. It might be said, if we confine ourselves to considering the Western world, that whereas the first stage is characterized by an increasingly irreligious or agnostic state of mind, the second is predominantly anti-religious; and while the first stage leads to scepticism, the second leads to an almost insane fanaticism; finally, to put the matter slightly differently, the first stage concludes with the complete isolation of man from all that is above him (in fact, from the divine power); the second stage exposes him to the demonic powers which exist, as it were, in the underworld of existence.

Inevitably, this offers an over-simplified picture of events, but, taken in broad outline, it throws considerable light upon our present situation and upon the choice which lies before us; if it were not for the belief in progress, which is ever at the back of our minds and affects all our thinking, we could hardly fail to realize that order and unity in human society can exist only when society is regulated, not by man's laws, which have only the authority of force behind them, but by the applications of eternal, unchanging principles to contingent events, applications which can be made only by a class of people whose vocation it is to achieve awareness of such principles and administered only by a class whose vocation it is to rule in the world of action.

Those to whom the notion that a state of affairs may yet arise in the Western world in which the Catholic Church might wield at least as great a power as she held in the Middle Ages seems quite beyond the bounds of possibility are inclined to overlook the extreme uncertainty of the times in which we live; our world may well be upon the brink of a complete break-down, and, should such a catastrophe occur, some form of authority would have to take charge of the situation and set about re-building Western civilization; it would take a daring man to prophesy whether such a new world would be more likely to take the form of a resurrected Christendom or of a vast Soviet Union.

I hope to have said enough to show why those who accept

the traditional view of life are bound, whatever changes they might wish to see in the structure of Catholicism, to look to the Catholic Church as the main source of hope for the Western world; the fact that they themselves may feel unable to embrace Catholicism and, indeed, that the Church would not receive them while they refuse to give the primacy amongst traditional doctrines to Christianity, need not in any way affect their attitude. But the moment has come to consider what may be the role, in the modern world, of those who find themselves in this rather unenviable position.

In the first place, their task is an intellectual one; but this does not mean that they will qualify as 'intellectuals' in the contemporary sense of the word. The extreme division which exists to-day between the intellectuals and the mass of ordinary people, particularly in the English-speaking world, is one of the most striking examples of that terrible isolation of group from group, that total lack of true social integration, which so effectively prevents the life-blood from circulating through modern society. This isolation necessarily breeds animosities and, in the widest sense, a snobbishness of a kind which could not exist in an integrated society, in which each man fulfils his vocation within the natural hierarchy, without arousing envy (since his vocation is his own, and no one else can fulfil it) and without indulging in envy. In such a vocational society there is a real sense of security and a complete lack of animosity as between the different social orders (each of which is giving what it is best qualified to give to the community as a whole) such as cannot survive in an industrial civilization, whether capitalist or socialist.

In our world, in which the very notion of a natural social hierarchy is lost, every group either fears or envies every other group; and it is, in part, a feeling of resentment that a certain group of people should possess a knowledge and tastes that savour of privilege that makes the *bourgeoisie* so suspicious of the intellectuals. But the isolation of the intellectuals is also due, to a considerable extent, to their own attitude and to the use to which they have put their special qualities; connoisseurs of all things human, sensitive with an indiscriminate sensibility, acutely aware of the minor profundities of life: yet troubled by their sense of isolation, embittered by the hostility of the Pharisee, the *bourgeois*; taking refuge either in the arrogant exclusiveness of a small clique or in the privacy of neurosis; for ever searching, yet afraid to find; in the midst of these preoccupations, they have neglected their true task, the task, not of 'thinking for themselves', but of understanding and of communicating that which they understand.

It is the fault neither of the *bourgeois* nor of the intellectual that 'highbrow' should have become so common a term of abuse; it is merely one more symptom of social disintegration; and such a process, once started, gathers velocity of its own accord; denied their rightful place in society, the intellectuals have become increasingly irresponsible (the same might be said of the aristocracy, or of what remains of what was once an aristocracy); less and less responsible, their position has become increasingly isolated.

It is essential that those who, believing in a universal truth which can be known and has been known the world over, are prepared to undertake the labour of understanding, should keep outside this vicious circle; that they should combine a justified intolerance of the ideals and ideologies which lie at the root of modern society with an unswerving tolerance for the men and women caught up in the circle, stamping out in themselves the animosities of group, class and race. It is their task to act as a bridge, when all the bridges are down; a bridge, in the first place, between East and West, but also between the partial and complementary truths buried under so many warring philosophies. It is for them to maintain the unity of truth against the diversity of error; and this they can do only by labouring themselves to become aware of that unity, that they may recognize it under the multiplicty of its disguises.

To think of this as a futile or ineffectual undertaking is to forget that the immediate results of any action (and by the term action we must understand, not only that which is outwardly done, but any movement of thought, will, or feeling) are only the most superficial, least essential of its fruits. It is not for us to concern ourselves with the results of our actions—this, indeed, is a platitude of all traditional doctrine, whether in the form in which it is stated in the Gita or in the form in which St. Thomas Aquinas states it, saying, 'God ordained that we should not be careful about that which is no affair of ours, viz.: the consequences of our acts, but did not forbid us to be careful about that which is our affair, viz.: the act itself'.

Even in the matter of actual, visible affects upon the field of history, the results of human action may be far wider in their scope than one might reasonably expect when considering the action itself; we have only to think of that old Bishop of Hippo who, fifteen centuries ago, persevered with his labour, a labour that was to provide the corner-stone of Christendom, when Rome had already been sacked and the barbarian clamoured at the gates of his own city; 'He looked beyond the aimless and bloody chaos of history to the world of eternal realities from which the world of sense derives all the significance which it possesses. His thoughts were fixed, not on the fate of the city of Rome or the city of Hippo, nor on the struggle of Roman and barbarian, but on those other cities which have their foundations in heaven and in hell . . .' (Christopher Dawson, *St. Augustine and his Age*). Augustine could not know how profoundly his work was to influence the form of the new civilization that arose upon the ruins of the old.

All sound and effective action is timeless, in that it is related less to the apparent exigencies of the present moment than to those 'eternal realities', and, whatever its results in time, it bears fruit, sweet or sour, in those 'other cities'. One man's love or hatred reverberates through all time; one man's attainment (in the Oriental sense of 'enlightenment') proliferates through all the spheres of being. Nothing can take place in isolation. So it is said that, at the moment of the Buddha's 'Great Awakening', there was a harrowing of hell, 'the hells were filled with light'. Or, if we turn to Judaism, the Chassids say, 'All worlds hang on his works, all worlds look and yearn for the teaching and good deeds of man'; and for them there is no human action that may not be used to foster the unity; 'Enoch was a cobbler; with each stitch of his awl that drew together the top and bottom leather, he joined God and his Shekhinah (the indwelling spirit)'. There are no private worlds, no walled pleasure-gardens; 'part and other part', says Plotinus, 'are wrought to one tone like a musical string which, being plucked at one end, vibrates at the other also'; nothing that we think or do can fail to have its due effect, and every effect spreads outwards like a circle widening on the surface of a pool.

It follows from this that the actions of those who strive, by whatever relative and convenient means may come to hand, to become aware of the truth (or of some part of the truth) which is the human heritage, are never fruitless, even though it may seem impossible to communicate what has been learned and even though the attainment may appear purely private and inward. And yet it cannot be too often repeated that we ourselves lack the means to determine what is or is not practicable at a particular stage in history; we cannot tell what changes and transformations, now germinating unseen, may be about to show themselves in the event; and this is specially true of the present moment, when certain of the forces which generated the world with which we are familiar appear to have exhausted themselves. It may seem improbable, but we cannot say that it is quite impossible, that the Western world should return to a traditional form of social organization, based, as such a society must be, upon principles which are recognized by all men and questioned by none. However remote this possibility, it must be taken into consideration.

It is for this reason that those who study the traditional doctrines, by whatever path they themselves may approach them, must keep in mind the Buddhist saying that, 'Whatever is not adapted to such and such persons as are to be taught cannot be called a teaching'; remaining sensitive to the currents of thought and prevailing tendencies of their time, they must be prepared, as far as they are able, to translate the universal truths into terms that correspond to the Western mind and character as they find it, without, in the process, adulterating them. It would scarcely be possible to exaggerate the difficulty of such a task; and yet those who achieve a real and effective knowledge of a certain order are said to receive that 'gift of tongues', whereby, in Guénon's words, a man 'always expresses himself in a form appropriate to the ways of thought of the men to whom he addresses himself'. To achieve such a degree of knowledge or, to be more precise, of personal realization, is therefore the one thing essential.

To translate into Western terms a knowledge which, in itself, lies beyond all particular forms may well mean, in practice, as we have seen, to translate it into Christian terms, and, by so doing, to inject new life into Christian doctrine, at one and the same time leading Christianity back to its origins and binding it more closely to the universal wisdom of which it is a particular application. We might therefore find a situation in which men who were not themselves Christians chose to speak in Christian terms and might even seem to preach Christianity; there would be nothing strange or false in such a situation, except in the view of those who are determined to deny all that lies beyond their own particular sphere of understanding.

But whatever the immediate prospects, uncertain, unpredictable as they are, the field of a knowledge which is much more than knowledge, of a love which escapes from the narrow bounds of human feeling, and of an action which is uninfluenced by fear of failure or hope of success, is wide and free, open to every being, in this age as in any other (in hell, as in heaven, according to the Hindus). And the fruit of such knowledge, such love, such action is certain. There is nothing desperate in our situation, unless we wish to think it so. Although for a time (and for a purpose) we are confined, storm-driven in a ship that may seem pilotless, yet our destination is sure; and, our course completed, we shall know freedom as the only truth, and truth as freedom. To be free, when all is done, is to know at last the joy towards which our longing and our lust so blindly strove; and to know that joy is the ultimate, fathomless peace.

INDEX

INDEX

INDEX

9 781597 310260

Made in United States
North Haven, CT
20 November 2024

60676783R00140